THE PROGRESS OF THE SOUL

The Interior Career of John Donne

Viri seraphici Joannis Donne Qua =
dragenarij Effigies vera, Qui post
eam ætatem Sacris initiatus Ec =
clesiæ Sti Pauli Decanus obijt.
Anō $\begin{cases} \text{Dōm } 1631° \\ \text{Ætatis suæ } 59° \end{cases}$

Lombart Sculpsit londi

John Donne in 1612, after an engraving by Pierre Lombart

THE PROGRESS

OF THE SOUL

The Interior Career of John Donne

BY RICHARD E. HUGHES

WILLIAM MORROW AND COMPANY, INC.

New York 1968

Contents

Contents

Prologue

And here I desire the Readers leave to remember . . . Mr. John Donne, who leaving Oxford, lived at the Innes of Courts, not dissolute, but very neat; a great Visiter of Ladies, a great frequenter of Playes, a great Writer of conceited Verses.

> (Sir Richard Baker, Chronicles of the Kings of England, 1641)

Newes here is none at all but that John Dun seekes to be preferred to be secretarie of Virginia.

> (John Chamberlain to Dudley Carleton, 14 February, 1609/10)

> The Muses garden with Pedantique weedes
> O'rspred, was purg'd by thee; The lazie seeds
> Of servile imitation throwne away;
> And fresh invention planted, Thou didst pay
> The debts of our penurious bankrupt age.
>
> > (Thomas Carew, "An Elegie upon the Death of the Deane of Pauls, Dr. John Donne," 1633)

He was earnest and unwearied in the search of knowledge, with which his vigorous soul is now satisfied, and employed in a continual praise of that God that first breathed it into his active body: that body which once was a temple of the

[7]

Holy Ghost, and is now become a small quantity of Christian dust: But I shall see it re-animated.

(Izaak Walton, *The Life of Dr. John Donne*, 1640)

This is authentic Donne, no doubt. Donne the dandy, Donne the indigent, Donne the revolutionary, Donne the satisfied inquirer. Authentic but not essential. More than half a century ago, Sir Herbert Grierson gave the proper lead. "For the historian," he wrote, "it is a matter of positive interest to connect Donne's wit with the general disintegration of mediaeval thought, to recognize the influence on the Elizabethan drama of the doctrines of Machiavelli, or to find in Pope's achievement in poetry a counterpart to Walpole's in politics. For the lover of literature none of these facts has any positive interest whatsoever. . . . For the lover of literature, literary history has an indirect value. He studies history that he may discount it. What he relishes in a poet of the past is exactly the same essential qualities as he enjoys in a poet of his own day—life and passion and art."[1]

The John Donne of the historical records must play the Vergil to the Dante of the essential John Donne. The historical Donne can direct us to the London of the 1590's, but he can't fully account for the *Satires*; he can take us into exile at Mitcham, but not into "The Anniversarie"; he can show us old St. Paul's, but not the core of the prebend sermons. No matter how fascinating is the Donne who once shivered in Pyrford, prowled in Somerset's garden, trembled in the pulpit, and snarled about a daughter's dowry, far more important is the mind which slowly reveals itself through its art. As an historical fact, the beruffed Donne is trapped in the late sixteenth and seventeenth centuries; but as a poet, Donne is a clear voice now.

In this century, two postwar societies adopted Donne; but they adopted only a small part of him, misunderstanding or

ignoring the larger part. It was the young Donne, the trench-
ant, anxious, ironic, and above all the fragmented Donne, to
whom we turned then, finding in his earlier kaleidoscopic
vision a paradigm of our own uncertainties and angers. There
is a fascination of the fragment in nearly everything the young
Donne wrote: we blunder into the intimacies of his songs,
and are forced to leave before the final scenes; or we enter the
theatre of his poetry too late and hear only the concluding
speeches. However, the thirst of this generation is not for
fragments, but for totalities. We have sensed, with Teilhard
de Chardin, that to be fragmented, to be *alone*, is to "cul-
minate in a dust of active, dissociated particles."[2] We crave
an entire vision, and for assurance we turn to communal
myths as "fixed points in a world of bewildering change and
disappointment,"[3] or to a physics wherein "mind no longer
appears as an accidental intruder into the realm of matter; we
are beginning to suspect that we ought rather to hail it as the
creator and governor of the realm of matter";[4] we entertain
concepts of man as "*intensely* aware of participation. . .
feel[ing] the centre of energy in himself identified with the
energy of which external nature is the image,"[5] or we entertain an awareness of love which sees that "the deepest need of
man . . . is the need to overcome his separateness, to leave
the prison of his aloneness."[6] The time demands some kind
of response to that "dust of active, dissociated particles," and
the present will surely be distinguished for both the frenzy
and the variety of its responses.

The great design that is relentlessly generated and eventually fulfilled in Donne's art is such a response. What we
witness in the whole of Donne's art is a mind discovering
itself, and in the process standing as a dramatization of
today's flight from loneliness and toward a fulfilling participatory experience. For the central fact of Donne is that he is a
man who expended himself entirely, who in grasping the

particularities of experience found himself clutching a universal. If the "truth of a work of art is both its adequacy to the basic structure of human experience and its correction and deepening of our understanding of this structure,"[7] then Donne's art is true. The "secret complicity between the infinite and the infinitesimal"[8] was an insight which Donne came to have, and as a major Christian artist he was aware of the tough edges of existence *within* which divinity was manifest. For all his learning, Donne's Christianity had little to do with commentaries and glosses and much to do with the Gospels and the epistles of St. Paul and St. John: the sense of the presential reality of Christ in the flesh and in the world. The discovery of that reality begins in and never leaves the contours of experience; and so sharp is Donne's awareness of those contours, and so human and contemporary-seeming the rhythm of Donne's pilgrimage from lonely particle to consummated totality, that his Christian art transcends doctrine and speaks meaningfully at large.

Professor TeSelle might have been speaking of Donne when she commented:

> Literature with its concrete, varied, and creative depictions of the basic structure of human experience, in both its cosmological and anthropological aspects, offers to the Christian invaluable acquaintance. It gives to the Christian, who is called upon to adhere totally to God in spite of the negative powers that appear to rule the world, an understanding of the depth and breadth of powers that his response must embrace if it is to be realistic. He must take into account those diseased and dying infants who trouble Ivan in *The Brothers Karamazov* (and feel for them as Ivan does) and that white whale which embodied all evil for Ahab in *Moby Dick* (and know in his heart the extent of that whale's rule as Ahab did). Literature also offers to the Christian, who is called

upon to love his fellows with a profound and appropriate love, an entrée into the crannies of the human heart that a realistic love cannot do without. What one can learn of the human heart from James or Faulkner or Tolstoy cannot be gained from history, psychology, or sociology books, or even, unfortunately, for most of us, from our own experience with our fellows, which is so stereotyped and patterned that we seldom see beneath the clichés of surface relationships . . . it is the peculiar function of literature both to discover and create the basic structure of human experience. This means creating autonomous visions of life and of the human heart—visions of life that see it as paradoxical, rich, and difficult, and visions of the human heart that see it as full of unexpected cliffs and valleys.[9]

We must, to be sure, be aware of those precise moments when the essential, the significant Donne entered the successive phrases of his own transformation from alien to participant in a totality (Grierson did not say that the literary scholar ignores history: he studies it so he may discount it). Thanks to the brilliance of Donne's editors, commentators, and biographers—a line that stretches from Walton to Edmund Gosse to Grierson, down to R. C. Bald, Helen Gardner, Evelyn Simpson, and a great many others—we now know that the semifigure who inhabits the *Holy Sonnets* is not much older than the figure who informs the later group of love poems; we know that the prose works of the agonized middle years are not separated from the sonnets; we know that the *Songs and Sonnets* is not an undifferentiated jumble of green animalism and erudite Platonizing. The stages of Donne's progress are reasonably clear. There are gaps, to be certain: within related groups of poems, the precise order of composition is cloudy; a large block of sermons remains undated; many of the verse letters can be only approximately dated.

The attempt to re-create the interior life of any great artist is a gamble, under even the best of circumstances. To attempt it in the case of Donne may well be hubristic. But the attempt will have been provoked by amazement and sympathy, and if not a cenotaph it can remain as a trophy.

> To'our bodies turne wee then, that so
>> Weake men on love reveal'd may looke;
> Loves mysteries in soules do grow,
>> But yet the body is his booke.[10]
>>> ("The Exstasie," ll. 69–72)

JOHN DONNE was born in London early in 1572. His father (who died when Donne was scarcely four years old) was a prosperous merchant, successful enough to be named Warden of the Ironmongers' Company—we would say director of a union or guild—a year before his death. At his death, he left a considerable fortune to his widow, the equivalent today of perhaps a quarter of a million dollars. But it was from his mother that John Donne received a less tangible but more perplexing inheritance: she was descended from the sister of Sir Thomas More, who had gone to the headsman's block in 1535 rather than renounce his Roman Catholicism for King Henry VIII's reformed church. John Donne was thus born into a distinguished family which was defined by law as renegade, suspect by the Protestant establishment, and barred from civil, ecclesiastic, or university careers; for to enter any career which had connections with the state meant taking the Oath of Supremacy, thereby according to the ruling monarch both religious and civil sovereignty. This was something the Catholic subjects of England would not do, for it meant denying the papal authority. Many years later, in a remark he made in *Pseudo-Martyr*, Donne noted that no one was more aware than he of having "endured and suffered more in their persons and fortunes, for obeying the teachers of Roman doctrine." The circumstances of Donne's birth closed off many an avenue of preferment and success.

Less than a year after her husband's death, Donne's mother married a second time. Donne's stepfather was Dr. John

Syminges, president of the Royal College of Physicians, and it may well be that Donne's precise, if limited, knowledge of physiology, which shows itself in several poems, was Dr. Syminges' bequest.

At the age of twelve, after being tutored at home "both in the mathematics and in all the other liberal sciences" as well as in "particular principles of the Romish Church" (this is Izaak Walton's account), Donne entered the University of Oxford, where he studied for three years. In 1587, he transferred to Cambridge, but in neither university could he proceed to a degree, for this would have required his subscribing to the articles of the English church. At this point, there were two obvious alternatives, neither one requiring Donne's declaration that he accepted Her Majesty, Elizabeth, to be the supreme governor in all spiritual, ecclesiastic, and temporal things: he might enter the profession of medicine (Dr. Syminges was a Roman Catholic, and had managed to achieve distinction) or the law. Donne chose the law.

It was probably in the spring of 1591 that Donne enrolled in Thavies Inn, London; a year later he transferred to Lincoln's Inn, proudly considered "the third University" by the fledgling barristers who studied there. How seriously Donne studied the law there's no way of telling: he had come into his patrimony (about £750) under his father's will while he was at Lincoln's Inn, so that he could well afford to put together the reputation he had for being not dissolute but very neat, a great visitor of ladies and frequenter of plays. He evidently studied more than the law, for Izaak Walton notes that he mastered the "grounds and use of physic," i.e., medicine, and his knowledge of French, Italian, and Spanish probably had its foundation in these years. He was supposed to have been the student in charge of Christmas festivities in 1594, but he was absent (and was fined by the school authorities) by reason of his traveling to the Continent, "first in Italy and then in Spain," according to Walton. He was back within the year, having taken on the job of tutoring a young gentleman, Thomas Danby. Donne's legal studies were at an end; but he had managed to reinforce a naturally astute intelligence with enough juridical terminology and patterns of argumentation to serve him well in both his poetry and his later controversial prose works. There was one somber note in Donne's law-student years: his younger brother Henry had been arrested for giving sanctuary to a Catholic priest, and had died of a fever contracted in prison.

Hanging loose upon society, so to speak, Donne in June, 1596, became one of the "gentlemen volunteers" who accompanied the Earl of Essex on a privateering (a euphemism for piratical)raid against the Spanish colony of Cadiz. The raid was, from the English point of view, a great success; and in the following summer Essex planned a similar attack against the Spanish ports in the Azores. Once again, Donne was among the volunteer recruits, but neither he nor anyone else got much glory from this "Islands Voyage." The Spanish treasure ships eluded the English, and Essex' fleet straggled home in October with its honor badly bent.

Early in 1598, Donne returned again to the Continent, this time as a confidential agent of Sir Robert Cecil, Her Majesty's chief Secretary of State, who was involved in negotiations with Henry IV of France. But this interim occupation was superseded by a much more promising post. During the Islands Voyage, Donne had met Thomas Egerton and Francis Woolley, the son and stepson, respectively, of Sir Thomas Egerton, Lord Keeper of the Great Seal of England and a member of Elizabeth's Privy Council. Donne needed a position, and Sir Thomas needed a competent secretary. There was nothing menial in Donne's place in the Egerton household: Sir Thomas, noted Walton, did not "account him to be so much his servant as to forget he was his friend" and

"esteemed his company and discourse to be a great ornament" to his own little court. The elder Egerton was possibly
the avenue to greater things for Donne, and at the same time
he was always an admired and respected friend.

It was while Donne was in the Egerton household that he
witnessed the downfall of the brilliant and illustrious Earl of
Essex. Dispatched into Ireland by Queen Elizabeth to put
down an insurrection, Essex instead had made peace with the
rebel leader Tyrone; then he had returned in September of
1599, against Elizabeth's commands. Angered by his failure,
the Queen placed Essex under house arrest and banished him
from court, with Egerton being assigned the task of acting as
prosecutor. If Essex had held his peace, he would probably
have escaped with censure and the official announcement of
Her Majesty's displeasure; but in February of 1601, Essex
marched through London with his armed retainers and was
thereupon labeled a traitor with designs against Her Majesty's
life. The result of that ill-conceived breaking out of custody
was execution for high treason, and Essex' head fell on February 25.

Through all this, disturbed though he must have been over
the downfall of his former commander, Donne continued to
prosper in Egerton's service; it's probable that he became a
Member of Parliament in October of 1601. But by December,
Parliament was dissolved, and Donne's short tenure as a
politician was over; and in the same month he secretly married Ann More, with disastrous consequences.

Ann, seventeen years old, was Egerton's niece and ward;
she and Donne had been in one another's company constantly
since 1600, when she had become (young though she was)
manageress of the household on Lady Egerton's death. Her
marriage to Donne was secret and, since Ann was underage,
illegal; and when her father, George More, heard of it, he had
Donne and his accomplices (Christopher Brooke, whom

Donne had met at Lincoln's Inn, the best man; and his brother Samuel, a clergyman who had performed the wedding) thrown into prison on charges of breaking both civil and canon law. Sir George furthermore demanded Donne's dismissal from Egerton's service and pressed hard for an annulment. The annulment was not granted, but the dismissal was. When Donne was released from prison on February 12, 1602, and was reunited with Ann, he was without a position, without a university degree, without professional status, humiliatingly forced to live on the charity of his wife's cousin, Sir Francis Woolley, who housed the wretched couple in his own home at Pyrford. The experience of poverty, degrading in any usual situation, had become a fact of Donne's life.

CHAPTER I

The Beginning,
1593– 1598

BEN JONSON interrupted his famous walking tour of Scotland to spend two or three weeks at Christmas time in 1618 with the Scottish poet William Drummond; and in the course of the garrulous evenings, Jonson required his host to believe that Donne had "written all his best pieces err he was 25 years old."[1] Jonson's critical opinions were usually peremptory but always cogent and delivered from a consistent point of view. Somewhere in Donne's earliest work, he detected an attitude of which he approved, and he applauded it. That attitude was a conservative and traditional response to his art and milieu. There are no innovative and original rhythm patterns in Donne's first phase: he stays cautiously within the confines of Jonson's own "bravest sort of verses," the heroic couplet, in all of the satires and in most of the early verse letters, and he adopts common song measures for his lyrics. His choice of large structures is significantly cautious: epistles, elegies, satires all came to Donne with the blessings of antiquity, revered and above all decorous, the darlings of the most reactionary of literary theorists. The stances which Donne assumes in the earliest poems are not invented but inherited: now he plays at being Ovid, now Persius, then Horace, Martial—amorist, satirist, epigrammatist. He wears his rue with a difference, but the basic pose is familiar.

For the young Donne was not really the iconoclast he's often made out to be, breaking old idols in wild isolation. Most of the idols had already been broken. We tend to push Thomas Carew's evaluations too far back. His "Elegie upon the Death of the Deane of Pauls, Dr. John Donne" has so insinuated itself into our perceptions of Donne that we think the young poet has already purged the Muses' garden, exiled the goodly train of gods and goddesses, and ruled the universal monarchy of wit. Not yet. It's a misplaced admiration that turns a young Donne into the bearer of mannerist doubt, metaphysical grief, bone-deep *Weltschmerz*, the whole load of *fin de siècle* weariness.[2] Apprentices still whistled, regardless of the metaphysical shudder. A scene in Jonson's *Every Man in His Humour* reminds us that the most pressing maladies of the late sixteenth century needn't always be taken seriously:

> *Matthew.* . . . Your true melancholy breeds your perfect fine wit, sir. I am melancholy myself divers times, sir, and then do I no more but take pen and paper presently, and overflow you half a score or a dozen of sonnets at a sitting . . .

> *Stephen.* I thank you, sir, I shall be bold, I warrant you. Have you a stool there to be melancholy upon?[3]

There's a bit of the Stephen in the early Donne, as there is in most young men. He is one of the most human of our poets, and we do him no favor if we forget his humanity and especially his youth in his early work. He was unsure of himself and uncertain of the identity he was to assume in the world. Eventually he achieved a magnificent identity through his art, but in the beginning he borrowed identities. The wonder of his earliest poetry is the skill with which he pours his embryonic self into ready molds and bit by bit creates angles and edges that were not in the originals.

Donne's electing to follow traditional models, strike established poses, and adopt recognized masks is a not unusual tactic for a young poet still unsure of his own métier; and in any case Donne could not succeed in suffocating his own distinctive voice in the borrowed accents of other poets. But it was not only the apprentice's unsureness which provoked his early imitativeness; it was a search for a kind of anonymity, a burying of his own personality in a throng of predecessors. Donne builds sanctuaries for himself in his earliest poetry, barricades to repel the invasion of the world against his own private pride. For he was not nearly as cocksure of himself as the Lothian portrait suggests, that unsigned painting which Donne left in his will to his friend Robert Carr[4] and which shows him staring level-eyed and composed from beneath a black melancholic hat. Donne was always more open-faced in his portraits than he was in his early poetry. Most of his work from 1593 to 1598 is a collection of facades.

At first, Donne's insulation of himself against the world was of a gregarious and sociable kind. He had the camaraderie of youth, and he could play at being caustic and aloof. There is much of the undergraduate sport of drawing a line between the wisdom of the young scholar and the grossness of the world-beyond-the-walls in the first two satires and in the "Epithalamion made at Lincolnes Inne."[5] In these poems we hear the green anger of the student rebel who portrays himself free of the grubbiness and posturings of the nonacademic. In the "Epithalamion," for instance, quite possibly the earliest of Donne's poetry, we observe Donne setting up distorting perspectives, creating a veritable trompe-l'oeil, where the apparent depth of the scene being portrayed is finally revealed as a sham, all presided over by the mocking laughter of the poet, who carefully keeps in the background. At first glance a nuptial song honoring bride and bridegroom, Donne's poem introduces images not consistent with the promises of delight and fulfillment usual in a wedding poem. Grim tokens of death and debasement appear: the bridal couch is "Like to a grave"; the opened chancery doors become a "leane and hunger-starved wombe"; the act of love becomes a disemboweling. Behind the glowing surface of a city wedding are dank corridors of revulsion; and at the end of the corridors is Donne, who, on closer examination, turns out not to be celebrating a real wedding at all but to be poking scabrous fun at all money matches whereby London merchants would consolidate their wealth by marrying their daughters into the right circles. For the "Epithalamion made at Lincolnes Inne" is a masquerade through and through, Donne's contribution to the Midsummer Revels staged by the young law students, part and parcel of the eternal warfare between Town and Gown.[6] Hidden deep within the masquerade is Donne himself, giving voice to the conventional young scholar's distaste for the pragmatic. This is all great fun, not so obvious as to be coarse and not so recondite as to lose its sting. Impressive too is the talent which refuses to let the outrage suffocate the sensual aspects of the imagined nuptial rites. There's no tunnel vision here; the bride may be only a fixture in this mangled version of love, but we're not permitted to overlook "that warm balme-breathing thigh." The combination of scorn, sensuality, and immediacy is vintage Donne, indicative already of his great mature manner. If the attitude of the "Epithalamion" is a commonplace of the young, the poetry certainly is not.

Another forecast of the later poetry is the way that Donne introduces the image of the "strange Hermaphrodite," the bride and bridegroom so completely joined that they become the androgynous One. Like Aristophanes in Plato's *Symposium*, Donne is toying with the notion of a bisexual unity; in the later poetry such a notion will be more than a toy.[7]

What is largely a game in the "Epithalamion" is more

serious in its near-contemporaries, the first two satires. The
basic pose of "Satyre I" and "Satyre II" is similar to that of
the "Epithalamion," for again we see the fresh scholar (now
pretending to be a grave elder philosopher) disdaining the
world of the market place and, added to it, the court. There is
even a fortress in the first satire, the refuge of the study,
which is a barricade against the world.

> Leave mee, and in this standing woodden chest,
> Consorted with these few bookes, let me lye
> In prison, and here be coffin'd, when I dye.
>
> (ll. 2–4)[8]

Donne will build many such fortresses—he will build them
out of eyes, and beds, and Bible texts; this is the first. The
great merit of this hermitage is its stability, for outside is all
flux and all change.

> Shall I leave all this constant company,
> And follow headlong, wild uncertaine thee?
>
> (ll. 11–12)

Of course, he does. He shuts the door on his strained-after
image (compounded of scholarship, asceticism, and a thirst for
quiet) and follows the fledgling courtier. The Donne in the
poem follows the Donne out of the poem; he accompanies
the man that Sir Richard Baker remembered. The personality
Donne wants to be confronts the personality he might be, as
though he recognized that he was a secret sharer of the
enemy's position. A personality begins to separate itself from
its creator, and even to look on its creator as the adversary.
The first satire is no schizophrenic idyll; it's a stock contest
between the sage and the fop. But to admit the obvious
doesn't prevent the poem from being the earliest dramatization of a recurrent theme in Donne's writings, the alienation
of the man within. In the "Epithalamion" Donne is fashion-

ably alienated from the iron age; that alienation is also in the first satire, but to it is added the alienation of two selves.

The paradox of simultaneous dual existence perhaps accounts for Donne's manipulation of time in this satire. For Donne tyrannizes over time; after 1601 he controls time, he contrasts linear time and atemporal time, real time and dream time, time that moves and destroys and time that remains and protects. Of all his successes and bequests to literature, his manipulation of time for symbolic purposes is not the least. Here, in his earliest work, he is conservative, and almost hesitantly controls and adjusts different kinds of time. But control and adjust them he does, so that narrative time and dramatic time overlap, contradict one another, complement and erase one another. The ambiguities of existence are matched by the ambiguities of time within the poem.

The satire begins in the dramatic present. The diatribe against the dandy who would lure him out of "this standing woodden chest" into the foppishness of the world continues in the present for sixty-six lines. At this point, the dramatic present ("Away thou fondling motley humorist," "I shut my chamber doore, and come, lets goe") is replaced by a durative present which fogs the difference between past and present:

> Now we are in the street; He first of all
> Improvidently proud, creepes to the wall,
> And so imprisoned, and hem'd in by mee
> Sells for a little state his libertie.
>
> (ll. 67–70)

Once in the street, it is the continuum of an ever-recurring presentness, not a dramatic presentness, which prevails. Every fine silken painted fool, every grin, smack, and shrug, by a slight manipulation of tense is made to seem naggingly persistent rather than single and thus endurable. Until line

eighty-two, we're treated to the impression that this foolishness has gone on and on, a limited repertory of absurdity.

From line eighty-three to the end, time sequences overlap
one another in dizzying succession. We return to the dramatic
moment of the opening, with an exchange of dialogue:

> Now leaps he upright, Joggs me, & cryes, Do you see
> Yonder well favoured youth? Which? Oh, 'tis hee
> That dances so divinely.
>
> (ll. 83–85)

The dramatic present is interrupted by the narrative past:

> Oh, said I,
> Stand still, must you dance here for company?
> He droopt, we went, till one (which did excell
> Th'Indians, in drinking his Tobacco well)
> Met us; they talk'd; I whispered, let'us goe,
> 'T may be you smell him not, truely I doe.
>
> (ll. 85–90)

The narrative past fades, the mock-dramatic persistent present returns, for twelve lincs: "He heares not mee . . . He
followes," and the fop comes at last to his final escapade, now
a figure in a narrative and at the same time an actor in a
miniature drama:

> He answered not, but spy'd
> More men of sort, of parts, and qualities;
> At last his Love he in a windowe spies,
> And like light dew exhal'd, he flings from mee
> Violently ravish'd to his lechery.
> Many were there, he could command no more;
> He quarrell'd, fought, bled; and turn'd out of dore
> Directly came to mee hanging the head,
> And constantly a while must keepe his bed.
>
> (ll. 104–112)

Past, present, and future are telescoped together in nine lines, capping the excursion into the complexities of time. What is real past, or where is real present, what persists and what evanesces is the issue which commands; and the relativism of time becomes an emblem for the conflict of roles within the poem. The foolish lover, the would-be courtier, is at the mercy of time; he must move in whatever time wrinkle the narrator chooses to assign him. The speaking voice, on the other hand, controls time, bending it to his will and making it dance to his music. The metronome of the couplet form provides the only static time in the entire poem.

In the androgyny of the "Epithalamion made at Lincolnes Inne" Donne let loose a major symbol of his later poetry; in the first satire he forecasts a technique he will quite spectacularly perfect in the third phase of his poetic life, the phase of the later poems of *Songs and Sonnets*.

It's difficult not to think of the second satire[9] as a companion piece to the first. These are the only two satires of precisely the same length; the mask that Donne puts on (rich in years, wisdom, and grace) is identical in each poem; and his targets in both satires have a curious resemblance to the Donne outside the poems. The first and second satires are, in a way, directed against Donne himself; they are ironically suicidal. In the first satire Donne skewers the very neat visitor of ladies. In the second satire this descendant of Thomas More impales "poor, disarm'd . . . Papists, not worth hate"; the author of "The Baite" contemns "One [who] would move Love by rithmes"; this man who revitalizes Ovid snaps at the writer

> who (beggarly) doth chaw
> Others wits fruits, and in his ravenous maw
> Rankly digested, doth those things out-spue,
> As his owne things.
>
> (ll. 25–28)

This fledgling lawyer, Master of Revels at Lincoln's Inn and author of the "Epithalamion," snarls at Coscus, "a Lawyer, which was (alas) of late/ But a scarce Poët."

The roll call of fools in the second satire is full and boisterous: rhymesters, theatrical poets, plagiarists, poetasters, shysters, libertines. Lively though the list may be, the second satire has none of the tautness of the first. It is merely a compendium, an assembling of leftover victims that the first satire missed. The second is to the first as the third book of *Gulliver's Travels* is to the other three, a gallery of follies raced through without any particular finesse. The controlled chaos of the first satire is missing here; the stunning juggling of time for symbolic effect is nowhere to be seen. One of the most prestigious of manuscripts, the O'Flaherty (Harvard College Library, MS. Eng. 966/5), and two somewhat less honorable manuscripts (British Museum, Add. MS. 25707, and Bridgewater MS., Huntington Library, MS. EL 6893) entitle the first satire as "Satyre the Second" or "Satyre 2." The nomenclature is tantalizing, tempting us to see the second satire as an experiment brought to a success in the first. But the two poems would seem to be irreversible: all seventeenth-century editors and the majority of the manuscripts rank them in one-two order, as here. A technique had been perfected in the first satire, and the fools that were left over would have to rest content being cut down by more traditional weapons of raillery; the second satire survives as the tamest of the five Donne wrote.

The ambivalences that appear in these early poems—conservatism and rebellion, egotism and self-laceration, involvement and seclusion—were partly forced on Donne the poet by Donne the recusant. So long as there was any lingering allegiance to the interdicted religion of Rome, Donne could operate only on the fringes of the world that was symbolized by the court. Defined by law as an outsider, he vented his disappointments by striking at the very thing he admired but could not join, the circle of power. With the exception of the third, all Donne's satires have one quarry: the court, its officers, its attendants and hangers-on, and its functions. The anticourt attitude is traditional enough in the first satire not to have stung severely; the court could not be entirely blamed for the fops that swarmed around it, and Donne merely rejuvenates Roger Ascham's sixteenth-century Italianate Englishman in the mercurial friend. But the second satire comes closer to the throne, and the polite ignoring of the Queen doesn't do much to temper the imprudence of the lines:

> to every suitor lye in every thing,
> Like a Kings favourite, yea like a King; . . .
> Bastardy abounds not in Kings titles, nor
> Symonie and Sodomy in Churchmens lives,
> As these things do in him; . . .
>
> (ll. 69–76)

The virulence comes in larger doses in the fourth satire:[10]

> As prone to all ill, and of good as forget-
> full, as proud, as lustfull, and as much in debt,
> As vaine, as witlesse, and as false as they
> Which dwell at Court, . . .
>
> (ll. 13–16)

> Aretines pictures have made few chast;
> No more can Princes courts, though there be few
> Better pictures of vice, teach me vertue.
>
> (ll. 70–72)

> At home in wholesome solitarinesse
> My precious soule began, the wretchednesse
> Of suiters at court to mourne, and a trance
> Like his, who dreamt he saw hell, did advance
> It selfe on mee, Such men as he saw there,

I saw at court, and worse, and more; Low feare
Becomes the guiltie, not the accuser; Then,
Shall I, nones slave, of high borne, or rais'd men
Feare frownes? And, my Mistresse Truth, betray thee
To th'huffing braggart, puft Nobility?

(ll. 155–164)

Goe through the great chamber (why is it hung
With the seaven deadly sinnes?).

(ll. 231–232)

The fifth, and perhaps the bitterest of the satires,[11] laments the grinding abuses of the law, and nearly obliges the aging Queen to accept the responsibility:

Greatest and fairest Empresse, know you this?
Alas, no more than Thames calme head doth know
Whose meades her armes drowne, or whose corne o'rflow.

(ll. 28–30)

It was quite possibly this accelerating contempt for court (and even crown) that at first blocked John Marriott's inclusion of the five satires in the 1633 edition of Donne's poetry. But the objection was silently withdrawn and the poems did, of course, appear. The servants of Charles I, devoted though they were to the mystique of royalty, doubtless saw no threat to the Stuart court in these raids of two reigns ago. The satires slipped by the Stationers' Register exception, and Marriott printed the poems.

But the *Elegies* was another matter. Five of the undoubted thirteen love elegies were prohibited from publication in 1633. Two of the expected poems appeared (but without proper dispensation by the licenser) in 1635, i.e., "The Bracelet" and "On his Mistris." Two more, "To his Mistris Going to Bed" and "Loves Progress," were printed in the last of the

seventeenth-century editions of the poetry, 1669, and "Loves
Warre" never appeared until 1802.[12]

It was not a flirting with political affairs that brought these
five elegies under the particular displeasure of the licenser, Sir
Henry Herbert, as was probably the case with the satires; nor
was it the brutal iconoclasm of the poems. If anything, the
elegies that Marriott was allowed to print outstrip the interdicted poems in their shock value. In "Tutelage," Donne
intimates that the sex act is equivalent to knowledge of good
and evil, and proffers himself as Creator and the woman as a
fleshly *hortus conclusus*:

> [I] have with amorous delicacies
> Refin'd thee, into a blis-full paradise.
> Thy graces and good words my creatures bee;
> I planted knowledge and lifes tree in thee.
> (ll. 23–26)[13]

"The Comparison" is calculatedly gross:

> Ranke sweaty froth thy Mistresse brow defiles,
> Like spermatique issue of ripe menstruous boiles.
> (ll. 7–8)

The plea for sexual license in "Change" is as firm and explicit
as possible:

> all beasts change when they please,
> Shall women, more hot, wily, wild than these,
> Be bound to one man, . . .
> Waters stincke soone, if in one place they bide,
> And in the vast sea are worse putrifi'd:
> But when they kisse one banke, and leaving this
> Never looke backe, but the next banke doe kisse,
> Then are they purest; . . .
> (ll. 11–13, 31–35)

The lessons in love that are woven into "The Perfume," "Jealousie," "Recusancy," and "Tutelage" (so credible that Edmund Gosse read them as autobiographical confessions) constitute a handbook of seduction and initiation into the society of Eros. The paradoxical praise of ugliness in "The Anagram" is as sadistic as Jonson's attack on a certain lady-in-waiting:

> Shee, whose face, like clouds, turnes the day to night,
> Who, mightier than the sea, makes Moores seem white,
> Who, though seaven yeares, she in the Stews had laid,
> A Nunnery durst receive, and thinke a maid,
> And though in childbirths labour she did lie,
> Midwifes would sweare, 'twere but a tympanie,
> Whom, if shee'accuse her selfe, I credit lesse
> Then witches, which impossibles confesse,
> Whom Dildoes, Bedstaves, and her Velvet Glasse
> Would be as loath to touch as Joseph was: . . .
>
>   ("The Anagram," ll. 45–54)

> I am no States-man, and much lesse Divine,
>   For bawdry, 'tis her language, and not mine.
> Farthest I am from the Idolatrie
>   To stuffes and Laces, those my Man can buy.
> And trust her I would least, that hath forswore
>   In Contract twice, what can shee perjure more?
> Indeed, her Dressing some man might delight,
>   Her face there's none can like by Candle light.
> Not he, that should the body have, for Case
>   To his poore Instrument, now out of grace.
>
>   ("An Epigram on The Court Pucell," ll. 25–34)

It was probably not the witty licentiousness that offended in the disapproved elegies, for those that were admitted into print aren't very far, if at all, behind them in their unabashed hedonism, their delight in sexual prowess, and their contempt for the physically unattractive. It is curious that four of the five renegade elegies explore the paradox of carnality and theology. In these four elegies we have the first appearance of a refrain of the later poetry, love as an exquisite passage from the profane to the sacred. Long before the great sermons on divine love, Donne will have put together a liturgy of human love. In these four elegies he toys with the paradox, but he will shortly put aside the playfulness. What will become for him canonical is for the moment strategically blasphemous.

The unique elegy here is "On his Mistris," and there is nothing occult in the reasons for its having been refused. The objection was probably to the lines:

> Th' indifferent Italian, as wee passe
> His warme land, well content to thinke thee page,
> Will haunt thee, with such lust and hideous rage
> As Lots faire guests were vext: . . .
>
> (ll. 38–41)

The two lines about the dildoes, bedstaves, and velvet glass in "The Anagram" were omitted in the 1633 edition, and the entire "On his Mistris" with its allusions to perversions was held in abeyance for two years, until the second edition of the poems. It's ironic that it should have been details of unnatural sexuality that stood in the way of early publication. Like Shakespeare, the Donne of the poetry had nothing but contempt for variations on the sport of love. He mocked Aretino's experimentalism in the fourth satire; he's definite about the "right true end of love" in "Loves Progress"; and in "To his Mistris Going to Bed" he specifies male dominance in the love act.

"The Bracelet" (perhaps the earliest of the elegies), on the other hand, is laced with theological parodies. Not only does Donne burlesque the whole idea of celestial hierarchies by

punning on "angels" as Elizabethan gold pieces and hiero-
phanies ("Pity these Angels yet; their dignities/Passe Vertues, Powers, and Principalities," ll. 77–78); but he assigns
to his mistress soteriological power, letting the woman play
the role of God the Father and the lost bracelet act out the
parts of Apostles, martyrs, and even Christ the Redeemer:

Shall these twelve innocents [i.e., the cost of the bracelet] by thy
    severe
Sentence (dread Judge) my sins great burden beare?
Shall they be damn'd, and in the furnace throwne,
And punisht for offences not their owne?
. . . But thou art resolute; Thy will be done.

(ll. 17–20, 79)

This is too close to sacred writ to have escaped Sir Henry-
Herbert.

The overlapping of human and divine analogues is more
subtly done in the other three outlaw elegies, "Loves Warre,"
"Loves Progress," and "To his Mistris Going to Bed," and the
subtlety grows out of the single emblematic figure who appears in all three poems. This is the figure of the pilgrim, a
spiritual type as old as Exodus and as recent as Spenser's
Guyon.[14] It's frustrating not to be able to date the third
satire[15] specifically, for there Donne gives a serious sketch of
the pilgrim, and it would be interesting to note Donne acting
as his own literary tradition. Certainly the third satire does
adapt the symbol of the man on an expedition to both serious
and satiric uses. The quest is for Truth, imaged as "Our
Mistresse faire Religion," existing but maddeningly inacces-
sible "On a huge hill,/ Cragged, and steep" (ll. 79–80). Only
the most venturesome searcher will find her out:

hee that will
Reach her, about must, and about must goe;
And what the hills suddennes resists, winne so.

(ll. 80–82)

The misguided fools—the Catholic Mirreus, the Protestant Crantz, the complacent Graius, agnostic Phrygius, and syncretist Graccus—are false pilgrims, substituting the claims of tradition, authority, or untested reason for the experiential search for truth. The primacy of existence is Donne's argument in the third satire, and he locates that argument in his pilgrim.

Was the generic idea of the search for truth then localized in the search for the truth of love? Did the remote woman of the third satire metamorphose into the sensuously explored woman of "Loves Progress"? Unfortunately, the priority of the third satire over the pilgrim elegies cannot be determined. The disavowal of authoritarian religion and particularly the breaking of affiliations with Roman Catholicism would certainly have occurred before the years with Sir Thomas Egerton, whose office as Lord Keeper would militate against having a Papist on his staff; but there is no strong evidence either for or against pushing the satire back as far as 1593. The only prudent course is to envision Donne preoccupied with the pilgrim figure, now as a seeker of the truth of religion, and again as a seeker of the truth of love, with an experienced apprehension of wisdom the common goal.

Once again there are fantasies in conflict. In the earliest "Epithalamion," and in the first two satires, there are covert images of a figure in sanctuary protecting himself from the world outside. The persona of those three poems is immured safely with his peers at the Inns of Court, in the hermitage of his study, in the enclosure of a Horatian golden mean. Now, and almost contemporaneously, we have the figure of the moving man, the explorer who has moved out of sanctuary and undertakes an exploration of experience. This figure traditionally inhabits religious literature, but Donne puts him on paths that are both religious (the third satire) and erotic (the "quest" elegies). The result is an aura of religiosity hovering over the most carnal of imagined episodes.

The briefest of the three elegies under discussion, "Loves Warre," concentrates on a military expedition as central image. The lady is the besieged city, the speaker the attacking army; and the phallic symbolism of all the machinery of war is given full display. The foreplay and the consummation of love are all analogized to the tactics of battle:

> Here let mee warre; in these armes let mee lye;
> Here let mee parlee, batter, bleede, and dye.
>
> (ll. 29–30)

Significantly (in light of what Donne will do with the motif in later poems), there is a disjunction between true and false warriors, lovers and nonlovers:

> Other men warre that they their rest may gaine,
> But we will rest that wee may fight againe.
> Those warres the ignorant, these th'experienc'd love;
> There wee are alwayes under, here above.
> There engines far off breede a just true feare,
> Neare thrusts, pikes, stabs, yea bullets hurt not here.
>
> (ll. 33–38)

"Loves Progress" is a swaggering subversion of the *Pèlerinage de la vie*, the pilgrim's progress to eternity. Working with the image of the cosmographer and navigator (entirely suitable for a poet who perhaps saw Sir Francis Drake and who knew the redoubtable pilgrim Thomas Coryat[16]), Donne the amorist explores the whole exciting map of the woman's body, from the face to the breast to the navel, and then, reversing direction to follow the fairer route from foot to "the Centrique part" of love, he docks at his own New Jerusalem:

> He's an infernall God, and under ground
> With Pluto dwells, where gold and fyre abound.
>
> (ll. 29–30)

As an explorer, Donne knows where the greatest treasures lie: the odyssey of ll. 41–66 finds Canary and Madeira wines in her lips, pearls in her teeth, the romance of Hero and Leander in her breasts, the riches of India in her trunk. But the excitement of all this adventuring makes him a pretty poor navigator, for taken geographically, it's a crazy route that begins at Jerusalem (the woman's brow, l. 45), sails almost due west to the Canary Isles (her lips, ll. 51–53) through the Mediterranean, then doubles back and moves north up the Aegean to the Dardanelles (her breasts, ll. 60–61), then south again to Jerusalem and an overland trip eastward to India (her trunk, l. 65), and then, still another reverse, back through the Mediterranean to the Atlantic Ocean (her navel, l. 66). "Loves Progress" is a topsy-turvy voyage to the Celestial City of carnal delight.

The pilgrimage that ends at a paradisal orgasm is more fully developed in "To his Mistris Going to Bed" than in any of the other elegies; and in the process Donne offers a tantalizing intimation of the mystique of love that develops throughout his career. The sense of love as self-immolation, love as an ecstatic auto-da-fé, makes its debut.

The city courtesan of the poem is early invested with sacerdotal powers, much like the lady of "The Bracelet" and "Loves Progress." She arrives like an angel, but an angel of flesh: "Thou Angel bring'st with thee/ A heaven like Mahomets Paradise" (11. 20–21). Her arrival transforms the bedchamber into a place of erotic worship, "love's hallow'd temple, this soft bed" (l. 18). She, too, is explored; she becomes both the journey and the quest:

> License my roving hands, and let them goe
> Behind, before, above, between, below.
> Oh my America, my new found lande, . . .
>
> (ll. 25–27)

Like the woman of the later *Anniversaries*, she is both the object and the wit, the thing discovered and the instrument of discovery.

As the speaker imagines her stepping from her clothes, the woman becomes pure spirit, stepping out of the fetters of the body. We hear an echo of the first satire:

> till our Soules be unapparrelled
> Of bodies, they from blisse are banished.
>
> ("Satyre I," ll. 43–44)

As celestial spirit, naked woman can now initiate lovers into the sacred mysteries forbidden to common men:

> Themselves are mystique bookes, which only wee
> Whom their imputed grace will dignify
> Must see reveal'd.
>
> (ll. 41–43)

The woman, promising Mahometan delights, is herself an *ecstasy*, angelic spirit standing forth (*ex stasis*) from the clothes-body. Once released, this houri transcends time and place, as all ecstatic states must:

> And whil'st our soules negotiate there,
> Wee like sepulchrall statues lay;
> All day, the same our postures were,
> And wee said nothing, all the day.
>
> ("The Exstasie," ll. 17–20)

The lover joins her in ecstasy; he transcends the material world (or expects that he will, if she would only hurry into bed). He yearns for the immersion of himself into the woman's body, which becomes the map to Paradise and then Paradise itself:

> How blest am I in this discovering thee.
> To enter in these bonds is to be free.
>
> (ll. 30–31)

Through her, the poet who had tyrannized over time in the first satire hopes to escape from time. The act of love (even under such businesslike conditions as the elegy hints at) becomes the fullest discovery of one's self and paradoxically the blissful extinction of self.

The idea that lovers inhabit a world different from the world of other men is here again, as it is in the related elegies and as it will be in the later love poetry. The difference between the attitude toward love here and in the later poetry is all in tone and belief: these earlier explorations of the idea are ironic, a hyperbolic exploitation of the concept for dramatic purposes. Later, it will be more restrained, barely ironic. For now, this is brilliant boudoir bawdry; it will become an article of a strong faith.

Through all the poetry of this early period there is a distinct sense of play acting. Even at his counterfeit best, Donne resists surrendering himself to the situation within the poetry. The scandalized idealist and the chest-thumping male are wonderful stage creations. In no sense at all is this indicative of a coldness or lack of passion. Rather, Donne seems to have taken extraordinary pains to preserve the distance between himself and the figure in the poems, as if he were reluctant to commit himself too deeply. There are moments when he comes very close to those scenes of the later poetry in which the stubborn creator is absorbed into the created personality. In later poems like "The Good-morrow" or "The Dreame" the shield between the world within and the world without is shattered, and such monistic interludes abound in the later work. But the interludes are achieved only by denying the distance between self and poem, and the early Donne is still too young, too egotistic, too aware of the solipsistic *I* to submit himself to anything, let alone his own creations. And so we have a bright parade of personae, actors in small dramas of fantasy that don't really impinge on the private territories beyond conscious fantasizing. The membrane between the private, concerned mind and the theatre of the poems is sometimes stretched extremely thin, as in the pilgrim elegies; but at no time in this period does it break. Even those elegies which clamor to be read as confessionals, as excursions of the literal self into verse (for instance, "On his Mistris" or "His Picture"), refuse to bend to such an interpretation; and all attempts to read the first as a tribute to Ann More or the second as a Cadiz valediction must fall to the ground. There is simply no internal or external evidence sufficient to support an autobiographical reading. Donne is terribly efficient in protecting himself from exposure in the early years.

This is just as true of the early works in the *Songs and Sonnets* as it is of the *Elegies* or the first of the *Satires*. In the lyric, as in the other genres with which he experimented, Donne achieves an anonymity by electing to wear masks and assume stances that were long in the public domain. It's no longer possible to see the Donne of "The Curse" or "The Flea" or "The Paradox" as the same man who "open'd Us a Mine/ Of rich and pregnant phansie."[17] The richness and pregnancy are indisputable, but that it was Donne who opened the mine is not true. At nearly every turn we confront the shadow of a prototype. Donne has several companions-at-arms, mute collaborators who can share responsibility for things said and attitudes adopted. As in the *Satires* and the *Elegies*, the figures of Horace, Martial, and Ovid stalk through the early poems of the *Songs and Sonnets*, and even Petrarch and his followers are not far removed from the scene.[18] There is even anonymity of technique: nine of the early lyrics are, either intentionally or functionally, associated with musical settings. The manuscripts which make up the Group II collection[19] indicate that "Goe, and catche a falling starre," "The Message," and "Sweetest Love, I do not goe" were all written to "certain ayres which were made before," while another manuscript notation states that "The Bait," "Communitie," and "Confined Love" were also specifically composed for a musical format.[20] "The Expiration" appeared, set for voice and lute, in Alphonso Ferrabosco's *Ayres* in 1609;[21] William Corkine published "Breake of Day," to be accompanied by voice and viol, in his *Second Book of Ayres* in 1612;[22] while William Lawes arranged a musical setting for "The Apparition."[23] There was no intention of intimacy in these poems; they were made deliberately accessible by being designed for the commonwealth of music. Giorgione's "The Concert" comes to mind: the central figure of that painting would be likely to reveal any intended intimacy, but the workman at the right of the canvas or the aesthete to the left would see to it that any intimacy would be clapperclawed to death. "The Concert" allegorizes the results of communal song, the depersonalizing of private emotion in the interest of harmony. And that is what happens in these nine songs of Donne—their obvious musicality is still another way of keeping himself carefully remote from the action of the poetry.

In "The Triple Foole," Donne expressed a concern over someone like Giorgione's middle subject. Having brought his love under the reins of music, and so symbolically controlled it, he now confronts the danger that it (and he) might be publicized in the performance:

> But when I have done so,
>   Some man, his art and voice to show,
>   Doth set and sing my paine,
>   And by delighting many, frees againe
>   Griefe, which verse did restraine.
> To Love, and Griefe tribute of Verse belongs,
> But not of such as pleases when 'tis read,
>   Both are increased by such songs:
> For both their triumphs are so published,
> And I, which was two fooles, do so grow three;
> Who are a little wise, the best fooles be.
>
>   (ll. 12–22)

Donne sees a wisdom in letting song control passion, but is anxious lest he be exposed. "Who are a little wise, the best fooles be," but it is a calculated risk. Such anxieties over revealing himself or surrendering any part of himself to scrutiny are strewn through these early lyrics.

Closely related to the distancing by music, as far as its effect is concerned, is a unique and never-repeated point of view in two of the songs ("Confined Love" and "Breake of Day"). The usual rule in Donne's poetry is for the fictive "I" to be unmistakably, even aggressively, masculine (with the foreseeable result that the poetry is sometimes mistakenly read as autobiography). But in these two instances, the speaker is a woman, and a total separation between the literal and poetic states is guaranteed. Part of the reason for this departure from usual practice is probably the intention to startle: there's something priapic in putting into the mouth of a woman the same libertine speech that characterizes "Change" or "The Indifferent" or "Communitie." (Jonson knew the trick, too, as witness the scurrilous tenth of his "Celebration of Charis in ten Lyrick Peeces," or "A Song Apologetique" and "In defence of their Inconstancie," both written "In the person of Woman-kind."[24]) But it's more than shock value that inhabits the point of view in Donne's two poems "in the person of womankind"; it's also a kind of anonymity.

In the early twenty-seven of the *Songs and Sonnets*,[25] Donne wards off any attempt to touch his privacy. In "The Curse" he turns away any maneuver to discover in the poetry a revelation of his extrapoetic world:

> Who ever guesses, thinks, or dreames he knowes
> Who is my mistris, wither by this curse.
>
> (ll. 1–2)

He gives away nothing of himself; imperiously, he only demands and takes. In "The Prohibition," he forbids that he
should be loved or hated; and he relaxes his interdiction only
so that love and hate can neutralize one another, leaving him
untouched and unscathed:

> Yet, love and hate mee too,
> So, these extreames shall neythers office doe;
> Love mee, that I may die the gentler way;
> Hate mee, because thy love's too great for mee;
> Or let these two, themselves, not me decay;
> So shall I live, thy Stage, not Triumph bee;
> Then, least thy love, hate and mee thou undoe,
> *Oh let mee live, yet love and hate mee too.*
>
> (ll. 17-24)

"The Indifferent" concludes with a malediction against any
woman who would try to possess and command him entirely:
"since you will be true,/ You shall be true to them, who'are
false to you" (ll. 26-27). The four poems addressed to the
god of love ("Loves Usury," "Loves Diet," "Loves Exchange," and "Loves Deitie") are all informed by the craving
to remain intact, unsurprised into any passion that would
make him vulnerable. "Loves Usury" seals a bargain which
will keep him free for now: submission to love is, Faust-like,
postponed to a latter age, but until then "let my body raigne"
(l. 5). "Loves Diet" exults over the fact that he has been able
to keep love from really touching him:

> I spring a mistresse, sweare, write, sigh and weepe:
> And the game kill'd, or lost, goe talke, and sleepe.
>
> (ll. 29-30)

In "Loves Exchange" he begs that if it should happen that he
fall victim to a beauty which "Can call vow'd men from

cloisters, dead from tombes" (l. 32), then let him forever be
ignorant of the fact that he has been so trapped:

> Let me not know that others know
> That she knowes my paine, least that so
> A tender shame make me mine owne new woe.
>
> (ll. 19–21)

He defies the god of love, he mocks him for his inability to
be a complete tyrant. Donne will not assent to any dismemberment of himself for love or by love, since "Rack't carcasses
make ill Anatomies" (l. 42). The progression of Donne's
argument in "Loves Deitie" is toward a protection of the
uninvolved self from all the snares of love. It is a sad destiny
to love one who does not return that love, and surely this was
not the original plan; but perhaps it's just as well, for under
the current laws I'm free to enjoy the sport and free to break
loose from love whenever I choose: it might be "A deeper
plague, to make her love me too" (l. 25).

Four of the poems in this early set capitalize on the double
sense of *elegy*, and combine the meaning of "lamentation for
the dead" and the meaning of "lyric of unrequited love."
These four are "The Apparition," "The Dampe," "The
Legacie," and "The Will." In each of them, the lover laments
for himself imagined as dead, excoriates the woman for having
induced his death by her cruelty, but then, in a most un-
Petrarchan way, rejoices that he has not been really wounded,
shaken, or diminished by love. "The Apparition" promises the
murderess that his ghost will come and exert unspeakable
powers over her. "The Dampe," after embroidering, for two
stanzas, the courtly and conventional image of the destroying
woman and the martyred lover, brushes it aside. The last
stanza rejects the hyperboles of love as extinction and demands only sexual congress: "Kill mee as Woman, let mee
die/ As a meere man" (ll. 21–22). "The Legacie" is a

masterpiece of misdirection and unexpected virulence against love. The poem begins as delicately and caressingly as any of the valedictions:

> When I dyed last, and Deare, I dye
>   As often as from thee I goe,
>   Though it be an houre agoe,
> And Lovers houres be full eternity, . . .
>   (ll. 1–4)

But by the end of the poem, the lament has become a snarl, and the legacy becomes a cozening and a denial that the woman ever truly invaded his susceptibilities:

> Yet I found something like a heart,
>   But colours it, and corners had,
>   It was not good, it was not bad,
> It was intire to none, and few had part.
> As good as could be made by art
>   It seem'd, and therefore for our losses sad,
> I thought to send that heart in stead of mine,
> But oh, no man could hold it, for twas thine.
>   (ll. 17–24)

"The Will" is a series of ironic reversals, all culminating in an attack on a beauty that threatens to overpower a lover. In the first stanza, he bequeaths treasures where they are not needed (eyes to Argus, tongue to fame, ears to ambassadors, tears to women and the sea); in the second, he leaves bequests not receivable by the heirs (constancy to the planets, truth to the Court, honesty to Jesuits, thoughtfulness to fools, money to a Capuchin); and so on, for five stanzas, and at each step he equates the absurdities of the will to the absurdities of love. Finally, having subverted the whole intention of any last will and testament, he ends by subverting love itself; and the

lament becomes a rejoicing that, once again, he cannot be
touched by love.

> Therefore I'll give no more; But I'll undoe
> The world by dying; because love dies too.
> Then all your beauties will bee no more worth
> Then gold in Mines, where none doth draw it forth;
> And all your graces no more use shall have
>   Then a Sun dyall in a grave.
>   Thou Love taughtst mee, by making mee
> Love her, who doth neglect both mee and thee,
> To'invent, and practise this one way, to'annihilate all three.
>   (ll. 46–54)

Noli me tangere with a vengeance.

When he is not making armor for himself against any love
which might threaten his own singularity, Donne is denying
his own humanity, and so denying all the vulnerability of
humanity. There are several poems of metamorphosis among
these lyrics where the personality of the poet dissolves, leaving
behind only an object or a wraith, immune to invasion by
another. In "The Expiration" he becomes a vapor; an epitaph
and tomb in "The Paradox." He is reduced to a portrait in
"Witchcraft by a Picture"; a shattered mirror in "The Broken
Heart." The surrealist logic of "The Flea" comes to a climax
in the assertion that after love the woman will "find'st not thy
selfe, nor mee the weaker now" (l. 24).

This insistence that one need not hand over an atom of
one's own self epitomizes the Donne of the first phase.
Throughout these earlier works in the *Songs and Sonnets*, he
holds himself intact, refusing to give away anything. Constantly, through his themes, his techniques, and points of
view, he builds a fortress around his own ego. The man in
these poems is proud to the point of arrogance, absolutely
refusing any compromise with those around him. And yet, for

all the tones of masculine dominance and delight in his insularity, this is also a threatened man. Sensitively aware of alarums and excursions against his own defenses, he protests rather too much about his own completeness and inviolability.

Those remaining poems of the first period, 1593-1598, are all roughly contemporaneous. The fourth satire was probably written in late 1596 or 1597; the fifth satire must have been written during the years of his service with Egerton (1598-1601), and the enthusiasm Donne expresses for

> You Sir, whose righteousnes she loves, whom I
> By having leave to serve, am most richly
> For service paid
>
> (ll. 31-33)

suggests a 1598 date: it has the ring of initial delight in a prized situation. The two verse letters to Christopher Brooke ("The Storme" and "The Calme"), as well as two to Sir Henry Wotton ("Sir, more than kisses" and "Here's no more news"), were all written between 1597 and 1598. It now seems probable that the funeral elegy "Sorrow, who to this house scarce knew the way" is to be dated 1595.[26] There are no prose letters that can be certainly dated in these years, nothing in propria persona. In only one of these is there the slightest sign that Donne's taut solitariness is being relaxed.

The funeral elegy, probably written to Lionel Cranfield on the death of his father, illustrates Donne's acumen in remarking to Robert Ker, much later, "I did best when I had least truth for my subjects."[27] It suffers from the same faults as do most of Donne's epicedes and obsequies, beginning with those on Lady Markham and Mrs. Boulstred, through that on Lord Harrington, down to the elegy on the Marquis of Hamilton in 1625. There is a note of strain, an overreaching for cleverness that suffocates any possible effect of personal grief. For this, of course, Donne cannot be blamed. He was a

dramatic poet, not a theatrical one; he could not "tear a
passion to tatters, to very rags, to split the ears of the ground-
lings, who for the most part are capable of nothing but
inexplicable dumb-shows and noise."[28] When he eventually
unleashes himself in his writings, he chooses his own occasions, not those handed to him.

"Sorrow, who to this house scarce knew the way" would be
an impressive elegy if we did not know that Donne wrote it.
The concept of a startling reversal of ordinary events (established in the first line) controls every detail in the poem.
Each image is basically a paradox, a microcosm of the opening
irony of the stranger Sorrow becoming heir to the dead man's
estate. Cranfield's life spoke loudly through his good works,
and now the survivors are left mute; his fortitude in life
forbade tears, and now the living are all tears. All who
depended on him must now wither through the same agent
that once supported them; having ventured their all in him,
they now lose all. His children are his portraits, but not really
portraits, rather mortuary statues, supplying him with a ready-
made mausoleum.

This is a forecast of what Donne will do so brilliantly in
"The Autumnal,"—the anatomizing of an opening motif in a
series of paradoxes. But "The Autumnal" goes beyond cleverness, and "Sorrow, who to this house" does not. It is a witty
execution of a difficult technique, a display of an artist's craft.
The objectification of grief belongs to the genre; in that lies
the therapeutic quality of all the rituals of death. It was a
genre that the Donne of these years could afford to experiment with, for it carried no threat of encroachment on
himself.

In the first of the verse letters to Brooke and the two to
Wotton, Donne carefully presents himself not as an involved
participant but as an observer. "The Storme" and "The
Calme" both describe horrendous moments of the Cadiz

voyage; in the first Donne portrays the scene in terms of "the others" on the voyage or else loses himself in the crowd of "we." He begins "The Storme"[29] by negating himself entirely: "Thou which art I, ('tis nothing to be soe)." As he describes the storm, it is *our* fleet, *our* sails, and *we* who watched the rising wind. It was the *I* which observed the tempest, but when the force of the storm hit the ship, it was the *others* who were coffined in their cabins or hideously gazed at the sea from the hatches or were being deafened by the clamor. It is as if Donne were at the eye of the storm, barely buffeted, but sharply observing all that happened around him. In a sense, "The Storme" is an emblem of Donne's whole career up to this moment.

It's altogether suitable that in our studying this most paradoxical of poets we should see "The Calme"[30] as a consummate paradox. The title belies its importance in the early canon. For the first time we have Donne standing undisguised and unaccompanied in his poetry, and at the same time admitting to a cast of mind that will shortly haunt his poetry. From ll. 39-43, Donne speaks directly of himself—not himself as a latter-day Ovid or Horace, or an Anglicized *secentismo* wit. Giving his reasons for having accompanied Essex' fleet to Cadiz, he writes:

> Whether a rotten state, and hope of gaine,
> Or to disuse mee from the queasie paine
> Of being belov'd, and loving, or the thirst
> Of honour, or faire death, out pusht mee first,
> I lose my end: . . .
>
> (ll. 39-43)

The rotten state and hope of gain: there speaks the voice of the earliest satires. The queasy pain of loving and being loved: the voice of the *Elegies*. The thirst of honor: the soon-to-be solicitor of Egerton, then Somerset, then Buckingham. But "faire death"? There had been symbolic suicides in the early satires;[31] there will be symbolic death in "Twicknam Garden," "The Canonization," and "A Nocturnall upon S. Lucies Day"; and *Biathanatos* is a decade away. For just an instant, "O, yes, my lord; he wore his beaver up,"[32] and a shared epistle reveals a secret usually kept from public sight. In the most turbulent of the early works, there is nothing so unexpected as the unmasking in "The Calme." Jonson admired the poem and recited, for Drummond's edification, the lines "and in one place lay/Feathers and dust, to day and yesterday" (ll. 17–18). But the poem is far more than bright patches of memorable images; it is the reverse of Donne's poetic method as he has practiced it so far. In everything else, he carefully externalizes himself: a borrowed posture, a dramatized locale, a rhythm, a dispassionate genre. Here, in "The Calme," he carries an outside scene into himself, and the torpid seascape becomes an internal landscape, an image of his and the human condition.

> How little more alas
> Is man now, then before he was? he was
> Nothing; for us, wee are for nothing fit;
> Chance, or our selves still disproportion it.
> Wee have no power, no will, no sense; I lye,
> I should not then thus feel this miserie.
>
> (ll. 51–56)

Here is the same bitterness that will manifest itself in the *Metempsychosis*, the same relinquishing of the pride and assuredness of the earlier poetry. Donne's several conversions never come like thunderclaps on the road to Damascus (even though he evidently thought of his greatest conversion as akin to St. Paul's[33]), but like scouting parties in advance of battalions. In "The Calme" is the first clear sign of the second stage of Donne's evolution.

To go from this epistle to those written to Wotton is to exchange the new manner for the old. "Sir, more than kisses" is an adaptation of the satirist's mask to the rules of a courtly game. Grierson demonstrated[34] that this poem is part of a group: Francis Bacon, in imitation of two epigrams in the Greek Anthology (readily available in the paraphrase versions included in both *Tottel's Miscellany*, 1557, and Puttenham's *Arte of English Poesie*, 1589), had written "The World," a poetic discourse on the relative merits of court, country, and city. Wotton showed Donne Bacon's poem; Donne turned his hand to the game; and Wotton then replied to Donne's poem. It is very likely, to move ahead several years, that Donne's "The Primrose" is part of a similar esoteric debate,[35] wherein Donne and Sir Edward Herbert "competed" in verse and argued for different definitions of love. "Sir, more than kisses" is the same kind of jousting, a tournament of wit. Such a literary debate was not intended to engage the whole personality, but to produce compelling sophistries and refurbished clichés. It is modified applause which admits that Donne mastered the rules of the game. We're not startled to learn that the city is a sepulcher, the country a desert, and the court a gathering of devils; and the triplets of the next epistle, "Here's no more news," advance not a whit from the conventional slandering of the court as we might find it all the way from Skelton to Rochester. These first two of the letters to Wotton are, for Donne, five-finger exercises, nothing more.

The fourth and fifth satires mark the end of Donne's first stage. The fourth was probably written between the voyages with Essex,[36] the fifth during his service with Egerton.[37] The works after this date are significantly different. The fantasies will take different shapes, new themes will appear; and by 1610 the contours of the early Donne are only faintly discernible in the personality who is created in the great valedictions or the controversial prose works. The fourth and fifth satires are the last utterances of the self-conscious renegade. The difference between them and the post-1601 works is the same as that between the Lothian portrait and the Isaac Oliver portrait, between a man partly hidden in shadow and a man fully revealed.

The mask of the renegade is most carefully adjusted in the fourth satire. It is characteristic of all the satires that Donne plays the outsider, the man who stands scornfully apart from the world he describes. This is a common satiric device, of course; but Donne is distinguished for the variety with which he can play the ironic commentator. First he is the scholar, then the Horatian sage, the skeptic, and the idealist. In the fourth satire he plays his most dangerous game, that of the recusant. The insulation which Donne sets between himself and the world is Roman Catholicism; this is the most insistently renegade of all the satires. There's little likelihood that Donne was literally a Papist as late as 1597, and so it is all the more revealing to find him brazenly parading as a Catholic in this poem. What better way to project himself as conspicuously unlike the foolish Town and Court than to pose as an outlaw?

The satire is packed with tokens of his contrived outlawry. He begins with an allusion to the Roman Catholic viaticum, the rites of final Communion: "Well! I may now receive, and die" (l. 1). He accepts the doctrine of Purgatory, in flat violation of Protestant doctrine:

> My sinne
> Indeed is great, but I have beene in
> A Purgatorie, such as fear'd hell is
> A recreation to, and scarce map of this.
>
> (ll. 1–4)

He jabs at the statute which penalizes anyone attending a Catholic mass (ll. 8–10); he shows disgust for all the strangers who have been washed into England by the tides of Continental religious persecution (ll. 17–19); and he throws a bitter glance at the priest-hunting magistrate (ll. 28–29). He speaks as a man steeped in the theological literature of the Renaissance, and drops casual allusions to the champions on both sides of the Catholic-Protestant controversy: Paolo Giovio, Laurentius Surius, and "Some other Jesuits" among the Catholics, Beza and "two reverend men/ Of our two Academies" among the Protestants (ll. 48, 55–7). He scores a palpable hit on those paid informers who sought out recusants, as he notices the fop who

> whispered by Jesu, so often, that A
> Pursevant would have ravish'd him away
> For saying of our Ladies psalter; . . .
> (ll. 215–217)

(and some of the manuscripts make the indictment even stronger: for "pursevant" they read "Topcliffe," i.e., Richard Topcliffe, the torturer of Robert Southwell, the Jesuit missionary and poet). Medieval iconography makes a brief appearance: the braggadocio at court has "a face . . . as ill/ As theirs which in old hangings whip Christ" (ll. 225–226), and the great chamber at court is "hung/ With the seaven deadly sinnes" (ll. 231–232). He concludes with a reference that clarifies his allegiance to the renegade minority:

> Although I yet
> With *Macchabees* modestie, the knowne merit
> Of my worke lessen: yet some wise man shall,
> I hope, esteeme my writs Canonical.
> (ll. 241–244)

The allusion is to the conclusion of II Machabees, which in the Douay Version reads: "I also will here make an end of my narration. Which if I have done well, and as it becometh the history, it is what I desired: but if not so perfectly, it must be pardoned me." The Roman Catholic tradition, until very recently, has been to accept the Books of Machabees as canonical, and Donne's "wise man" is an allusion to those church councils which have insisted that these two books belong to the canon of Sacred Scripture. The Anglican Church, on the other hand, defines Machabees as apocryphal, and the sixth of the Thirty-nine Articles states that "the Church doth read [the Apocryphal books] for example of life and instruction of manners; but yet doth it not apply them to establish any doctrine."[38] Donne's intimation that the Machabees are canonical sharpens the force of the analogy which he throws over the entire satire. Elizabeth's court is imaged as the court of Antiochus, wherein the sanctuary of God's chosen people was defiled and their kingdom despoiled; and the Catholic minority is identified with the Israelites, who ultimately rose from their humiliation and resanctified the holy places.

The device of providing a Biblical analogy at the very end of the satire is a brilliant stroke. Suddenly what had been a more or less anticipated diatribe assumes allegorical proportions. The court filled with strangers, the toadying courtiers, the gossip mongerers, the attendant ladies, the effeminate hangers-on, the braggarts, and the guards summons up memories of Jerusalem sacked, where "the virgins and the young men were made feeble, and the beauty of the women was changed. Every bridegroom took up lamentation: and the bride that sat in the marriage bed, mourned . . . and the city was made the habitation to strangers, and she became a stranger to her own seed, and her children forsook her" (I Machabees 1: 27–40). Standing on the edge of all this rapine is Donne, the exiled Israelite who waits for God's wrath to fall.

It's difficult to take any of this more seriously than the first two satires. Donne was no Savonarola, and there's more high comedy than moral outrage in the poem. The fourth satire looks ahead not to Bunyan but to Dryden, not to a serious equation between revelation and society but to a mock epic equation. It is an interesting and effective experimentation, but one which Donne will not repeat. The personality of a prophet, even a burlesque prophet, is not one which Donne chose to adopt for any length of time.

The similarities between the fourth and fifth satires encourage the notion that they were written quite close to one another. The basic image of the raped court appears again; the outrage against the informer is repeated; and Donne draws on the Old Testament for his concluding analogies. In the corrupted courts of England, beauteous Law has been turned into a strumpet, and the legalistically choked courts are trying to outdo Aaron in the complexities of their office. As high priest of the Israelites, Aaron was clothed in truly wondrous garments, "a breastplate, and an ephod, and a robe, and a broidered coat, a mitre, and a girdle. . . . And thou shalt put in the breastplate of judgment the Urim and the Thummim; and they shall be upon Aaron's heart, when he goeth in before the Lord" (Exodus 28:4,30). This Jezebel of English law wants still more glory, and ends up being smothered under formalities:

> Thou had'st much, and lawes Urim and Thummim trie
> Thou wouldst for more; and for all hast paper
> Enough to cloath all the great Carricks Pepper.
>
> (ll. 83–85)

The end result is that the law, in forgetting its dignity and becoming an instrument of persecution, will suffer the fate of Haman in the Book of Esther. Haman, a proud officer under King Ahasuerus, was enraged when Mordecai, one of the persecuted Jews, refused to bow down to him, and made plans to hang him from a gallows fifty cubits high. But Mordecai had defended the King by revealing a plot against him, and so the delicious irony of the book of Esther is accomplished: "Behold also the gallows fifty cubits high, which Haman had made for Mordecai, who had spoken good for the king, standing in the house of Haman. Then the king said, Hang him thereon. So they hanged Haman on the gallows that he had prepared for Mordecai" (Esther 7:9–10). As in the fourth satire, Donne represents himself as the dispossessed Jew, now as Mordecai; his warning to the throne is the satire itself. Egerton by implication is Harbonah, the chamberlain of Ahasuerus, who sees to it that true justice is executed against Haman.

Donne's characterization of himself is quite different from earlier versions. While he is still the outcast, he is also an active participant in the battle against folly. The tone of the invective is very unlike that of the other satires. "Thou shalt not laugh in this leafe, Muse" (l. 1). Nor will he only look on and berate, but like Mordecai he will act. "I . . . now be-ginne/ To know and weed out this enormous sinne" (ll. 31–34). Perhaps Donne was emboldened by his service with Egerton to think of himself as an active reformer; at any rate he was shortly to serve in the exceedingly brief Parliament of 1601. But there is nothing to indicate that Donne undertook any reforms as an M.P.—in fact, there's no record that he uttered a word. The approaching marriage to Ann More and the subsequent expulsion from Egerton's household put an end to Donne's career as a militant power at court. This fifth satire is the first and last time in all of his poetry that he will consider the role of the activist. He will, in certain of the prose letters, petition for such a role, but as a character in the literary canon he disappears once and for all.

From this moment on, external events will play an even more important part in Donne's creation of himself. He will be driven even more deeply into the laboratory of his poetry, and deprived of an identity in the public world, he will forge an identity in the private world of his imagination. There is a certain leisureliness in the evasive maneuvering of this first phase. Exiled by reason of his recusancy from university, ecclesiastic, or civil advancement, and by reason of his pride from compromise, he tended to dramatize his alienation, an alienation which was a good deal more psychological than it was social. But yet he had the time and above all the resiliency of his youth to forestall any panic in his search for himself. He tries on personalities with the aplomb of a man looking for a suitable wardrobe in Savile Row, and he discards them with the same ease as he dons them. In the years to come, however, Donne approaches his art not as an accumulation of artifacts and masks, but as a process, a continual and determined probing for the truth of himself.

FOR TWO YEARS, Donne and his wife remained at Pyrford in Surrey, dependent on the kindness of Sir Francis Woolley; and his letters and those of his poems which can be reasonably assigned to these years reflect his melancholy and depression. When Donne was at last able, sometime after 1606, to establish a household of his own at Mitcham, from which he could commute to London, it was a mean and cramped place. When Donne referred to it, it was "my hospital at Mitcham."

Between the residency at Pyrford and the move to Mitcham, Donne was abroad again, traveling in company with Sir Walter Chute. It's not altogether clear why Donne undertook the voyage of 1605, but he was probably trying to locate himself in some situation, either as secretary or tutor, so that he could support his already growing family (Ann eventually bore him twelve children, seven of whom survived). But it was not with Sir Walter that Donne began his ascent to at least a minimal security, but with Thomas Morton, Dean of Gloucester from 1607 and future Bishop of Durham.

The pamphlet warfare between Anglican and Catholic had been heightened by the discovery, in November of 1605, of the Gunpowder Plot, in which Catholic saboteurs had planned to dispose of King and Parliament and the Protestant power group in the forthright way of explosives, set to go off when King James was in attendance at Parliament. The plot was discovered, the conspirators were executed, and Anglican charges against the Catholics swelled in number and urgency.

Thomas Morton was one of the chief spokesmen for the Anglican position; he needed the assistance of a scholarly researcher; and Donne sorely needed a post. From 1605 to 1607, Donne was Morton's collaborator.

Morton could hardly have found a better assistant. Raised in a Catholic context, trained early in Catholic doctrine, already well versed in the apologetic and polemic literature of both sides of the quarrel, and familiar with the tactics of legal argumentation, Donne, if not yet a devout Anglican, was certainly no longer an adherent of Catholicism.

The cooperation between the two men was eminently successful. King James was so impressed by Morton's defenses that, in 1607, Morton was appointed Dean of Gloucester. For Donne, unfortunately, it meant the end of a livelihood, for the new Dean could not reasonably be expected to continue as a publishing warrior. Morton encouraged Donne to follow him into the ministry, to accept Holy Orders; but Donne would not, pleading that his own conscience was still so perplexed that he dare not take such an irrevocable step. Eight years were still to pass before Donne would take Morton's advice.

A great part of Donne's artistic activity over the next three years was devoted to that perplexity of conscience. In 1607, he sent to Lady Danvers (before her second marriage, Magdalene Herbert), mother of the poet George Herbert and a valued friend to Donne, the collection of sonnets known as La Corona; and by late 1609 or early 1610, he had completed twelve of the Holy Sonnets. These poems are a testament to Donne's rigorous searching into his own spiritual condition, a necessary prelude to his eventual decision to be ordained. There were works in prose, too. In 1608, probably, Donne completed Biathanatos, a mocking disquisition on suicide; Pseudo-Martyr, Donne's contribution to the debate between Catholic and Anglican, was published in 1610. In the time between these two prose treatises, Donne met Lucy, Countess of Bedford, who over the years became his patroness—often demanding and unpredictable, but a patroness nevertheless. By 1610, Donne's worldly position was not so desperate as it had been in 1602, but it was still precarious enough: he had tried in 1608 to be appointed to a governmental post in Ireland, and in 1609 he had been hoping for an appointment as Secretary of the Colony of Virginia. But the turning point of Donne's life was destined to take place not in the Countess of Bedford's little court at Twickenham, not in Ireland, and not in Virginia.

In December, 1610, Elizabeth Drury, the only child of Sir Robert Drury, died at the age of fourteen. Donne may have met Sir Robert through Anne Donne, the poet's elder sister, who was married to William Lyly, a frequent inhabiter of the Drury household in Suffolk. However well Donne knew Sir Robert, he had never seen Elizabeth; but he sent his future patron a brief "A Funeral Elegie" lamenting the young girl's death. The poem was not insincere, but Donne's motives were probably mixed: the patronage of Sir Robert might be less demanding and more rewarding than the patronage of the Countess of Bedford. From 1610 to 1621, Donne was provided with a small house in Drury Lane in London. This was not charity: Donne paid rent to Sir Robert for the accommodations, and in any case the patron received more credit from the poet than the other way around.

For "A Funeral Elegie" was accompanied by the long poem The First Anniversary, nominally a lament in much fuller terms for Elizabeth Drury, but more profoundly Donne's most searching examination of himself. When the Drurys traveled abroad in 1611–1612, Donne was with them; and while in France, he completed The Second Anniversary, once again a eulogy of Elizabeth but also a completion of his self-examination.

When Donne returned to England, he contributed an elegiac poem to the collection *Lachrymae Lachrymarum*, a volume of verse laments honoring Prince Henry, the Prince of Wales, who died in 1612; and shortly thereafter he celebrated the marriage of the Prince's sister, Princess Elizabeth, in "An Epithalamion, or Marriage Song." There was nothing time-serving in either of these poems: Donne, like most of his generation, had looked to Prince Henry as a brilliant guarantor and defender of Protestant England; and the wedding poem for the Princess Elizabeth acts as a counterbalance against the national grief over the death of her brother. But one work of 1613 shows Donne still hesitating over the course he will follow: a second wedding poem, this time directed to the Earl of Somerset on his marriage to Frances Howard, was an unabashed claim on the powerful Earl's attentions. Donne hoped that Somerset could engineer for him a post as clerk of the Privy Council, but the plan did not materialize. There's no way to gauge how strong was Donne's disappointment over this setback, but his letters make it clear that he had solicited for the post in every way short of actually debasing himself. However, when Somerset failed him, Donne had another alternative—not an alternative of desperation, but a genuine second choice that he could make without regret now that circumstances pointed that way. On January 23, 1615, he was ordained a priest by Dr. John King, Bishop of London.

CHAPTER II

The Initial Prose
and the *Songs and Sonnets,*
1598–1605

I T'S CURIOUS, in a way, that Donne held his *Paradoxes* and
Problems in such favor. These sophistic and ironic evapo-
rations were his earliest attempts in prose; and it's evident
that Donne at first was unable to expand or explore in this
medium. Most of these mock casuistries (eleven paradoxes
and ten problems) had been printed in the same year as the
first edition of the poems, 1633; by 1652, when their publication had been taken over by Donne's son, twelve paradoxes
and seventeen problems had come to light. Only two of these
pieces can be located after the turn of the century: Problem
VIII, "Why Venus-Starre Onely Doth Cast a Shadow?" and
a problem not printed until 1899 by Sir Edmund Gosse,[1]
"Why was Sir Walter Raleigh thought the fittest Man, to
write the Historie of these Times?" All the others were most
likely written shortly before 1600. Behind them lies the
Latin and Italian tradition of the paradox so discernible in
Donne's own early poetry.[2] But to anyone coming from the
poems, which pulsate with a presence within them (even
though that presence is recluse or counterfeit), these prose
pieces seem absolutely characterless, witty but insubstantial.
And yet, Donne was oddly solicitous about them. He might,
in one letter, condescend to them as "but swaggerers—quiet

enough if you resist them. If perchance they be prettily gilt, that is their best, for they are not hatched. They are rather alarms to truth to arm her, than enemies: and they have only this advantage to scape from being called ill things, that they are nothings."[3] On the other hand, as late as 1621 he was inquiring of Sir Thomas Lucy, "Why do you say nothing of, my little book of Cases,"[4] by which he presumably meant either these same problems and paradoxes or, remotely possible, a similar later and nonextant collection. In the same year he wrote to Henry Goodyer and in the course of the letter mentioned his imminent appointment to the Deanship of St. Paul's and inquired for "my Cases of conscience,"[5] which he seems to have loaned Goodyer, along with some of his sermons. It seems most peculiar that this elder Donne should have bothered himself over such ephemera. Several alternatives ask to be considered. Was Donne preparing an edition of his poems and/or prose in 1621, and so wrote to Lucy and Goodyer to send him back his materials? Or had he felt compromised, in this year when King James would appoint him to St. Paul's, by the not-so-muted anti-Scots barbs of some of the early prose?[6] Had the scurrility of some of the paradoxes proved embarrassing, and now Donne wanted them out of the way? An undated letter to his father-in-law, George More, shows some anxiety: "Though their unworthinesse, and your own ease be advocates for me with you, yet I must adde my entreaty, that you let goe no copy of my Problems, till I review them. If it be too late, at least be able to tell me who hath them."[7] Or was Donne perhaps referring to some other collection of "cases" altogether in 1621? There would have been many opportunities for him, as a minister trained in the law, to have gathered together the more interesting of moral problems brought to him by his parishioners of Sevenoaks or St. Dunstan's. All such alternatives are credible, but unprovable. There's nothing in Donne's canon that fits the category of "my . . . book of Cases" so well as the *Paradoxes and Problems.*

Donne's concern is an encouragement to look more closely at this initial prose of his. There are some few moments in the content of the work when he adverts to themes never far from his mind. The second paradox, "That by Discord things increase," is a good digest of Empedocles, but it also describes his own creativity. His allusion in the ninth paradox to the "*Allegorical death* of entering into *Religion*" marks the first appearance of a concern that continues to nag at him as late as 1619, when he catalogued in "To Mr. Tilman after he had taken orders" what it means to renounce the world for the sake of religion. The eleventh paradox reads like a gloss on ll. 49–72 of "The Exstasie": "My *Body* licensth my *soule* to *see* the Worlds *beauties* through mine *eyes; to heare* pleasant things through mine *eares;* and affords it apt *Organs* for the convenience of all perceivable delight."[8] From the pursuit of the fleshly mistress in the *Elegies* to the search for the Bride of Christ in the 1619 sonnet "Show me deare Christ," the evanescent woman is a recurring image in Donne's work; and in the first paradox he wryly notes that "Every Woman is a *Science*; for hee that plods upon a Woman all his life long, shall at length find himself short of the knowledge of her."[9]

But it is not the content of the *Paradoxes and Problems* that's so important. If it was these prose pieces that Donne was recalling in 1621, he was remembering them not for their themes but for the angle of vision they embody. Slight though they are, they still were "made rather to deceive Time than her daughter Truth."[10] They show Donne uninterruptedly, albeit shallowly, glimpsing the depths of ambivalence in the world. It's one thing to create paradox sporadically, as Donne has been doing up to this point, and something else again to rely on paradox as the sole instrument. Paradox belongs to both rhetoric and philosophy. In the first phase, Donne is a rhetorician, and in his later career, a philosopher of paradox.[11]

The rhetoric of paradox assumes there is a controlling power in language sufficient to warp reality into unexpected shapes. This sense of the residing strength of language is the generator, among other things, of the epigram. Drummond thought Donne could have been the best of English epigrammatists,[12] and that master of the form, Ben Jonson, often quoted from Donne's epigrams.[13] Grierson printed nineteen epigrams as decidedly Donne's and hinted there are probably more ("There is no use burdening Donne with more of this kind than he is already responsible for"[14]). Most of these were probably written before 1600, but it's also likely that Donne continued to write them at odd hours and largely for his own amusement. They are the sort of brief triumph of language, ranging in size from a couplet to eight or ten lines, that allows a man to catch an idea on the fly, freeze it, and then drop it. Even so reserved a poet as Dryden, who put epigrams at the very bottom of all poetry in his *Discourse on Satire*, composed the epigram on Milton for the 1688 edition of *Paradise Lost*; and when Jacob Tonson displeased him (late payment for work done, probably), Dryden dashed off a satirical epigram and sent it by messenger to Tonson with the words, "Tell the dog that he who wrote these lines can write more."[15] If Donne did continue to write epigrams, Grierson is probably right: there's no point in adding to the canon more than he's responsible for. Like many of the paradoxes, the epigrams are characterless, indistinguishable from any good instances of their kind. Here, for example, is Ben Jonson:

To Alchemists

If all you boast of your great art be true;
Sure, willing povertie lives most in you.

On Old Colt

For all night-sinnes, with other wives, unknowne,
Colt, now, doth daily penance in his owne.

> To Foole, or Knave
> Thy praise, or dispraise is to me alike,
> One doth not stroke me, nor the other strike.[16]

Here is Donne:

> A lame begger
> I am unable, yonder begger cries,
> To stand, or move; if he say true, hee *lies*.

> Antiquary
> If in his Studie he hath so much care
> To'hang all old strange things, let his wife beware.

> Phryne
> Thy flattering picture, *Phryne*, is like thee,
> Onely in this, that you both painted be.

> Klockius
> *Klockius* so deeply hath sworne, ne'r more to come
> In bawdie house, that hee dares not goe home.[17]

The effect of these epigrams of Donne's depends on the protean quality of single words: *lies, old strange things, painted, bawdie house.* The words are powerful enough to capture two separate entities and bring them together under one command:

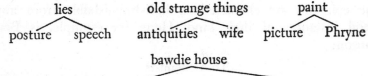

This blurring of lines between discrete entities by a turn in the language is rhetorical paradox, and Donne had employed it with eminent success in the early poetry. The "Epithalamion made at Lincolnes Inne" depends on such paradox for its peer-group humor; the delicious bawdry of "Loves Warre" and "Loves Progress" depends on it; the arguments of "The Flea" and "Confined Love" depend on it. The reshaping of reality to fit the contours of a word is rhetorical paradox, and between 1594 and 1598 Donne develops what is probably the supreme English mastery of the technique. The epigrams are the least of his successes in the genre, the pygmy versions of a device that grows into a full-bodied drama in poems like "The Dampe" or "The Will." But deep in the structure of the Elegies and the early group of the Songs and Sonnets is such paradox, masculine language domineering over feminine reality.

Philosophic paradox, in all its varieties, does not create ambiguities, it perceives them. It does not assume that language can overpower and control reality, but exactly the opposite: reality is so sinuous, so complex, that it slips through the coarse net of language. Language becomes not a container of reality, but an imperfect medium through which we see reality, as through a glass, darkly. The word is no longer conceived of as a two-handed engine, with separate items of experience held fast, one in each fist:

> Compassion in the world againe is bred:
> Ralphius is sick, the broker keeps his bed.[18]

Supine Ralphius ◄——— keeps his bed ———► Repossession by
a broker

Instead, the word is precariously balanced on the razor edge that separates two items, each intent on preserving its own identity, refusing to bow to the control of language, all the while clamoring for their ambivalence to be recognized:

> That All, which alwayes was all, every where;
> Which could not sinne, and yet all sinnes did beare;
> Which could not die, yet could not chuse but die.
>   (The Progresse of the Soule,[19] ll. 74–76)

Here, reality simply eludes the precise word, and the Petruchio-Kate, language-reality equation of rhetorical paradox is totally reversed.

Most of Donne's paradoxes and problems were written before the disastrous year of 1601, when Donne could still look on the contrary world from a fairly safe distance. The wit of the paradoxes lies in Donne's ordering ambiguity into existence with a pun or an oxymoron, thus gaining a splendid rhetorical effect. But contrariness and ambiguity Donne came to see more profoundly after 1601 and after the *Paradoxes and Problems*, are in the very fiber of things; and he could no longer maintain that safe aloofness. The elemental fact of ambivalence is that it demands coexistence and complementarity. The paradoxical bride in Donne's later sonnet "Show me deare Christ" is declared to be both "chaste" and "open to all men": her very paradoxicality demands that she be both simultaneously. The lovers of "The Exstasie" cannot be you and *I*, they must be *we*. The hemispheric eyes of "The Goodmorrow" must not be two, but one; the legs of the compass in "A Valediction: forbidding Mourning" must be joined, complementarily. The more ambivalent Donne's vision becomes, the less singular and alone he becomes. In his earliest work, Donne practiced alienation and protective masquerade, but as his sense of paradox increases, he relinquishes his own isolation. The deeper he looks into the abyss of ambiguity, the closer he comes to Meditation XVII and "I am involved in mankind."

Donne's vision of reality escaping from the control of man's voice did not come all at once; nor did that vision's companion, the denial of singularity. Donne's writing in this second period, from 1598 to 1605, is divided. Part of his creativity is released in a satiric recital of the destructive consequences of schism: this is *The Progresse of the Soule*. The other part of his genius devotes itself to the allied issue, the annihilation of the proud egoist of the early poetry. This murdering of a persona is begun but aborted in the later part of the *Songs and Sonnets*, and achieved in the religious poetry.

Donne reaches a critical point in 1610. After that date, the two trails of genius join. To arrest a reality which is hurtling beyond the reach of reason and language, Donne infuses himself intuitively and communally into that reality. The *Anniversary* poems are the first complete proclamation of the Donne who destroys himself to be born again within the world, and the *Devotions*, the *Sermons*, and the last hymns are the products of the phoenix-Donne. There is an essential rightness in this second and preparative phase beginning with a collection entitled *Paradoxes and Problems*.

Admittedly, these prose pieces are a frail enough beginning. They're generally waspish and bad-tempered, as is the "Essay on Valour," which was probably composed at the same time.[20] In the essay we can detect the frustrated intellectual carping at a society which pays him no mind: "To be accounted handsome, just, learned, or well favoured, all this carries no danger with it . . . and all women take delight to hold him safe in their arms who hath 'scapt thither through many dangers."[21] Such truculence against an effeminate society (which ignores *real* virtues, i.e., his own) lasts as late as the *Catalogus Librorum Aulicorum*, the Rabelais-inspired mockery of pretensions to learning. Written probably before *Biathanatos* (1608?) and perhaps as early as 1603, this little Latin satire was recast by Donne in 1610 or 1611.[22] Like four of the satires, it is aimed at the court, and specifically at the courtier whose chief business is "meals and amusement." Knowing how busy such a creature is, the commentator deigns to provide him with a list of thirty-four synopses of useful knowledge that should be a palatable substitute for true knowledge. In the process Donne mocks many of the

ideas that will elsewhere grip his imagination: Pythagorean-
ism, Neoplatonism, cabalism, each possessing creeds of self-
extinction and immersion into an Absolute. But meanwhile
Donne sports with catalogue item 6, "That the Book of Tobit
is canonical; in which, following the Rabbis and the more
mystical of the Theologians, the hairs of the tail of his Dog
are numbered," and by a little judicious twisting of the dog's
tail, "letters are formed which yield wonderful words, by
Francis George, a Venetian";[23] or item 8, "The Judaeo-
Christian Pythagoras, proving the Numbers 99 and 66 to be
identical if you hold the leaf upside down, by the super-
seraphical John Picus," or item 14, "A Bundle of Oaks, or,
The Art of grasping Transcendentals, by Raymond Sebun-
dus."[24] Franciscus Georgius, Pico della Mirandola, and Raymond of Sebond make honorable appearances in the *Essays in
Divinity*, and they were not always figures of whimsy for
Donne. They all shared the belief that under the flux of
contradictory reality there resided a pattern which man might
perceive and participate in, and Donne will take this idea
seriously, not mockingly.

But it is not the prose which brings us close to Donne, but
the poetry. He turns instinctively to verse to probe into ideas
and passions. The two earliest poems of this period make a
perfect *coincidentia oppositorum*. "The Autumnal," probably
written about 1600,[25] is a rhetorical paradox; *The Progresse
of the Soule* (1601) is a philosophical paradox, Donne's first
extended analysis of world-deep ambiguity.

"The Autumnal" is the best of the verse compliments
which Donne paid to his friends and patronesses. There is
none of the laboring for effect that we find in the addresses to
Lucy, Countess of Bedford, or to the Countesses of Huntingdon and Salisbury. For the next twenty-seven years, from this
poem to his commemorative sermon, Donne's devotion to the
remarkable Magdalene Herbert doesn't flag. This first poem

to her escapes Dryden's censure that "[Donne] affects the metaphysics, not only in his satires, but in his amorous verses, where nature only should reign; and perplexes the mind of the fair sex with nice speculations of philosophy, when he should engage their hearts, and entertain them with the softnesses of love."[26] The seven later verse epistles to the Countess of Bedford and those to the Countess of Huntingdon and the Countess of Salisbury do not. In too many of those later compliments, Donne clumsily plays the gallant, and ingenuity has to take the place of real engagement. In "The Autumnal,"[27] however, the obeisance to Mrs. Herbert is not an occasion for vexatious philosophizing, it is the entire issue. Donne is still considering paradox a rhetorical control over reality. The poem is an exorcism, a driving out of the devils of aging through paradox. The gallantry is a complete success just because Donne is so poised and so in command of Mrs. Herbert's beauty. He consecrates and refashions her beauty in an incantation of paradox. After an invocation whereby Mrs. Herbert becomes an autumnal deity, a Cereslike goddess of bounty from whom "Affection . . . takes Reverences name" (l. 6), Donne proceeds paradoxically to argue out of existence any possible blemish. She's no longer in her Golden Age, for that age has fled; but it is only Age that has fled, and not the Gold, and so she becomes "gold oft tried, and ever new" (l. 8). As a young beauty she was torrid, but now her heat has cooled; but since an excess of heat is equivalent to pestilence, who would wish for more heat? The wrinkles in her face are ugly only through nomenclature; if we agree to call them not graves but Love's tombs, then they lose their ugliness. The magic of the word disposes of all decrepitude: youth is noon, revelry, and drunkenness; this being the case, then middle age must be calm evening, counsel, and discreet banqueting. We desire what is long sought; age is gained only after a long time; age must be desirable. We love what is fragile and likely to vanish; in age, beauty has reached its fragile vanishing point; so we must love aged beauty. All these paradoxical enthy-memes are hortatory: Donne traps a situation in a series of truncated syllogisms, and orders the situation to do his bid-ding. No Scholastic could have done it better.

Donne concludes his exorcism by erecting word barriers against any intrusion by senility. Having frozen Mrs. Herbert's beauty at its ideal station, he denies entrance to "Winter-faces, whose skin's slacke" (l. 37). He concludes by reversing the direction of love as he had defined it in "Loves Progress." There, the natural movement of love is upward; here, it is downward. The anatomical voyages of the *Elegies*, with their heavy-breathing haste, are replaced by a much quieter journey.

> Since such loves naturall lation is, may still
> My love descend, and journey downe the hill,
> Not panting after growing beauties, so,
> I shall ebbe on with them, who home-ward goe.
>
> (ll. 47–50)

This is an anticipation of the image in *The Progresse of the Soule*:

> For though through many streights, and lands I roame,
> I launch at paradise, and I saile towards home.
>
> (ll. 56–57)

There is no other work of Donne's so provocative of debate or so productive of conflicting interpretations as *The Prog-resse of the Soule* (1601). It has been variously defined as a Catholic satire against Elizabeth,[28] a testament of libertin-ism,[29] a pendant to the anti-Jesuit prose satire *Ignatius His Conclave*, and a satirical prelude to the *Anniversaries*.[30] It has been described as occasioned by the fall of Essex[31] and by Donne's impending marriage;[32] as both satiric history[33] and spiritual self-examination.[34] Ben Jonson was certain that the poem, if completed, would have concluded with Calvin, and Grierson was equally certain that it would have ended with Queen Elizabeth. Such judgments, sometimes conflicting but more often complementary, obscure what I believe to be a central consistency in the poem, fragment though it may be. *The Progresse of the Soule* is a major turning point, Donne's recognition that paradox is not something he may administer to reality in the interest of wit, but something which resides in temporal reality. In the poem we see something very like " 'existential disappointment,' a disappointment which penetrates into the very existence of man."[35]

Whatever may have been the immediate occasion of the poem, its central consistency is provided by an Augustinian sense of a world disjointed by rebellion against divine fiat. More exactly, Donne's controlling principle is analogous to the Augustinian view of history; and even more exactly (and incautiously, perhaps), I believe *The Progresse of the Soule* to be based ultimately on St. Augustine's account of the conflict between the two kingdoms. In Books XV–XVIII of *The City of God*, Augustine traced in considerable detail the evolution of two hostile cities, from the time that Abel prefigured the celestial city and Cain prefigured the earthly city down to the completion of both histories in Christ. Augustine's account of the progress of Abel-Cain, eternal-temporal, redemption-death, is welded to a characteristically trinitarian view of history. Book XV treats of universal history from the beginnings to Noah; Book XVI, from Noah to Abraham; and Book XVII, from Abraham to Christ, whereupon the successive books identify Christ as the fulfillment of history. Augustine continually stresses the snarled relations between the two cities: history runs its course, he says in the first chapter of Book XVIII, not in light but in shadow. But the Incarnation of Christ is the signal for the absolute distinction between the two cities, and Christ as Judge will gather all

kingdoms to himself and thrust the unregenerate into the
infernal pit (Book XVIII, chapter 54). The Apocalypse will
be the solution of the conflict between the two kingdoms.

Donne begins his poem with a similar trinitarian view. He
sings (with Pauline overtones of the post-Mosaic superse-
dence of the Law through Christ) of "times before the law/
Yoak'd us, and when, and since" (ll. 3–4), that is, before
Moses, the Mosaic dispensation, and since Moses (see St.
Paul, Galatians 2: 16–19). It is a version of history which he
continues to use: in a sermon preached at Whitehall in 1626
Donne noted, "In all the two thousands yeares of Nature,
before the Law given by Moses, And the two thousand yeares
of Law, before the Gospel given by Christ, And the two
thousand of Grace which are running now, (of which last
houre we have heard three quarters strike, more then fifteen
hundred of this last two thousand spent). . . ."[36] At the
same time, he begins with a reference to Seth (and the
fragment ends with the name of Seth). The poem will be

> A worke t'outweare Seths pillars, bricke and stone,
> And (holy writt excepted) made to yeeld to none.
>
> (ll. 9–10)

Seth is an essential figure in Augustine's history. Cain is the
founder of cities in The City of God (Book XV), as he is in
Donne's poem:

> wonder with mee,
> Why plowing, building, ruling and the rest,
> Or most of those arts, whence our lives are blest,
> By cursed Cains race invented be,
> And blest Seth vext us with Astronomie.
>
> (ll. 513–517)

It is Augustine's puzzle, with which he concludes his eigh-
teenth book, the good things that accompany the damned

city. But Cain is the archetype of the reprobate City of Man, and so are Japheth and Esau. Abel, on the other hand, is the archetype of the City of God.

> Abel, as white, and milde as his sheepe were,
> (Who, in that trade, of Church, and kingdomes, there
> Was the first type). . . .
>
> (ll. 404–406)

When Abel was murdered by Cain, the later-born son of Adam, Seth, became the surviving celebrant of the celestial kingdom and erected the pillars to which Donne refers as testament to the wisdom of the heavens (and so initiated astronomical studies).[37] Enos, the son of Seth, became the symbol of the redeemed man (City of God, Book XV, chapter 21), the type of resurrection. The promise of resurrection and of triumph over Cain extends through Abel, to Seth, to Enos, to Shem, to Abraham, and is completed in Christ (City of God, XV, 17–18). The soul whose progress Donne undertakes to describe is Augustine's history, the war between Seth and Cain, the puzzle-filled conflict between sacred and profane, eternal and temporal, unity and division.

The Progresse of the Soule begins with "a deathlesse soule" which existed before creation, and which will outlast creation. In the second stanza Donne scorns the sun, which is younger in time than this soul, and which will be quenched long before this soul:

> Yet hast thou not more nations seene then shee,
> That before thee, one day beganne to bee,
>   And thy fraile light being quench'd, shall long,
>   long out live thee.
>
> (ll. 18–20)

Were the poem complete, this eternal soul, historia, would perhaps have shown itself in the two races of Seth and Cain;

as it is, only half of the pedigree is sketched out, that half which is sin, death, Cain, and the temporal world. But there is another half, that which is Seth's. The soul of history existing before time, dividing itself, and showing forth in the world through Seth and Cain is purely Augustinian. In the eleventh book of *The City of God*, Augustine argues that the two cities originated before time, in the separation of the faithful and fallen angels; and that God's division of light from darkness at the beginning of time symbolized that elder schism. The pristine unicity of God's law had been shattered outside time, and time began with a symbolic remembrance of that first rebellion. The first command of creation, the original *Verbum*, was, "Let there be light," "And God saw the light, that it was good: and God divided the light from the darkness" (Genesis 1:3–4). Time began with schism, which is older than time; and history begins with paradox, the simultaneous existence of contradictory states.

In the Christian tradition, the paradox is resolved in the Incarnation, the doctrine of the God-Man, Christ as the Logos or the Word who retrieves the original unity by absorbing both halves of the cosmic dichotomy into himself. In stanzas VII and VIII, Donne contrasts the soul of history as it appears in the secular order and as it appears in the Incarnation. The seventh stanza locates that half of the soul of history which derives from the will of the fallen angels, and he appropriately equates it with innovation and flux:

> For the great soule which here amongst us now
> Doth dwell, and moves that hand, and tongue, and brow,
> Which, as the Moone the sea, moves us; to heare
> Whose story, with long patience you will long;
> (For 'tis the crowne, and last straine of my song)
> This soule to whom *Luther*, and *Mahomet* were
> Prisons of flesh; this soule which oft did teare,

And mend the wracks of th'Empire, and late Rome,
And liv'd when every great change did come,
　　Had first in paradise, a low, but fatall roome.

This is the schismatic soul, created by the rebellion of Lucifer
and thrust into human history in Eden. Its opposite, the soul
of unity, is in the Incarnate Christ (stanza VIII):

　　Yet no low roome, nor then the greatest, lesse,
　　If (as devout and sharpe men fitly guesse)
　　That Crosse, our joy, and griefe, where nailes did tye
　　That All, which alwayes was all, every where;
　　Which could not sinne, and yet all sinnes did beare;
　　Which could not die, yet could not chuse but die;
　　Stood in the selfe same roome in Calvarie,
　　Where first grew the forbidden learned tree,
　　For on that tree hung in security
　　　　This Soule, made by the Makers will from pulling
　　　　　free.

The Incarnation closes the circle of history and reproduces
the pre-existent unity of the Word of God. The identity of
Paradise and Calvary is the central conceit of the "Hymne to
God my God, in my sicknesse," and here is the first appearance of the image in Donne's poetry. The Augustinian pattern is the Word dichotomized by the reprobate will of the
fallen Angels (Book XI), the re-enactment of Will disputing
the Law in Eden (Book XIII), and the reassembling of the
Word through Christ (Book XX). Donne telescopes this
history by locating the tree of death (the forbidden fruit of
Eden) and the tree of life (the cross) in the same place, so
that the divided and reunited souls of history share a coincident symbol.

　　Having flirted with the contrariness of existence in the
Paradoxes and Problems, Donne undertakes in this satire to

contemplate the ubiquity of paradox in human history. Along with Augustine, he considers that it is the perversity of created will which frustrates an original beneficent design. It is a poem not of despair but of disappointment. The soul of history finds its way from eternity into the world but, as Donne says in the introductory *Infinitati Sacrum*, no matter how dulled it becomes, "her memory hath ever been her owne," and she will recall both her origin and her destiny.[38] The origin and the destiny is the Word as it was in the beginning. This soul, schizophrenic since the revolt of the angels, has been entrusted to the race of Cain, which will continue the rebelliousness of the fallen angels and make capital of the broken Word; but a recollection of the aboriginal unity is kept alive by the race of Seth, with its guardianship of the original wholeness and power of the Word. *The Progresse of the Soule* was to have been a mock epic poem dealing with the war between the children of light and the children of darkness, an ironic narration of the success of the descendents of Cain and the destroyers of design: this would have been "the crowne, and last straine of my song." If completed, *The Progresse of the Soule* would have been a more massive onslaught on the foolishness of the world than he had accomplished in the satires and a full account of how thoroughly the world is out of joint for having denied the original Wisdom. The design of indicting the madness of the world as seen in its entire history may have been hopelessly ambitious, but it did not lack a firm conceptual center. At the heart of Donne's design is Augustine's metahistory.

(Seth's generation has its defense in the other "Progress of the Soul," *The Second Anniversary*. The sense in which Donne completed the 1601 *Progresse* by the 1611 "Progress" will be dealt with later; in the meanwhile it might be appropriate to suggest that Donne's position in *The Progresse of the Soule* is comparable to what Paul Tillich describes as a "boundary situation." Intent on the total negativeness of a situation, Donne is later forced to look beyond the world for positive meaning, and this is the dialectic of the two *Progresses*. For Donne, what Tillich identifies as "the vacuum of disintegration" becomes a "sacred void" that he attempts to fill in the years after *The Progresse of the Soule* and does, ultimately, fill.[39]) For as much of *The Progresse of the Soule* as he completed, Donne successfully illustrates how thoroughly Augustine's divisive soul of history has penetrated into the world. After three introductory stanzas, wherein he touches on the eternity of the soul (I, II) and its ubiquity (III), Donne stresses that the poem will not be only a recording but a self-examination and that he, like the soul of the poem, is caught in the world but yet has a memory of another time.

> For though through many streights, and lands I roame,
> I launch at paradise, and I saile towards home.

This uniting of his own history with universal history (a theme he will rejoin in the *Essays in Divinity*, and wonderfully complete in the *Anniversaries*) leads me to believe that the cryptic lines in the *Infinitati Sacrum*, "shee is hee, whose life you shall finde in the end of this book," refer to Donne himself.

Stanzas VII and VIII contrast incomplete soul and total soul, human history versus Incarnation; and in stanza IX, the prelude gives way to the narrative proper.

The soul of rebellion is propelled into human affairs in Eden. Adam's and Eve's eating the forbidden fruit is treason, since that particular tree was "Fenc'd with the law" (l. 82). Immediately the consequence of treason was released into the fiber of existence, and "Man all at once was there by woman slaine" (l. 91). The paradox of transmitted death appears much later in one of Donne's first sermons to King Charles. At Whitehall in 1626 Donne preached:

> Adam sinnd, and *I* suffer; I *forfeited* before I had any *Possession*, or could claime any *Interest*; I had a *Punishment*, before I had a *being*, and God was displeased with *me* before *I* was *I*.[40]

From that instant of rebellion in Paradise, the soul of denial and sundered unity filled every part of creation. The soul leaves the apple and inhabits the mandrake (vegetable), and from there it populates a variety of animals, and so filters into all the inhabitable elements: sparrow (air), fish (water), amphibian swan (water-earth-air), elephant, mouse, wolf (earth). Then it moves into the scale of rationality. Imprisoned in the body of a wolf, the soul of divisiveness approaches the tent of Abel and impregnates one of his herd dogs. Significantly, the offspring is caressed by Abel's sister and wife, Moab, even as later on the ape is caressed by Siphatecia. But there is no issue from the congress of the soul and Moab: Abel's race is not invaded by the contradictory soul. When, however, the soul is in the "toyfull Ape," Siphatecia is made pregnant, and she gives birth to Themech; and Themech is both wife and sister to Cain, cofoundress of his line and equal partner in the establishment of the City of Man. The fragment ends with Cain and with the assertion,

> There's nothing simply good, nor ill alone,
> Of every quality comparison,
>   The only measure is, and judge, opinion.
>   (ll. 518–520)

To say that these concluding lines are Donne's expression of a faith in libertinism and his revocation of universal law is only half true. Donne is admitting lawlessness without espousing it. These lines follow immediately on the description of the

contentious soul passing into the race of Cain, just after it has
been denied admittance into the race of Abel and of Seth.

> and fast there by one end,
> Did this Soules limbes, these limbes a soule attend;
> And now they joyn'd: keeping some quality
> Of every past shape, she knew treachery,
> Rapine, deceit, and lust, and ills enow
> To be a woman. *Themech* she is now,
> Sister and wife to *Caine, Caine* that first did plow.
>
> (ll. 503–510)

The soul of unrule is now in control, building its cities,
domineering over all the parts of existence, while the untouched heirs of Seth are exiled from a realm of coherence
and order that they still remember. The theme in Donne is
not entirely new; in the early poetry he sometimes played at
being Seth the incorruptible (in the *Satires*) or Cain, Lord of
Misrule (the *Elegies*). But the vision is more somber here,
more earnest for all its satiric intent, predicating as it does a
divisiveness deep in universal history.

Most of the later poems of the *Songs and Sonnets* are
flights from the divided soul of this *Poema Satyricon*. In the
love poetry Donne creates a world of fantasy where the
ambiguities and the paradoxes are solved by the unitive experience of love. These poems may have been inspired by Ann
More, or by his exile from city and court, or by his eccentric
studies of these years; but such information is largely irrelevant, and may even be misleading.[41] Irrelevant, because all of
Donne's poetry was based on experience, but that triggering
experience was always converted into drama that outran its
origins. Misleading, because the later works in the *Songs and
Sonnets* are not uniquely of the post-marriage years: they deal
with an issue of his earliest poetry and of *The Progresse of the
Soule*. They are Donne's supreme secular treatment of the

problem of alienation, loneliness, and ambivalence. In them Donne achieves, for a brief time, a profane solution to the problem; and shortly thereafter he achieves a sacred solution. In the later group of the *Songs and Sonnets*, we watch Donne step out of the confusing history of the *Progresse* and occupy an ahistorical and reassembled realm of unity.[42] We watch Donne surrender the fantasy and fall back into a bitter awareness of a sundered and contradictory existence. A Prospero-like entry into an Eden, the invasion by reality, and the breaking of enchantment is the enclosing structure of these love poems.

The exact sequence of these twenty-seven poems is problematic, but by no means chaotic.[43] It is a reasonable hypothesis that, between 1602 and 1605, Donne wrote twenty-four poems. Within these twenty-four, there are clusters of poems which share common themes, metrical patterns, and preoccupations. It is certainly true that these clusters might be broken up, should further evidence for dating appear; but at the moment it is more credible to imagine Donne working steadily at one idea and then moving on to another issue than it is to see him as returning sporadically and undesignedly to an idea he had laid aside. There is always a teleological process visible in what Donne wrote. So, acknowledging that truth is the daughter of time and admitting that there can yet be no finality on the point, I propose to arrange the poems of 1602–1605 as beginning with "The Exstasie," "Negative Love," "The Undertaking," "Image and Dream," and "A Feaver." These are all poems of hesitancy and transition, cautiously exploring an awareness of love quite different from that in the early love poetry but controlled by the conservative verse patterns of Donne's early period. Sometime afterward (perhaps as late as 1605) come four valedictions, each examining the theme of separation and dismemberment (emblems of the crisis faced in *The Progresse of the Soule*), and, not necessarily later than but contiguous in many ways to the valedictions, four debates on the nature of love and the role the woman must play ("Aire and Angels," "Loves Growth," "Loves Infiniteness," and "A Lecture upon the Shadow"). Five poems read like a test of the consequences of such a debate ("The Good-morrow," "The Anniversarie," "The Sunne Rising," "The Canonization," and "The Dreame"), while three poems ("The Dissolution," "The Relique," and "The Funerall") cooperate to give a symbol of the absolute limits of those consequences. This is not necessarily a chronological order; there is no way of determining that. But whatever the time sequence, it is clear that Donne grapples with various phases of disunity in sets of poems rather than in isolated single pieces. The whole fantasy collapses in "The Blossome," "Loves Alchymie," and "Farewell to Love," and Donne is forced back, but now without illusion, into history and the unpatterned human situation.

(The three remaining poems of the late twenty-seven are probably not part of this quest. "Twicknam Garden" is probably post–1607; "The Primrose," 1613; and "A Nocturnall upon S. Lucies Day" evidently belongs to 1617.)

By 1607, and very much so by 1613, Donne no longer takes seriously his secular response to universal ambiguity. It has become a conceit only, an outmoded image that he gamesomely adjusts to fit situations of patronage or rejects altogether. After 1605 the need to escape from the cruel polarity of history brings him to sacred myth, where time, place, and paradox are abolished.

The suggestion has been made[44] that "The Exstasie" was part of a literary debate in which Sir Edward Herbert and Donne, working within a tradition already inhabited by Sidney, Wither, and Fulke Greville,[45] wrote rival poems on the definition of love. The traditionalism of "The Exstasie" has been reinforced by demonstrations of how completely the poem is saturated with Neoplatonic lore:[46] Marsilio Ficino, Leone Ebreo, Petrarch, Bruno, and Castiglione have all been located in the background. The impression is left that "The Exstasie" is in part a learned revival, a resurrection of the verse tournament of courtly love. If so, never has a literary exercise played so important a part in a poet's intellectual development; for not only has Donne transformed the tradition in which he wrote,[47] he also introduces the motif which dominates his love poetry, his religious poetry, and much of his devotional prose. In "The Exstasie" the singular, ego-protecting, and dominating male will that stalks through the early poetry disappears. In its place is a figure who so completely submerges himself in another that his own identity is lost. With that loss of identity comes a surge of unitive experience and the sense of a world existing apart from all the conflicts and dilemmas of history. Many of the ingredients had been surveyed before, but all whimsically: the androgyny of love in the "Epithalamion made at Lincolnes Inne," the private commonwealth of passion in "Loves Warre," transcendent desire in "To his Mistris Going to Bed." In "The Exstasie" these same themes are brought together seriously, and they constitute Donne's apprehension of a personal omega point.[48]

The tense of "The Exstasie" is crucial to Donne's insight. As in the first satire, but for different purposes, there are crossing time schemes in the poem. The different senses of time in "The Exstasie" are locked into an accelerating awareness of the mystery of love. The first twenty-eight lines are unique in Donne's love poetry: they are recollective, not dramatic, located in past time. In these same twenty-eight lines the two lovers have begun their drift into the synergy, the completed oneness of love, but have not yet achieved it. They are still one another, two distinct personalities. They have been yoked by the lower and the higher physical avenues

of love—"Our hands were firmly cimented . . . Our eye-
beames twisted" (ll. 5, 7)—but their souls "(which to advance their state,/ Were gone out)" (ll. 15–16) are still
distinct from one another: they are "Our *soules*," and not yet
"That abler soule" (ll. 15, 43).

From lines twenty-nine to forty-eight, narrative is replaced
by direct address, and a present tense evolves within the
framework of past tense:

> This Extasie doth unperplex
> (We said) and tell us what we love,
> Wee see by this, it was not sexe,
> Wee see, we saw not what did move.
>
> (ll. 29–32)

As the tense evolves from past into present, so the realization
of total unity grows sharper: love has annihilated the separateness of souls and created one soul which "Defects of
lonelinesse controules" (l. 44) and which resists all mortality,
"For, th' Atomies of which we grow,/ Are soules, whom no
change can invade" (ll. 47–48).

As the lover makes his plea for the final and consummate
surrendering of one to another, the joining of bodies as
completely as souls so that all vestiges of the defect of
loneliness are controlled, the tense changes for the third and
last time, and lines forty-nine to seventy-six are all in the
present tense. Change, flux, and death belong to time, and
time is halted in an eternal present the moment total union is
anticipated. Present time in the early love poetry is always a
dramatic device; from "The Exstasie" onward it is both
dramatic and mythic, an instant of truth which resists all
temporality.

Such mythic time is, of course, an arresting feature of most
Christian liturgies; and Donne is eventually drawn into the
theological dimensions of the concept. The idea of a self-

effacing love which transcends all time and exists as both historical and ahistorical reality is dramatized in the Incarnation, perpetuated by liturgy, and is the focus of Donne's religious experience. Here, in "The Exstasie," human love serves the same end as divine love.

The calculated blasphemy of "To his Mistris Going to Bed," where carnality is divinized, is a pale prelude to the earnestness of the idea in "The Exstasie." To transfer a sacred element to secular love, Donne makes use, at considerable risk to the unity of the poem, of a technique that has been either overlooked or misunderstood. I refer to the "third figure" in the poem. The figure is first imagined in ll. 21–28:

> If any, so by love refin'd,
>> That he soules language understood,
>> And by good love were grown all minde,
>>> Within convenient distance stood,
>
> He (though he knew not which soule spake,
>> Because both meant, both spake the same)
>> Might thence a new concoction take,
>>> And part farre purer then he came.

He's resummoned in ll. 73–76:

> And if some lover, such as wee,
>> Have heard this dialogue of one,
>> Let him still marke us, he shall see
>>> Small change, when we'are to bodies gone.

Donne is by no means the only Renaissance artist who has used the motif of the "observer." In El Greco's "Healing the Blind Man," ca. 1573, the composition of the painting divides into three areas: in the center, Christ performing the miracle; on either side of him, a gesticulating group of men. Standing somewhat apart from the group on Christ's right, anachronis-

tically dressed in Renaissance garb, a young man gazes out of
the painting, directly into the eyes of the beholder. He is not
a part of the action; he stands behind it, and by his uncom-
promising gaze he draws the audience into the painting with
him. In "The Despoiling of Christ," ca. 1584, El Greco uses
the figure to the right of Christ (again, an anachronism in
Renaissance armor) in the same way as the young man in
"Healing the Blind Man." In "The Martyrdom of St.
Maurice and the Theban Legion," ca. 1584, there are two
such figures, both to the left of Maurice; in "The Burial of
Count Orgaz," 1586, a young boy (a portrait of the artist's
son, Jorge Manuel) stands to one side of the action, pointing
with his left hand to the body of the Count but staring
directly at the beholder.

Titian, in the "Madonna of the Pesaro Family," 1526,
shows us another boy, kneeling among several figures in
adoration, but looking away from the Madonna and directly
out of the canvas. Pontormo in the "Madonna and Saints,"
"The Visitation," and "The Holy Family" (ca. 1514–1520)
presents foreground figures detached from the action of the
painting and appealing directly to the audience. Puligo, in
"The Adoration of the Kings"; Caravaggio, in "The Madonna
of Del Rosario"; Paolo Veronese, in "St. Anthony Abbot
Enthroned with St. Cornelius and St. Cyprian"; Correggio, in
"The Madonna of St. Sebastian," all make use of an observer
essentially unrelated to the action of the painting. "The
Exstasie" is similar to these paintings in composition, and
Donne's intended effect is analogous to these "observer"
paintings. The link between the fictive world and the literal
world, the observing figure is the mind in transit from the
profane world outside to the sacred world inside the art. The
"observer" technique is characteristic of Renaissance religious
art: a phenomenon which reinforces the religious overtones of
Donne's title. If the beholder resists being drawn into the

scene of sacred activity through the agency of the "third" or "other" figure, if he fails to adopt the sympathetic posture of the actors therein, then he must remain alien to the scene and set apart from the experience of unity within poem or painting.

The third figure completes the illusion of a world set apart by love. He steps from the secular order into the framed world of love just as the lovers step from time into an enduring present. When the third figure leaves the consecrated area, he will "part farre purer then he came," just as the lovers when they re-enter time will not be harmed by time: "Let him still marke us, he shall see/ Small change, when we'are to bodies gone." The conceptual rhythm of the poem is, first, a movement away from the real and ambivalent world that is populated by such contradictory fixtures as the carnal pregnant bank and the innocent violet's reclining head; the entry into a world of suspended time and sacred space;[49] and a return to the world, regenerated by this Æson's bath of love.

Only rarely does Donne entertain the idea of remaining eternally in the timelessness and spacelessness of total love. There is no return into the world in "The Undertaking," "The Sunne Rising," nor in "A Lecture upon the Shadow"; but in all other of the love poems, he does, as in "The Exstasie," walk back into real existence after having been absorbed into a transcendent experience. In this, he resembles Marvell rather than Vaughan. Vaughan's retreat from the disassembled world is total, but Marvell's is momentary. There is a re-entry pattern in Donne and Marvell, but not in Vaughan.

> Meet mee at London, then,
>   Twenty dayes hence, and thou shalt see
> Mee fresher, and more fat, by being with men,
>   Then if I had staid still with her and thee.
>   (Donne, "The Blossome," ll. 33–36)

Let us roll all our Strength, and all
Our sweetness, up into one Ball:
And tear our Pleasures with rough strife,
Through the Iron gates of Life.
Thus, though we cannot make our Sun
Stand still, yet we will make him run.
    (Marvell, "To his Coy Mistress," ll. 41–46)

Come, come, what doe I here?
    Since he is gone
Each day is grown a dozen year,
    And each houre, one;
        Come, come!
Cut off the sum,
By these soil'd teares!
(Which only thou
Know'st to be true,)
Dayes are my feares.
            (Vaughan, "Come, come, what doe I here?"
                                            ll. 1–10)

This stubborn return to the flux of existence is most significant of Donne's temper. It is what gives such immediacy to
his poetry and such sacramental depth to his religious experience. His strong sense of the *it is* characterizes English humanism. The Italian Renaissance, as distinct from its English
counterpart, took more seriously "the *summa* complex" and
was considerably more entranced by a holoscopic epistemol-
ogy. The *Summaries* of the twelfth-century Peter Lombard,
the thirteenth-century *Summa Aurea* of William of Au-
vergne, *Summa Universa Theologiae* of Alexander of Hales,
Summa Theologica of Thomas Aquinas, and the fifteenth-
century *Summa Theologica* of Antoninus are all expressions
of the holoscopic sense, a de-emphasis of accident and a
glorification of genus. This thirst for a *symmetria prisca* that
smooths over the tough wrinkles of experience dominated

Continental humanism but never made much headway in English humanism.

This amazing vision of unity that decries flux, of form that resolves all accidents, of a symbolic center for all phenomenological fragments is ubiquitous in the Italian Renaissance. It appears in such things as the hubristic compendia of Mirsilio Ficino, first with his *Theologica Platonica*, then with his Plotinian and Hermetic studies; with Pico della Mirandola, his nine hundred theses and his work with the mystic unity of the Jewish cabala; and with Gian Baptiste Alberti, who may be fairly taken as the epitome of the concordant artist-philosopher. Often called "The father of the Renaissance," Alberti, in the metaphysical and artistic assertions in his studies on architecture, sculpture, and painting (*De Re Aedificatoria*, ca. 1472; *De Statua*, 1464; *Della Pittura*, 1436), summarized the holoscopic inclinations of the Continent. It was he who revived the doctrine of Polyclitos and the "golden section," the "modulism" of Vitruvius, and the mystic Pythagorean belief in the symbolic unity of all experience. Two of his architectural plans have been especially singled out as significant of the Italian Renaissance: his design for the Church of St. Andrea challenged the logic of the traditional basilican church, and his design for the Church of St. Sebastian provided the model for all central churches.[50] In both plans, we see metaphysical vision at work.

The basilica-type church (which is the basic design of the Gothic cathedral, and is what St. Peter's became, through the meddling of Carlo Moderna with the design of Bramante and Michelangelo) has a ground plan of atrium, narthex, central nave and side aisles, a transept, and the apse. From the atrium to the apse and altar is a succession of columns and arches, lighted from above through the clerestory. Its symbolism is wonderfully manifest: atrium is purgative, narthex is baptismal, nave and aisles are journey, transept and apse are unitive.

The emphasis is on *movement toward*, and *progression through*, finitude (the columns and arches). The whole line of perspective is *toward* the altar, and the visitor is conceived of as the member of a marching column, passing through sequential experience to a point of rest. All this changes with Alberti's churches. There is only one central point, only one person can stand there at a time, the proper movement is not *march* but *station*, and instead of the multitude of detail there is the covering dome. The stationary point arched over by an enclosing dome is a microcosm, a concrete manifestation of the holoscopic vision. It is the metaphysic which encloses all singularity. Behind the unrecessed formalism of much Italian Renaissance art lies the Albertian vision.

But current with and counter to this holoscopic sense of reality is the meroscopic: the awareness of multiplicity, of an infinitude of unresolved singularities. Like the holoscopic, it is a pervasive sense: it is present in the nominalism of Occam, in the fourteenth-century Siennese and Florentine painting of Duccio, Simone Martini, and Giotto; in the Gothic cathedrals of the twelfth and thirteenth centuries; in the works of the fifteenth- and sixteenth-century Flemish painters such as van Eyck and Brueghel; in the works of Holbein, Dürer, Bosch. It is an art which eschews or subordinates a metaphysic, and which is aware of the riot of the finite. It is Gothic realism, naturalism, gargoylism; the little dog which intrudes into the otherwise shimmering dream vision of Chaucer's *Book of the Duchess*, the Friar's lisp, the Monk's sweat, the Wife of Bath's gap teeth, the Miller's warty nose, the demand of the *it is*. While Italy was marveling over the Florentine Academy and the broadcasting of the texts of antiquity, England was nearly destroying herself in the Wars of the Roses, and the trailing pike took priority over Plato. When the arts began again with the Tudor reign in 1485, it was the recovery of the past that was the first order of the day. The chronicles of

Polydore Vergil, the translation of Froissart's chronicles by Lord Berners, William Caxton's publications of the history of the Trojan wars, the Arthurian legends, the Robin Hood legends: these are all attempts to link up not with the classical past but with England's own past. When classical influence did come to the English court in the reign of Henry VIII, it was with remarkable differences from the way it came to the Medici court. The Oxford Reformers—Grocyn, Linacre, Colet, William Lyly—modeled themselves on the Florentine Academy, but they produced not a *summa* but functional Greek and Latin grammars. John Colet was the English Ficino—and he established a new direction in Biblical exegesis by ignoring the mystic, allegorical, and symbolic and lecturing on the literalism of St. Paul's epistles. Sir Philip Sidney achieved a stunning synthesis of Aristotle and Plato in his *Apologie For Poetrie* (1581), but admitted he was most stirred by the indigenous ballad of Chevy Chase. Edmund Spenser undertook to absorb Plato's *Symposium* and Aristotle's *Nichomachean Ethics* into the English stream, and he revived the spirit of Chaucer in *The Shepheard's Calendar*, Celtic realism in the midst of the *Epithalamion*, and northern grotesquerie in *The Faerie Queene*. Sir Thomas Elyot and Roger Ascham both took up the Renaissance theme of the "Mirror for Princes," which extends from Plato's *Republic* through Xenophon, Plutarch, and Marcus Aurelius to Castiglione, and both produced English courtesy books as iconoclastically English as Christopher Wren's later London churches, which surmounted the classical architectural orders with a uniquely English steeple. The Tudor monarchs evolved a theoryless system of government; Queen Elizabeth and her archbishop, Matthew Parker, formulated a contradictory but workable liturgy; Francis Bacon assembled a coherent philosophy without the aid of, and even the attack on, metaphysics and hypotheses.

There is a common denominator at work here, an idea which underlies such diverse phenomena as the Thirty-nine Articles, the failure of Euphuism, Shakespeare's parodies of pastoralism, Holbein's court portraits, Stowe's *Chronicles* and Camden's *Annals*, Spenser's eclogues and Dekker's handbooks. It is the challenge of experience that refuses to be stylized out of existence. The exciting collision with irreducible disorder is characteristic of a very great part of English Renaissance thought. It is also characteristic of John Donne in all his phases. For all its contradictions and discords, the world held Donne in thrall. For that reason his art is immeasurably greater than it would have been had he turned away from the tense dialectic of fragment versus unity and time versus eternity.

The four poems which are putatively contemporaries of "The Exstasie" all have a common element: they all search into the contours of earthly and perishable love for some sign of transcendence and endurance. In these four ("Negative Love," "The Undertaking," "Image and Dream," and "A Feaver"), Donne balances the terrestrial and transitory against the ethereal and immutable, and hunts for the instant of rest. In "Negative Love," he counterposes a love which "on eye, cheeke, lip can prey" to a love "which soare[s] no higher/ Then vertue on the mind to'admire" (ll. 2, 3–4). These conflicting loves are so disparate and yet so compelling that each surrenders itself to the other and disappears; and such a love can only be defined in the terms of mystic theology, the *via negativa* of a Pseudo-Dionysius:

> If that be simply perfectest
> Which can by no way be exprest
> But *Negatives*, my love is so.
>
> (ll. 10–12)

The notion of a love so fragile that it cannot be positively defined, and so ineffable that to express it is to destroy it, is the theme of "The Undertaking." The perfect love which he contemplates is as clear, as dazzling, and as indestructible as that mysterious specular stone that Pliny described in his *Natural History*, known only to the ancients, irrecoverable now, but emblematic of brightness and eternity. This love is beyond the reach of reason, so that if the profane world were told of it, they would not understand it and "Would love but as before" (l. 12). The sense of a priesthood of love, suggested first in "To his Mistris Going to Bed," and fulfilled in the mysterious "some lover, such as wee" of "The Exstasie," comes into play; and it is only the initiate who could possibly comprehend. The laity, which "colour loves, and skinne,/ Loves but their oldest clothes" (ll. 15–16); the Platonic kingdom of loveliness is within, forgetful of the sexuality of Hee and Shee (l. 20). Unutterable, this love must be guarded in silence.

> And if this love, though placed so,
>   From prophane men you hide,
> Which will no faith on this bestow,
>   Or, if they doe, deride:
>
> Then you' have done a braver thing
>   Then all the Worthies did,
> And a braver thence will spring,
>   Which is, to keepe that hid.
>   (ll. 21–28)

The vision of a woman as being, not, as in the *Elegies*, a fleshly prey, but the possessor of a flame that outlasts mortality and corruption appears in both "Image and Dream" and "A Feaver." The woman in the latter poem is virtually the *anima mundi*. If she should die, "The whole world vapors with thy breath" (l. 8), and her departure from the world would be the apocalyptic fire. But such a death is unthinkable, for she exists not in perishing matter at all, but in eternal spirit; and even if she were corruptible, she still promises immortality.

> And yet she cannot wast by this,
>   Nor long beare this torturing wrong,
> For much corruption needful is
>   To fuell such a feaver long.
>
> These burning fits but meteors bee,
>   Whose matter in thee is soone spent.
> Thy beauty, 'and all parts, which are thee,
>   Are unchangeable firmament.
>
> Yet 'twas of my minde, seising thee,
>   Though it in thee cannot persever.
> For I had rather owner bee
>   Of thee one houre, then all else ever.
>   (ll. 17–28)

In "Image and Dream," Donne makes a sharp distinction between evanescent love and enduring love. The physical beauty of the woman is equated with dullness, with pain, and with brevity. The sense-perceived image of her has so over-borne his mind that his heart "is growne now too great," and "our sense/ Strong objects dull" (ll. 6, 7–8). Her physical presence encourages "tears and pain" (l. 20), but her remembered beauty, summoned up in fantasy, is far more desirable. The dream vision has no memory of pain.

> When you are gone, and Reason gone with you,
>   Then Fantasie is Queene and Soule, and all;
> She can present joyes meaner then you do;
>   Convenient, and more proportionall.

> So, if I dreame I have you, I have you,
>   For, all our joyes are but fantasticall.
> And so I scape the paine, for paine is true;
>   And sleepe which locks up sense, doth lock out all.
>
> (ll. 9–16)

Only in "The Undertaking" is there a flight from the world and the flesh; otherwise Donne is poised between matter and spirit. In "The Exstasie," "To' our bodies turne wee then"; in "A Feaver," "For I had rather owner bee/ Of thee one houre, then all else ever"; in "Negative Love," the coincidence of sense and mind gives simple perfection. Now here, in "Image and Dream," there is the characteristic re-entry into the world, the completion of the rhythm of the love poems.

> But dearest heart, and dearer image stay;
>   Alas, true joyes at best are dreame enough;
> Though you stay here you passe too fast away:
>   For even at first lifes Taper is a snuffe.
>
> (ll. 21–24)

The magnificent valedictions of this period epitomize Donne's systole and diastole of love. The recoil from post-Paradise chaos, the participation in a fantasized love that denies fragmentation, and a return to profane existence is a tempo that infiltrates these four poems of parting. The very choice of *valediction* as the metaphoric situation is impressive, to say the least. Having established, in "The Exstasie" and its companion poems, that the universe of love is fulfilled in the flesh, Donne pushes this awareness to the breaking point. What if the fulfilling flesh were absent? Could the unity of love survive being disembodied? The valedictions explore the question, not in the arid rhetoric of debate, but in the context where it belongs: fully realized human drama. When read together, these four poems create a polyphonic effect, with their distinct variations on a single theme. The optimism of "A Valediction: forbidding Mourning" is challenged by the anxiety of "A Valediction: of Weeping." The trust placed in the woman in "A Valediction: of the Booke" is counterbalanced by fear in "A Valediction: of my Name in the Window." There is a full orchestration of moods: solicitude in "forbidding Mourning," uneasiness in "of my Name in the Window," assurance in "of the Booke," and commiseration in "of Weeping." The only static elements are the situation itself in each poem and the figure of the woman, who could be moved from one poem to the other without harm. This is not a flaw: the issue of separation and of the power of the woman to metamorphose time into eternity are the cruxes of these poems, and for that matter of the later poetry as a whole. She must remain fixed as the enigma around which the inquiry revolves.

Izaak Walton presumed that at least one of the valedictions was provoked by a literal parting from Ann Donne; and it now seems most likely that Donne was, as a matter of fact, traveling abroad in 1605–1606, and that he had to leave his wife before the birth of their son George, in May of 1605.[51] There are other indications that the valedictions are to be associated with such a literal separation. Much later, in "A Nocturnall upon S. Lucies Day, being the shortest day," Donne seems to identify Ann with the weeping woman of these poems (ll. 23–27). Also, in "A Valediction: of Weeping" there is a striking conceit that gains in poignancy if we imagine that Donne is addressing himself to Ann practically on the eve of her confinement with her third child (as she indeed was in May of 1605). The valediction opens:

> Let me powre forth
> My teares before thy face, whil'st I stay here,
> For thy face coines them, and thy stampe they beare,

> And by this Mintage they are something worth,
>   For thus they bee
>   Pregnant of thee; . . .
>   (ll. 1–6)

It's a deft and surprising reversal: not only is she pregnant by him, but his tears have become pregnant by her. Donne contrives thus to stress still further the communal nature of their love: even this we share.

But history accounts for, doesn't explain, Donne's work. To say that Ann More Donne is within the poetry does not preclude there being more than Ann. Out of raw fact Donne creates private worlds that may have begun in a literal context but then are autonomously enclosed in his art. In the valedictions, Donne may very well be describing an impending channel crossing; but he is also describing a return to the ambiguities of existence. The images of water, slaughter, and tempest are ensigns of the flux of history that he defined in *The Progresse of the Soule,* and the woman (an idealized Ann perhaps, provided such a rubric doesn't overliteralize the poems) he leaves is his phantasm of unity. The valedictions all confront the question, can the experience of love survive in the City of Man? Each poem is an exhortation, not only to the woman, but to his own need, and the reply is: it must. Donne's *Anniversary* poems accept the *occasion* of a real death (Elizabeth Drury's) and then move far beyond the occasion; it is quite possible that the valedictions accept the occasion of a literal parting; they certainly move beyond domesticity or Gravesend dock.

Something of the bravery of "The Undertaking" is captured in the valedictions "forbidding Mourning" and "of the Booke." The mood in all those poems that radiate from "The Exstasie" is certainty in the presence of mystery. In "Negative Love," the sensationalists and idealists of passion are abandoned, deserted for a love which is ineffably beyond theirs:

> I never stoop'd so low, as they
> Which on an eye, cheeke, lip, can prey,
>   Seldome to them, which soare no higher
>   Then vertue or the minde to'admire,
> For sense, and understanding may
>   Know, what gives fuell to their fire:
> My love, though silly, is more brave,
> For may I misse, when ere I crave,
> If I know yet, what I would have.
>
> (ll. 1–9)

The arcana of "The Undertaking" cannot be shared:

> So, if I now should utter this,
>   Others (because no more
> Such stuffe to worke upon, there is,)
>   Would love but as before.
>
> (ll. 9–12)

Reason and Fantasy are both summoned, dismissed, recalled, and finally united in "Image and Dream" in the effort to cope with the magnitude of love; and the perplexities of "what we love" or the doubts of the "wrangling schools" do not hamper the affirmations that cascade through "The Exstasie" and "A Feaver." Exploratory though they are, and stubborn in their pursuit of love's definition, there is nothing of the backing and filling that we find in the debate poems ("Aire and Angels," "Loves Growth," "Loves Infiniteness," and "A Lecture upon the Shadow").

This affirmative mood continues in the valedictions "forbidding Mourning" and "of the Booke." The by now familiar contrast between the laity and the initiates, the profane and the sacred, the broken and the whole provides the movement within each poem. In "A Valediction: forbidding Mourning," the lovers are absolved from all the sensational agonies of the dull sublunary lovers. "Like gold to ayery thinnesse beate"

(l. 24), they are together even when riven by parting. Their complementary compass-love insures their being the emblem of eternity, that Hermetic sphere whose center is everywhere and circumference nowhere that so delighted Thomas Browne.[52] "A Valediction: of the Booke" continues the combat against metempsychosed history, the soul of division and death:

> I'll tell thee now (deare Love) what thou shalt doe
> To anger destiny, as she doth us, . . .
>
> (ll. 1–2)

The woman of the poem first appears as a sybil, then as a galaxy of poetesses (Corinna, Lucan's wife, and Phantasia[53]), and finally, along with the lover, as a compendium of prophecy and poetry, a sacred book. As their love shames all other loves, so the book which they have become shames all other sacred texts.

Donne's ingenuity in specifying a bibliography of mystery gives some slight notion of his far-flung literary researches in these post-marriage, pre-Morton years.[54] Donne, in these years, had turned to esoterica: Neoplatonism, cabalism, Hermeticism, the occultism of transcendent philosophy. He evidently recognized in their heterodoxy reinforcements of his own disquiet over the puzzle of existence. Doctrines which the several gnostic philosophies hold in common read like a gloss on Donne's mind and art as they are developed after *The Progresse of the Soule*: a primordial catastrophe when a divine unity was shattered; the memory of that unity which torments the surviving fragments; the yearning for oneness as a cosmic ache; the tantalizing intimations of a recoverable unity in a hieroglyphic universe; the preservation of that memory by the elect; the image of a woman as the *typos* of oneness and wholeness; and, to point to Donne's valediction, the existence of a sacred text which shows the way.[55] We need not hunt for chapter and verse in the *Enneads*, the *Zohar*, or the *Asclepius* as sources of Donne's own phantasm of unity. The fascination such works have exerted and continue to exert is due to the way they impinge on that part of the mind that has watched logic attempt to explain mystery and been baffled. They are all symbolizations of a mythic faculty, and under their speciously different terminologies lies a common, shared insight: the intuition that man is involved in a drama of loss and discovery,[56] and that he is naturally equipped with a yearning for safety and revelation.[57]

The occult traditions of East and West were not the sources of Donne's longing. He was alert enough to his own intuitions not to need *Hermetica* as the catalysts of insight. But he was able to use the several gnostic philosophies as articulations of his own felt emptiness, and as a storehouse of expressive symbols of exile and reunion. They provide him, for a time, with a voluble and confident myth. Source studies have shown how wide Donne was casting; the poems of 1602 to 1605 show marks of Ficino's *Commentary*, Leone Ebreo's *Dialog of Love*, Paracelsus, Lipsius' commentary on the *Myriobiblion* of Photius, Franciscus Georgius, Pico della Mirandola, not to mention the more conservative Aristotle and Aquinas.[58] "A Valediction: of the Booke," for instance, has overtones of the *Corpus Hermeticum*. Participants in the sacred mysteries can pass through swift and dangerous waters, which are symbols of the world (*Corpus Hermeticum*, Libellus VII); the lovers can outwit destiny and history ("Valediction," ll. 1–2; *C.H.*, Libellus XII); they possess a wisdom that is closed to the noninitiate ("Valediction," ll. 23–26; *C.H.*, Libellus XIII); the union of lovers is a paradigm of eternity ("Valediction," ll. 35–36; *C.H.*, Libellus I); the revelation they possess is total and includes all wisdom ("Valediction," ll. 23–27; *C.H.*, Libellus XVI).[59] Donne's poem is structured, like most of the *Corpus Hermeticum* and the

Latinized Hermetic book, the *Asclepius*, as a master-disciple discourse, and Donne assigns to love most of the qualities of the sacred book of Hermes Trismegistus: it is eternal, hieroglyphic, encyclopedic, sacerdotal. Indeed, the book of their love is so revelatory that it resolves all the quiddities traced out in "The Exstasie" or "Negative Love": the abstractionists of love, the materialists, and the typologists may all find their sacred texts contained here:

> Here Loves Divines, (since all Divinity
>   Is love or wonder) may finde all they seeke,
>   Whether abstract spirituall love they like,
> Their Soules exhal'd with what they do not see,
>   Or, loth so to amuze
>   Faiths infirmitie, they chuse
>   Something which they may see and use;
>   For, though minde be the heaven, where love doth sit,
> Beauty'a convenient type may be to figure it.
>
> (ll. 28–36)

Two of Donne's earlier targets, lawyers and statesmen, are introduced as *exempla* of the outsiders, those who cannot understand the mystique of love and can never be privy to its magic. The lawyer will pragmatically examine "by what titles Mistresses are ours" (l.38), and the statesman will fail equally in his analytic approach to this suprarational cult:

> Love and their art alike it deadly wounds,
>   If to consider what 'tis, one proceed.
>
> (ll. 48–49)

But to these creatures of the world, who are trying to reduce mystic cabala to practical alchemy, love will remain a closed book, frustrating all their attempts to crack the code: "In this thy booke, such will their nothing see,/ As in the Bible some can finde out Alchimy" (ll. 53–54). The valediction con-

cludes with what is nearly a digest of several poems of this
period:

> Thus vent thy thoughts; abroad I'll studie thee,
>> As he removes farre off, that great heights takes;
>> How great love is, presence best tryall makes,
> But absence tryes how long this love will bee;
>>> To take a latitude
>>> Sun, or starres, are fitliest view'd
>>> At their brightest, but to conclude
>> Of longitudes, what other way have wee,
> But to marke when, and where the darke eclipses be?
>
> (ll. 55–63)

A present trial of greatness describes the five "consequence"
poems ("The Good-morrow," "The Anniversarie," "The
Sunne Rising," "The Canonization," and "The Dreame"),
while endurance tested by absence describes both the valedictions and the three poems of dismembered love ("The Dissolution," "The Relique," and "The Funerall"). The sense of
the compactness of the poems of 1602–1605, the impression
of Donne exploring every nuance of love, is heightened by this
nine-line capsule résumé or forecast of his other poems.

The two remaining valedictions are unique in that they
both reveal that misgiving which reaches its climax in "Loves
Alchymie" and "Farewell to Love." Ever since "To his Mistris Going to Bed," Donne has imposed on the woman a
double task: she must be both the initiator into the mystery
of love and the mystery itself, priestess and temple at the
same time. In that elegy, the woman begins as the map to
Paradise, and finally is Paradise; in "A Valediction: of the
Booke," she begins as poetess and ends as poem. In "A
Valediction: of Weeping" and "A Valediction: of my Name
in the Window," Donne wavers in his faith that the woman

is capable of containing and guarding the mystery. Even in his most bitter and disenchanted states, Donne never underestimates the shattering brilliance of present sexual love; but he grows less optimistic about woman's love being able to endure "the dark eclipses" of separation. The interplay of images of day and night, brightness and darkness, symbolizing the explosiveness of sexual love as opposed to the calm of enduring suprasexual love, operates in all but three ("Loves Infiniteness," "Aire and Angels," "Loves Growth") of the non-valedictory poems of this period. That there should have to be such a dichotomy runs counter to the equipoise achieved in "The Exstasie" or "Negative Love" or "Image and Dream"; but the doubts that provoke such a clash are woven into the nervous valedictions. The dismembered unity which Donne attempts to repair through love makes its appearance even within love. The road to the repudiations of "Farewell to Love" begins here.

"A Valediction: of my Name in the Window" is a return to paradoxical argument as Donne practiced it in "The Flea." Even the movement of the poem is reminiscent of that youthful sleight of hand: a surprising analogy is so carefully developed that its very implausibility begins to diminish, and just as we've been persuaded to admit the cogency of the image, Donne demolishes it. In no other love poem of this second group does Donne essay this creation and then smashing of a paradox; his usual mode is to create and then maintain to its farthest extent a single intact conceit. It is as if, in this poem, Donne is attempting the same sort of exorcism of a demon as in "The Autumnal." The fear is captured in a verbal icon, the icon is destroyed, and along with it the fear. If so, the spell didn't work; but in the meantime it provides a firm structure for the valediction.

The poem is a series of metamorphoses. The window pane of the first stanza, on which the lover engraves his name, becomes first a microcosm of the lover himself: the glass is as transparent as he, and the gouges in the glass are surgical incisions which reveal his whole anatomy.

The engraved name then becomes a charm against all evil spirits, sufficient to ward off any intruder, e.g., a rival lover; and eventually becomes his mana, an effluvium that will work its way into the woman's unconsciousness and always keep her mindful of him. Then, suddenly, Donne repudiates the image. It has been uncomfortably swinging to a demonstration of the woman's weakness, and he hurriedly reverses himself.

> But glasse, and lines must bee,
> No meanes our firme substantiall love to keepe;
> Neere death inflicts this lethargie,
> And this I murmure in my sleepe;
> Impute this idle talke, to that I goe,
> For dying men talke often so.
>
> (ll. 61-66)

"A Valediction: of Weeping" also hovers on the edge of recognizing ambiguities even in love. The overt imagery of the poem is all optimistic, a tender sharing of grief between man and woman. Their love transforms their tears into stamped coins, into entire worlds; their sighs rival the winds of a storm in their destructiveness. But underneath this canopy of compliment is the faintest shadow of a doubt. These lovers are not "Like gold to ayery thinnesse beate"; their separation might be the end of their love. "So thou and I are nothing then, when on a divers shore" (l. 9). The woman's tear may be an emblem of grief, a coin, a globe; but it may also be a moon, the waxing and waning symbol of infidelity. The woman may be not the antidote to the world into which the lover is stepping, but the world itself in disguise, harboring all the death-dealing flux of existence:

O more then Moone,
Draw not up seas to drowne me in thy spheare,
Weepe me not dead, in thine armes, but forbeare
To teach the sea, what it may doe too soone;
Let not the winde
Example finde,
To doe me more harme, then it purposeth.

(ll. 19–25)

Such flickers of doubt set these valedictions apart from their companions, and mark them as preludes to the later poems of rejection.

The four debate poems ("Aire and Angels," "Loves Growth," "Loves Infiniteness," and "A Lecture upon the Shadow") are probably the most legalistic, the most closely reasoned, of all Donne's love poetry. An aura of Scholastic *sic et non* inquiry hovers over them, a near-Thomistic awareness of alternatives and adversaries that must be reckoned with before a conclusion can be reached. They are not as subtly ingenious as the "Elegie upon the untimely death of the incomparable Prince Henry" (1612), but of all the love poems these come the closest in method and purpose to Donne's controversial prose works. Donne is always something of the grand inquisitor in his later poetry, but never more so than in these searches for the endurance of love.

It might seem at first that these four poems are adjuncts to "The Exstasie," in that they too examine "the metaphysic of love" and probe into the theme of resolution: body and spirit, flux and permanence. In a sense, this is true. The delicate balance that was reached in "The Exstasie" must, precisely because of its delicacy, be continually dramatized, and the diaphanous bond between contraries needs to be reassuringly felt. But they are not in any sense repetitions of "The Exstasie." Between it and them intrudes the problem of separation.

The creation of an eternal present, in which all the perturbations of time are suspended and a primeval unity is captured in the flesh, is the dream of the earliest poems of this period. But what if that single everlasting day of love were broken into, and the space of love stepped out of? Could the unity of love survive? Two of the valedictions affirm that it could, but two entertain doubts. Solar unity of total love, and dark eclipses of absent love: this now becomes the issue. Both aspects are examined in the debate poems; then solar love is the subject of five poems ("The Good-morrow," "The Anniversarie," "The Sunne Rising," "The Canonization," and "The Dreame"), while the dark eclipses are the subject of three poems ("The Dissolution," "The Relique," and "The Funerall").

In "Aire and Angels," Donne resolutely fuses a whole series of perplexities as antique as the satires and as immediate as the valedictions. How does love exist? In what sense do I exist? Does woman complement man, and if so, how? Can there be any love beyond the basic fact of male and female, something which both includes and transcends sexuality? The isolated romantic of the satires, scorning all contact, and the engrossed sensualist of many of the elegies and the early poems in the *Songs and Sonnets* are both denizens of "Aire and Angels," the first with his "lovely glorious nothing" (l. 6) and the second with his "scatt'ring bright" collection of lips, eyes, and brows (l. 22). But behind the two definitions of love that are first proposed in the poem (a disembodied yearning versus physical delight) a deeper question lurks. What is it *to be?* There are two poles set up in the poem: on the one hand *nothing*, and on the other hand *surfeit*. Each is a possible sphere wherein a man might hope to find satisfaction. But the argument of "Aire and Angels" is that neither satisfies. Of the first,

> Love must not be, but take a body too,
>   And therefore what thou wert, and who,
>   I bid Love aske, and now
>   That it assume thy body, I allow,
>   And fixe it selfe in thy lip, eye, and brow.
>   (ll. 10–14)

But the reaction away from *nothing* is a move toward *surfeit:*

>   Ev'ry thy haire for love to worke upon
> Is much too much, some fitter must be sought;
>   For, nor in nothing, nor in things
> Extreme, and scatt'ring bright, can love inhere.
>   (ll. 19–22)

The equilibrium between the two is the same *discordia con-cors,* the conjoined duality of body and spirit, of "Negative Love" and "The Exstasie."

>   Then as an Angell, face, and wings
> Of aire, not pure as it, yet pure doth weare,
>   So thy love may be my loves spheare;
>   Just such disparitie
>   As is twixt Aire and Angells puritie,
>   'Twixt womens love, and mens will ever bee.
>   (ll. 23–28)

Donne has been establishing equations throughout the poem, as so:

>   Angels = men = nothing
>   Air = women = substantial sphere

For love to take "limmes of flesh, and else could nothing doe" (l. 8), man must have the incarnate experience of a woman, she must become his love's sphere.

The most dramatic thing about the poem is not that Donne is repudiating the surfeit carnal love of his earlier period, but that he is rejecting the appeal that *nothingness* had for him earlier. His angelic = nothing is submerged into the woman's air = action, and this is something of a major conversion in Donne's attitude. Earlier, Donne was caught by the seductiveness of *nothing*, and beginning with the first two satires, he identified *nothing* and *potency*. Pure potency is vitiated in act, and Donne played with both the sexual and philosophic nuances of the terms. Superficially he is most male in the violent *Elegies*, his masculinity is paraded in the act of love. But he really gives up very little: in the act of love that the woman provides, he does not surrender his intact and still unshaped self. The woman in the *Elegies* was only a stage, incapable of activating anything but sexual potency. As far as getting him to commit part of himself, and so to transform himself, she was inadequate. The same is true of the woman in the early group of the *Songs and Sonnets*: she could provoke no involvement, break through no barriers; she could not help to create the man. In "The Prohibition," for instance, the great passions of love and hate cancel one another out, leaving the lover as neutral as he was before he and the woman confronted one another.

In the poems of this period, she becomes something more; the woman becomes the vehicle of philosophic potency passing into act. It is through her that the residing power *to be* becomes existent. As Donne said of her in "A Valediction: of my Name in the Window,"

> all my soules bee,
> Emparadis'd in you (in whom alone
> I understand, and grow and see,) . . .
> (ll. 25-27)

Before the poems of 1602-1605, Donne was entranced by being *nothing* as the surest invulnerability; by the time of the religious poetry, he is aiming at *nothingness* as the prelimi-

nary of spiritual rebirth. But in this period, and very much so
in "Aire and Angels," he renounces the idea, and accepts love
as a better surrogate.

"Loves Growth" is very like "Aire and Angels," but it is
more precise in the way that it explores the two dimensions of
potency and *act*. It begins with a variation on the *nothing-
surfeit* clash of "Aire and Angels." Now, it is *immutable*
versus *mutable*:

> I scarce beleeve my love to be so pure
>   As I had thought it was,
>   Because it doth endure
> Vicissitude, and season, as the grasse; . . .
> (ll. 1–4)

The movement toward solution is much more rapid than in
any of the other conjugate poems, i.e., "The Exstasie" or
"Aire and Angels"; the collaboration of the two poles is
achieved by the end of the first stanza.

> Love's not so pure, and abstract, as they use
> To say, which have no Mistresse but their Muse,
> But as all else, being elemented too,
> Love sometimes would contemplate, sometimes do.
> (ll. 11–14)

The second stanza is given over to developing the germinal
idea of "Aire and Angels," the woman's ability to bring into
existence what had been latent, potency passing through act
into life:

> Gentle love deeds, as blossomes on a bough,
> From loves awaken'd root do bud out now.
> (ll. 19–20)

At the center of ever-widening love, which was immanent but
uncreated, is the woman veritably the *axis mundi* and the
agent of potency becoming act:

If, as in water stir'd more circles bee
  Produc'd by one, love such additions take,
  Those like to many spheares, but one heaven make,
For, they are all concentrique unto thee;
And though each spring doe adde to love new heate,
As princes doe in times of action get
New taxes, and remit them not in peace,
No winter shall abate the springs increase.

(ll. 21–28)

The creative power of the woman thwarts the somber note of
the poem's opening, "[love] doth endure/ Vicissitude, and
season, as the grasse." As in "The Anniversarie" or "The
Sunne Rising," love and the woman can control even the
debilitating effects of the seasons.

"Loves Infiniteness" acts as a counterbalance to the refrain
of *nothing* as it dominates in "Aire and Angels" and "Loves
Growth." Its impetus is provided by what might be identified
as musical paradox, i.e., contrapuntal melody. Using counterpoint as a superb embodiment and melodic solution of conflict, Donne pursues the sense of *all* as rigorously as he has
been pursuing *nothing*. The *all* chimes through the poem
without intermission:

If yet I have not all thy love,
  Deare, I shall never have it all; . . .

(ll. 1–2)

If then thy gift of love were partiall,
  That some to mee, some should to others fall,
    Deare, I shall never have Thee All.

(ll. 9–11)

Or if then thou gav'st mee all,
  All was but All, which thou hadst then.

(ll. 12–13)

> The ground, thy heart is mine, what ever shall
> Grow there, deare, I should have it all.
>
> (ll. 21–22)
>
> Yet I would not have all yet,
> Hee that hath all can have no more, . . .
>
> (ll. 23–24)
>
> But wee will have a way more liberall,
> Then changing hearts, to joyne them, so wee shall
> Be one, and one anothers All.
>
> (ll. 31–33)

The drumming insistence of the *all* is counterweighted by the equally insistent disjunctives that run through the poem: *if, nor, yet, if, or, but, for, yet, yet, since, if, but.* There is a fugal quality established, a constant refrain (*all*) that endures through all the atonality of the harsh and staccato interruptions.[60] The survival of a rhythmic pattern helps the structure of the poem. Each of the three stanzas is made up of two open quatrains and a tercet, and the rhyme of all three tercets is patterned around *all*:

> partiall
> fall
> All
>
> general
> shall
> all
>
> liberall
> shall
> All

At the end of each hesitating stanza, packed with the discordant notes of the monosyllabic *buts, yets, ors,* and *ifs,* is the repeated musical refrain capped by *all.*

But this is not the limit of Donne's structuring principle.
He relates melodic counterpoint to conceptual paradox. The
opening quatrain of the first two stanzas includes the rhyming
on *all,* and is answered, each time, by a quatrain that includes
a rhyming of *thee* and *mee.* In these two stanzas, the nega-
tives are rampant, and the infinity of love is most elusive:

> yet . . . not . . . love
> never . . . *all*
> cannot . . . move
> nor . . . *fall*
> > thee
> > spent
> yet . . . *mee*
> > ment
>
> or . . . *all*
> but . . . then
> but . . . *shall*
> > men
> > teares
> > mee
> > fears
> for . . . *thee*

In the third stanza, the elusiveness of love's infiniteness is
overcome:

> But wee will have a way more liberall,
> Then changing hearts, to joyne them, so wee shall
> > Be one, and one anothers All.

> (ll. 31–33)

In this last stanza, there is no *mee-thee* rhyme; its disappear-
ance is simultaneous with the triumph of *All* over the discords
of the poem.

The stichomythia of love, where selfishness argues with

selflessness, sexual delight argues with transcendent rapture, separateness argues with unity, and temporariness argues with infinity, is embodied here in a musical form. The paradoxes of love are represented by a fuguelike interweaving of dissonant ideas, and at the end all the discords are submerged in the infinite music of love. Neither the structure nor the logic of the poem creates the melody of infinity by simplistically denying the dissonances; rather, the music is made by them. The final chord of "Loves Infiniteness,"

> we shall
> Be one, and one anothers All

is not at all the same as

> When love, with one another so
> Interinanimates two soules,
> That abler soule, which thence doth flow,
> Defects of lonelinesse controules.
> ("The Exstasie," ll. 41–44)

Nor is it the same as the "simply perfectest" of "Negative Love" nor the forgetfulness of the Hee and Shee of "The Undertaking." Those poems, the earliest and most optimistic of Donne's flights from the divided soul of the world, all end in utter silence. Safe from clanging existence, "wee said nothing, all the day"; love "can by no way be exprest"; and I "have done a braver thing . . . which is, to keepe that hid." But there is no silence in "Loves Infiniteness"; instead, crashing polyphony. The line between the noise of the world and the silence of love, over which the observer of "The Exstasie" was invited to step, grows thinner and thinner.

The last debate poem, "A Lecture upon the Shadow," shares the uncomfortable ambiguities that make their reluctant appearance in "A Valediction: of Weeping" and "Loves

Infiniteness." Under a cover of bravado and affirmation of the strength of love runs a stream of images and ideas that contradict the bravery. The tension between the splendor and the fugacity of love is the controlling element in this loveliest of the debates.

The poem is, characteristically, a dramatic monologue; but whereas the listening woman was only recurrently noticed in the other debates, she is very much a presence here. There is a shower of plural pronouns, continually pulling the speaker back to the woman and away from the intricacies of his meditation. There is a great quiet in the poem, almost the stillness of "The Exstasie."

"A Lecture upon the Shadow" occupies that land of growing doubt which stretches between "A Valediction: of the Booke," on the one hand, and "The Anniversarie" and "The Sunne Rising," on the other. In the "Valediction" the depth of love was gauged by viewing its sun at zenith; in the latter poems, the sun is senescent, an affront to love, hardly an adequate index to love's powers. Its contrary nature, peripherally touched on in "Loves Growth," is brought completely into the open in "A Lecture upon the Shadow," and its contradictory nature as both an adequate symbol of love ("A Valediction: of the Booke") and a mocker of love ("The Sunne Rising") is tested.

As the "Lecture" begins, there is an identity between love and the sun:

> Stand still, and I will read to thee,
> A Lecture, Love, in loves philosophy.
>> These three houres that we have spent,
>> Walking here, two shadowes went
> Along with us, which we our selves produc'd;
> But, now the Sunne is just above our head,
>> We doe those shadowes tread;

> And to brave clearnesse all things are reduc'd.
>   So whilst our infant loves did grow,
>   Disguises did, and shadowes, flow
> From us, and our care; . . .
>
> (ll. 1–11)

But from this instant, there must be two suns: "but, now 'tis not so" (l. 11) that the sun of our love and the literal sun can be the same. Love must create its own sun, not "westwardly declining" like the other.

>   Except our loves at this noone stay,
>   We shall new shadowes make the other way.
>
> (ll. 14–15)

If ever the sun of our love should begin to decline, we must hide that knowledge from one another.

>   As the first were made to blinde
>   Others; these which come behinde
> Will worke upon our selves, and blind our eyes.
> If our loves faint, and westwardly decline;
>   To me thou, falsly, thine,
> And I to thee mine actions shall disguise.
>
> (ll. 16–21)

For the sad fact is that even the blazing noon of love is ephemeral.

>   The morning shadowes weare away,
>   But these grow longer all the day,
>   But oh, loves day is short, if love decay.
>
> (ll. 22–24)

There is only the tiniest flicker between the zenith of love and its nadir.

Love is a growing, or full constant light;
And his first minute, after noone, is night.

(ll. 25–26)

Love shares with the sun its brave clearness, but it also shares the shortness of its noon. As in "Loves Growth," love may expand, but as it does it shares in the vicissitudes of all growing things. Around it are the shadows which are made by itself and which threaten to extinguish it. The double vision of the hope and disappointment of love is as poignant as anything Donne ever wrote.

The metaphors of passion = sun, tested endurance of love = eclipse continue to operate so persistently that eight of the love poems create a dialogue effect. "The Good-morrow," "The Anniversarie," "The Sunne Rising," and "The Dreame" all treat of a time-arresting, primarily physical love, in settings of dawn, awakening, or light. "The Dissolution," "The Relique," and "The Funerall" are all concerned with a love that survives physical separation, in settings of darkness and death. One of the poems, "The Canonization," totters between present light and future eclipse. The impression of Donne using his poetry as a laboratory of meditation, probing into an enigma in extended, purposeful, and related groups of poems, continues to assert itself.

Not since the most erotic of the elegies has Donne so successfully re-created the intoxication that comes with sexual satisfaction as he does in the four *aubades* of this group. The voice that is heard is positively drunken in its swaggering, scornfully dismissing anything that mocks or threatens to demean the triumph of love. There is nothing of the post-coital ennui of "Farewell to Love" in "The Sunne Rising," but instead a raucous male chest-pounding. The twitching expectancy of "come, Madame, come" is recaptured in "The

Dreame," while astral and political hierarchies are subverted by love in "The Good-morrow" and "The Anniversarie." In "The Dreame" and in "The Good-morrow," the world of fantasy and imagination pales before present delight, in a reverse of the situation in "Image and Dream":

> Enter these armes, for since thou thoughtst it best,
> Not to dreame all my dreame, let's do the rest.
> ("The Dreame," ll. 9–10)

> If ever any beauty I did see,
> Which I desir'd, and got, 'twas but a dreame of thee.
> ("The Good-morrow," ll. 6–7)

Enjoyed love is a blaze of light, an illuminated sphere of perfection and immutability:[61]

> My face in thine eye, thine in mine appeares,
>   And true plaine hearts doe in the faces rest,
> Where can we finde two better hemispheares
>   Without sharpe North, without declining West?
> ("The Good-morrow," ll. 15–18)

> Shine here to us, and thou art every where;
> This bed thy center is, these walls, thy spheare.
> ("The Sunne Rising," ll. 29–30)

> As lightning, or a Tapers light,
> Thine eyes, and not thy noise wak'd me; . . .
> ("The Dreame," ll. 11–12)

And yet, for all the ferocious delight, there is still, as in "Loves Infiniteness" and "A Lecture upon the Shadow," a counterbalance in all these poems, a hard sense of threat. Images of change and of treason jostle with images of eternity and fidelity. In "The Good-morrow," love is given a condition to fulfill:

If our two loves be one, or, thou and I
Love so alike, that none doe slacken, none can die.

(ll. 20–21)

"The Anniversarie" hints at the possibility of a broken pledge:

Who is so safe as wee? where none can doe
Treason to us, except one of us two.

(ll. 25–26)

The climax of "The Dreame" is the woman's movement
toward shattering the union:

Comming and staying show'd thee, thee,
But rising makes me doubt, that now,
    Thou art not thou.
That love is weake, where feare's as strong as hee;
    'Tis not all spirit, pure, and brave,
If mixture it of *Feare, Shame, Honor*, have.
Perchance as torches which must ready bee,
Men light and put out, so thou deal'st with mee,
Thou cam'st to kindle, goest to come; Then I
Will dreame that hope againe, but else would die.

(ll. 21–30)

Intimations of approaching death give a resonance to the
theme of immediate delight in both "The Anniversarie" and
"The Canonization":

Two graves must hide thine and my coarse,
If one might, death were no divorce.
Alas, as well as other Princes, wee,
(Who Prince enough in one another bee,)
Must leave at last in death, these eyes, and eares,
Oft fed with true oathes, and with sweet salt teares; . . .

("The Anniversarie," ll. 11–16)

> We can dye by it, if not live by love,
> And if unfit for tombes or hearse
> Our legend bee, it will be fit for verse;
> And if no peece of Chronicle wee prove,
> We'll build in sonnets pretty roomes;
> As well a well wrought urne becomes
> The greatest ashes, as half-acre tombes,
> And by these hymnes, all shall approve
>   Us *Canoniz'd* for Love.
>   ("The Canonization," ll. 28–36)

Most importantly, there is a new attitude toward the mystery of love, which is no longer conceived of as an objective body of doctrine known to the magi of love. The sense of a closed apostolate of love, a blessed sanctuary which shuts out the noise and confusion of the world is evident in the poetry which followed upon *The Progresse of the Soule*. In "The Undertaking," the lover has discovered the mystery; "The Exstasie" is a descant upon the orthodoxy of that mystery; "A Valediction: forbidding Mourning" capitalizes on the contrast between closed mystery and public ignorance; while "A Valediction: of the Booke" asserts the bibliothetic reality of mystery. It is possible that the image of Seth is still operating through these poems, for he was thought of as the inheritor of sacred wisdom, the guardian of that vision of unity that had been shattered by Cain. Whereas the descendants of Cain are left with shards, fragments, and public Babel, the descendants of Seth silently preserve the sacred truth of oneness and sanctitude. Hidden though such wisdom had to be, it nevertheless is *real*, a promise that could be found.

But there is none of this in the *aubades*. Any mystery of love which controls the defects of loneliness must be created by the lovers themselves. There is no sign of a doctrine discovered, only a self-assembled brilliance. The closed universe of love does not reflect any geography of order that lies beyond temporal disorder and incoherence. It is every bit as solipsistic, as desperately self-centered, as the little lonely worlds that Donne built in the earliest poetry. The only difference is the resident woman, but she is continually on the verge of leaving, always about to frustrate the salvific role she must play. She must be monitored: love as I do, do not betray me, do not leave me. Those intrusions of doubt that are noticeable in the valedictions "of Weeping" and "of my Name" are, if anything, stronger in the *aubades*.

It is this element that gives to Donne's light imagery in these poems its greatest effect. The daytime of love has to be assembled by the lover in defiance of all the normal laws of light and shadow. The light of these poems is like that in Caravaggio's "Vocation of St. Matthew" or Tintoretto's "Presentation of the Virgin"; it is mannerist light, generated by no conceivable force of nature and obeying none of the usual laws of optics. It is an incandescent world which

> no tomorrow hath, nor yesterday,
> Running it never runs from us away,
> But truly keepes his first, last, everlasting day.
> ("The Anniversarie," ll. 8–10)

It "no season knowes, nor clyme,/ Nor houres, dayes, months, which are the rags of time" ("The Sunne Rising," ll. 9–10). The blaze of love is as manipulatable and as plastic as the light in a Vermeer portrait, dominating the whole surface of the represented object:

> Shine here to us, and thou art every where;
> This bed thy center is, these walls, thy spheare.
> ("The Sunne Rising," ll. 29–30)

But for all the unearthly brilliance of this light, it lives on the edge of shadows, a frail taper that can be easily snuffed out by infidelity or by death:

Call us what you will, wee 'are made such by love;
Call her one, mee another flye,
We'are Tapers too, and at our owne cost die.
                    ("The Canonization," ll. 19–21)

Perchance as torches which must ready bee,
Men light and put out, so thou deal'st with mee,
Thou cam'st to kindle, goest to come; . . .
                    ("The Dreame," ll. 27–29)

The palpable sense of death that puts an end to this exceedingly tenuous light is converted by Donne's imagination into an affirmation that love can survive the dark. As he had said in "A Valediction: of the Booke," an eclipse can be the measurement of the endurance of love. So in "The Anniversarie," death is converted into such a triumphant trial:

When bodies to their graves, soules from their graves remove.
And then we shall be throughly blest, . . .
                                    (ll. 20–21)

In "The Canonization," love will so completely triumph over death that he and the woman will pass into hagiography. Three poems ("The Dissolution," "The Relique," and "The Funerall") transform death into a demonstration of love's power to endure. They are the absolute terminus of Donne's flight from postlapsarian chaos along the route of human love; they are all attempts to follow love beyond death and to persuade himself that death doesn't matter.

In *The Progresse of the Soule*, Donne had put together a bestiary that showed how all the elements of creation had been poisoned by paradox and division and death, and in "The Dissolution" he complains of the burdensomeness of the elements; only when he can, projectilelike, flee such impediments can he overtake a fantasy-mistress lost in fantasy-death:

My fire of Passion, sighes of ayre,
Water of teares, and earthly sad despaire,
  Which my materials bee,
But neere worne out by loves securitie,
Shee, to my losse, doth by her death repaire,
  And I might live long wretched so
But that my fire doth with my fuell grow . . .
   This death, hath with my store
    My use encreas'd.
And so my soule more earnestly releas'd,
Will outstrip hers; As bullets flown before
A latter bullet may o'rtake, the pouder being more.
     (ll. 9–15, 20–24)

In "The Relique," as in "The Canonization," the real depths of love will be known only in death, and the sacral sense of love's mystery will not be recognized until then. "The Funerall," very much as in "Image and Dream," envisions a love free of all pain and all anxiety; and the release from inquietude can come only in death: in life, the woman meant the bracelet of hair to be a source of pain, but now it has become a brave emblem of love vanquishing sorrow.

These three poems, like most of Donne's poetry, are auto-rhetorical, orations delivered at himself and dramas staged for himself, persuasions to believe in the reality of love as a way back to a shattered Eden. But the persuasions grow more and more aware of the adversaries, the confirmations less and less confident, the *exordia* shriller. The whole campaign collapses in "The Blossome," "Loves Alchymie," and "Farewell to Love." From the confidence of "The Exstasie," then the apprehension of ambivalence in the debates, the fears in the *aubades*, Donne arrives at a weariness of trying to devise a philosophy of human love out of shifting dreams that are mocked by experience. These three poems are a sad and bitter surrender to the divisiveness of the world.[62]

"The Blossome" looks back to the startling reversals of "Woman's Constancy" or "Goe, and catche a falling starre" in the way that it establishes a line of argument and then ironically veers off to a conclusion that is both anticipated and unexpected. We suspect we're going to be surprised, but we're not sure just when. As in a Punch and Judy show, violence hangs in the air, we can see the pandybat being flourished, but we still jump when it comes down. The last four lines of "Womans Constancy" or the double surprise of "If thou findst one, let mee know . . . Yet doe not, I would not go" are prime examples of the delayed-action rancor; and "The Blossome" is at least as successful, if not more, in its irony.

The poem begins as a saccharine lament, a lovesick analogizing of blossom and heart, a stuttering ancestor of Waller's perfect "Go, lovely rose." But whereas Waller will convince with his analogy, Donne's poem parodies the emblem. The blossom, like his heart, has grown in the sun (of his mistress' favor) and both will die in the winter (of her coldness). As he leaves on a journey, in this travestied valediction, he will leave blossom and heart behind. Having constructed this pastoralism, Donne now demolishes it, and at the same time demolishes the spirit of his own valedictory poems. What need is there to leave a heart behind, since all the woman cares for is country matters:

> Practise may make her know some other part,
> But take my word, shee doth not know a Heart.
>
> (ll. 31–32)

It is the libertine note that Suckling heard, and Carew; it is not the note of

> Our two soules therefore, which are one,
>   Though I must goe, endure not yet
> A breach, but an expansion,
>   Like gold to ayery thinnesse beate.

"Loves Alchymie" reduces the whole quest for the mystery of love to

> Oh, 'tis imposture all:
> And as no chymique yet th'Elixar got,
> But glorifies his pregnant pot,
> If by the way to him befall
> Some odoriferous thing, or med'cinall,
> So, lovers dreame a rich and long delight,
> But get a winter-seeming summers night.
>
> (ll. 6–12)

The long travail for love's long day becomes only this, "the short scorne of a Bridegroomes play" (l. 17). In "Farewell to Love" the place once filled by the phoenix, the eagle, and the dove is taken now by *homo post coitum triste*. The sun so central to Donne's *aubades* is taken entirely from man and given only to beasts, who alone can borrow solar energy: according to Franciscus Georgius (mocked in the *Catalogus*, but now an evidence-producing witness), cocks and lions are *solares*, joining in the sun's vigor.[63]

> Ah cannot wee,
> As well as Cocks and Lyons jocund be,
> After such pleasures? . . .
>
> (ll. 21–23)

The sun itself, which Donne had transformed into the icon of eternity, becomes an emblem of naked sensuality, an aphrodisiac and nothing more.

> And when I come where moving beauties be,
> As men doe when the summers Sunne
> Growes great,
> Though I admire their greatnesse, shun their heat;

Each place can afford shadowes. If all faile,
'Tis but applying worme-seed to the Taile.

(ll. 35–40)

These three bitter poems are not love poems at all; they are palinodes. There must be some question left about the actual order of Donne's grouped poems: reliquaries, valedictions, aubades, and debates might have occurred in several possible sequences, but any proposed sequence shows the same honest search for a reconstructed Paradise. But I'm convinced these three explosive lyrics are the coda, angry denunciations of his own fantasies. They constitute a return to the shattered reality of The Progresse of the Soule:

my minde
Shall not desire what no man else can finde,
I'll no more dote and runne
To pursue things which had, indammage me.

("Farewell to Love," ll. 31–34)

CHAPTER III

The Middle Years
1605–1609

A LL BUT THREE of the later songs and sonnets were probably
completed by 1605. After that date, Donne's energies
were pretty well taken over by his work with Thomas Morton.[1]
"The Primrose," however, is probably as late as 1613,[2] and
"Twicknam Garden" was written sometime after 1607. "A
Nocturnall upon S. Lucies Day, being the shortest day" most
likely was composed in 1617.[3]

"Twicknam Garden" is a parody, perhaps a clever adaptation of stock Petrarchanisms to a command by Lucy, Countess of Bedford. As a preacher, Donne could do great things on
command; and those sermons specifically ordered by King
James and King Charles[4] are not the least of his pulpit
successes. His poetry was another matter. He is always at his
best when he is talking to himself, and at his weakest when
he's performing by request. "A Funeral Elegy," the obsequies
of the middle years, even the epithalamia on the Princess
Elizabeth and on Somerset, while certainly not a waste of
shame, are not the expense of spirit that made Donne great.
This is true of "Twicknam Garden," which, except for one
image in the first stanza, has very little to do with the Donne
of the best poetry. The poem seems to have been provoked,
even requested, by the Countess. Something of a minor

poetess, she asked Donne's opinion of her own verses, and perhaps even set wit contests, with herself and "her" poets competing on single topics.[5] "Twicknam Garden" may have been such a "contest poem." A decree from one's patroness to act the disappointed lover in the Countess' own garden would help explain the tameness and the conventionality of the poem. (It would also be in keeping with the Countess' love of masking and charades, for which she was notorious until her rather spectacular conversion.[6]) The parade of Petrarchan details, from the sigh-blasted lover, through the sympathetic landscape, the cascade of tears, and the final not-terribly-convincing shriek over the mistress' cruelty, is very unlike the Donne of the valedictions or the *aubades*. It is only in the lines,

> And that this place may thoroughly be thought
> True Paradise, I have the serpent brought
> (ll. 8–9)

that we have a momentary return to a major theme: the lost Eden, forfeited by a fall from grace, and irrecoverable by human means. The lines encapsulate the despair of "Loves Alchymie" or the dilemma of "A Lecture upon the Shadow," and antedate the mood of the divine poems. Apart from this single flash, "Twicknam Garden" is a public poem, finely executed like all his public poems, but detached from Donne's central mode.

The work of the years between "Twicknam Garden" and the completion of *The Second Anniversary: Of the Progres of the Soule* is all controlled by the problem of extinction, the theme that has fitfully appeared in Donne's poetry from the beginning. During these years, and without respite, Donne invades every conceivable issue of the theme: the persistent but suicidal attractiveness of it, the moral dimensions, the social consequences, and above all extinction as a prerequisite

of rebirth and resurrection. Once in orders, Donne will brilliantly and recurrently preach on the resurrection—Christ's,
mankind's, his own—and he will adopt St. Paul as a type of
himself. The impressively personal fervor with which Donne
elaborates on the resurrection in his sermons owes much to
the writings of 1607–1612, wherein Donne sometimes joyfully
and sometimes reluctantly assimilated the idea into his own
being. The identification with St. Paul perhaps begins in these
years; from 1607 onward it is possible to trace the strain of the
Epistle to the Romans: "For if we have been planted together
in the likeness of his death, we shall be also in the likeness of
his resurrection" (Romans 6:5).[7] The little death and the
desired rebirth that human love had offered him were tried,
debated, finally rejected in the secular love poetry; another
death and a different rebirth are tried, debated, and finally
accepted in these years. There's no sudden conversion to
Pauline Christology: it's only after great trial that Donne accepts Christ as the successor to the woman who has failed him
as the guide to Paradise, All the writings of these five years—the
religious poetry, the contemplative prose, the controversial
works—are a rehearsal for the two Anniversary poems. These
poems are the climax of the evolution of Donne, and they
exhibit the whole constellation of his major themes: the
ubiquity of disorder, self-identification, the role of love, release from the chaos of history. "Every instant has the possibility of being an eschatological instant,"[8] and Donne's instant was supremely achieved in the Anniversary poems.

There are none of the tremors of the eventful poems in
either the prose or verse letters of these years, nor in the three
funeral elegies of 1609. As always, Donne dropped his vizor
when he spoke in propria persona, and revealed himself only
in the symbolic structures of his own choice. When convention, need, or expediency dictated the terms of his craft, the
essential Donne withdrew and left a homunculus behind to

speak what was expected to be spoken. In the years between 1601 and 1612, Donne wrote nineteen verse letters to friends and acquaintances;[9] from the same period Donne's son preserved some sixty prose letters, to which must be added many that John Donne Jr. never included in his 1651 edition.[10] As documents of Donne's public fortunes, the letters are of great value. As records of his deeper and truer biography, they are useful only in that they make clear the disjunction between the two Donnes. From the prose letters we can follow the quixotic story of Donne's marriage, the collision with Sir George More, and the slow reconciliation; his early thirst for a place at court; his friendships ("my second religion") with Henry Goodyer, George Gerrard, Robert Ker, Mrs. Cokayne. We can watch the progress from delight to disenchantment with the Countess of Bedford, and observe his concern for *Biathanatos*, the *Paradoxes and Problems*, the *Anniversary* poems. But Donne was more often a gossip than a philosopher in his prose letters, and his epistolary habits are every bit as frustrating as Dryden's: each maintains a perverse silence on the major issues of his art, and only infrequently gets behind penumbral matters.

The verse letters are a bit more illuminating, but not much.[11] The group of letters to Thomas and Rowland Woodward are models of encomiastic verse that sometimes briefly and unexpectedly throw light on the Donne within the major poetry. For instance, there are allusions to Donne's concept of poetry as the real theatre of his experience. He mentions "My verse, the strict Map of my misery."[12] In poetry "is a cherishing fyer which dryes in mee/ Griefe which did drowne me,"[13] and even a type of Eden itself, "Delicious garden where all sweetes are sowne."[14] The three early epistles to the Countess of Bedford ("Reason is our Soules left hand," "You have refin'd mee," both probably 1607, and "You that are shee," probably 1609) are positively embarrassing in the way they convert some of Donne's most important motifs to the demands of patronage. The first of these concludes a run-through of the woman-as-divinity image with an unabashed reference to "all the good which you can do me here." The Countess as the fulfillment of his own solar symbolism is unconvincingly paraded in "You have refin'd mee"; and the convulsions of "You that are shee," wherein Donne praises both the surviving Countess and her recently dead friend (either Lady Markham or Mrs. Boulstred[15]), are incredible. As representatives of a courtesy tradition, the verse letters of this middle period deserve respectful attention, but not as poetry which engages Donne's whole mind.

Grierson's judgment that Donne's "Elegie on the Lady Marckham," "Elegie on Mrs. Boulstred," and "Language, thou art too narrow" "were frankly addressed not so much to the memory of the dead as to the pocket of the living,"[16] harsh though it may be, is substantially correct. The smell of the lamp (and the humiliation of poverty) that hangs over all three elegies is chastened at times by such a powerful image as

> But as the tide doth wash the slimie beach,
> And leaves embroder'd workes upon the sand,
> So is her flesh refin'd by deaths cold hand.
> ("Elegie on the Lady Marckham," ll. 18–20[17])

In the main, however, the very sizable amount of time expended on these letters and elegies, sometimes out of friendship and sometimes out of need, is a dissipation of the thrust toward real insight that characterizes the best of Donne's work.

It's with a sense of relief that we rejoin the mainstream of Donne's genius in the poetry and prose of these years. It's painful to watch Donne stalled in the purgatory of patronage while he's launching at paradise. The stages of Donne's discovery of himself and a self-absorbing kerygma are much clearer in these years. There is little doubt that we must move from the *La Corona* (1607) as the starting point. It is most likely that "A Litanie" was written in 1608,[18] as was "Upon the Annunciation and Passion falling upon one day." There are some uncertainties about the date of *Biathanatos*, but *ca.* 1608 seems a likely choice.[19] Twelve of the *Holy Sonnets* were probably written in 1609, and four others shortly thereafter, almost certainly before *The First Anniversary*.[20] *Pseudo-Martyr* was completed in 1609, though not published until 1610,[21] while both the Latin and English versions of *Ignatius His Conclave* appeared in 1611.[22] *An Anatomy of the World* was written in 1611, and *Of the Progres of the Soule* in 1612.[23] Thus far, the route we must retravel with Donne is clearly marked.

There are three exceptions to this rule of certainty: "The Crosse," "Resurrection," and the *Essays in Divinity*. The first two present little difficulty. Free cogitations, they might have been written at any time after 1607; I would, without too much hesitation, place them close to that date, given the inquisitiveness of "The Crosse" and the similarity between the night-sun image of several of the poems in the *Songs and Sonnets* and that image as it appears in "Resurrection." This last is the most tenuous of reasons, I admit; the fact that "Resurrection" is a fragment makes it impossible to see the full scope of Donne's intentions, and impossible to be any more precise.

But if the exact location of these two poems is an indifferent matter, such is not the case with the *Essays in Divinity*. These somber and often moving incursions into the meaning of creation and salvation contain major elements of Donne's expanding vision, and their place in his evolution is important.[24] But their date of composition is uncertain. Edmund Gosse assumed they were written just before his ordination in 1615.[25] Mrs. Simpson has argued for a date later than the *Anniversary* poems,[26] and she offers a large body of circum-

stantial evidence to support her thesis: the unorthodox philosophers of the *Catalogus Librorum* are present in Donne's
text (but so too are Augustine and Thomas Aquinas); there
are several verbal links with the *Anniversaries;* there is a
kinship with the *Holy Sonnets* (for whose dates Mrs. Simpson had only Grierson's authority and edition); there are
parallels between some early sermons and the *Essays.* But
there are objections that might be made to all the evidence:
Donne was making use of St. Augustine as early as 1601,
Aquinas is represented in "Aire and Angels," and the various
cabalist and Hermetic philosophers were being read before
1605. It is as plausible to see the *Anniversaries* as continuing
ideas first appearing in the *Essays* as the other way around.
Grierson thought the holy sonnets were as late as 1617, but
since the majority of them were written before 1610, kinship
with the *Essays* suggests a date before the *Anniversaries,* not
later. It was not uncommon for Donne to use images in his
sermons years after he had first developed the image; for
example,

> A busie Wit hath taken the pains to survey the possessions
> of some Princes: and he tells us that the *Spanish* King hath
> in *Europe* almost three hundred thousand miles, and in the
> new world seaven millions, besides the borders of *Africk,* and
> all his Ilands: And we say, the Sun cannot hide himself
> from his Eye, nor shine out of his Dominions.
>
> (*Essays in Divinity*)[27]

> If some King of the earth have so large an extent of Dominion,
> in North, and South, as that he hath Winter and Summer to-
> gether in his Dominions, so large an extent East and West,
> as that he hath day and night together in his Dominions,
> much more hath God mercy and judgement together.
>
> ("Preached at Pauls, upon Christmas
> Day, in the Evening. 1624")[28]

Mrs. Simpson's very great authority is formidable, and her suggestions are not to be taken lightly. Still, I cannot accept her circumstantial evidence as compelling. It seems to me that the *Essays in Divinity* could equally well have preceded the *Anniversary* poems, and are even more meaningful when read as preludes to those poems.[29]

The *Essays in Divinity* reads like a paradigm of Donne's thought between 1607 and 1610. As in several of the holy sonnets, the primary emphasis is on destruction and rebirth; as in *La Corona*, Donne attempts (without entire success) to embody his own state of mind in a traditional and extrapersonal rubric. In other words, thematically and structurally the essays resemble the pre-*Anniversary* works and show Donne laboring at what may be defined as the central task of these years: the conversion of his secular anxieties into a spiritual crisis, and the search for a form which will objectify and universalize what up to now had been subjective and singular. Donne does not put off the mood nor abandon the real objects of his secular poetry, i.e., himself, mutability, and unitive experience. Rather, he becomes aware of the spiritual dimensions of the same ideas. Recognizing that the terrors and the aspirations of the earlier years are not altogether his private property, Donne begins to accept the communality of his own tremors; and he looks for a structured expression which will be true to both the experiential and the communal aspects of his thought. He does ultimately find such a structure in the sermon, a form which allows him to live in the divided but like worlds of self and others; and the writings of 1607–1610 are all movements toward this discovered form.

The *Essays in Divinity* clearly reveals the early stages in this pattern. The essays are, first of all, intensely personal, in the sense that they press hard against the very theme which surfaces recurrently in his poetry, that is, the fascination with nothingness, the extinction of the self and rebirth into a state free of the nightmares of history. They are, secondly, an attempt to fit this private quest into a much greater framework, to share his burden with mankind. Nominally, the subjects of the essays are the first verses of Genesis and Exodus. It is true that Donne contemns the whole rabbinic-Alexandrian tradition of allegorical exegesis, and aligns himself more with the literally inclined Antiochene tradition:

> They therefore which stub up these severall roots, and mangle them into chips, in making the word of God not such, (for the word of God is not the word of God in any other sense then literall, and that also is not the literall, which the letter seems to present, for so to diverse understandings there might be diverse literall senses; but it is called literall, to distinguish it from the Morall, Allegoricall, and the other senses; and is that which the Holy Ghost doth in that place principally intend:) they, I say, do what they can this way, to make God, whose word it is pretended to be, no God. They which build, must take the solid stone, not the rubbish.[30]

But in putting aside the fourfold method of analysis, Donne still sees himself as a mirror of both Genesis and Exodus. In his exordium he refers to, among others (John, Matthew, and Solomon), Lazarus and St. Paul of First Corinthians: to the one who returned from the dead, and to the epistle which stresses the communion of all men. The article of Genesis which Donne is most insistent upon is that God created the world from "Nothing," and Donne moves away from the text to worry at the idea of "Nothing": the opinions of Scotus, of the commentator Benedictus Pererius, of Bede, of Augustine; the Old and New Testaments; the conflicting testimonies of Lucretius, Boethius, Zoroaster, Francesco Piccolimini—they are all surveyed. The issue for Donne is not cosmogonic, but human:

. . . know ye by how few descents ye are derived from Nothing? you are the Children of the Lust and Excrements of your parents, they and theirs the Children of *Adam*, the child of durt, the child of Nothing. Yea, our soul, which we magnify so much, and by which we consider this, is a veryer upstart then our body, being but of the first head, and immediately made of Nothing: for how many souls hath this world, which were not nothing a hundred years since? And of whole man compounded of Body and Soul, the best, and most spirituall and delicate parts, which are Honour and Pleasure, have such a neighbourhood and alliance with Nothing, and even now when they are, they are Nothing, or at least shall quickly become Nothing.[31]

Mankind is a redramatization of Genesis, and in the prayer that concludes the first book of the *Essays*, Donne asks that creation happen again in his own condition.

And as, though thy self hadst no beginning thou gavest a beginning to all things in which thou wouldst be served and glorified; so, though this soul of mine, by which I partake thee, begin not now, yet let this minute, O God, this happy minute of thy visitation, be the beginning of her conversion, and shaking away confusion, darknesse, and barrennesse; and let her now produce Creatures, thoughts, words and deeds agreeable to thee. And let her not produce them, O God, out of any contemplation, or (I cannot say, *Idaea*, but) *Chimera* of my worthinesse, either because I am a man and no worme, and within the pale of thy Church, and not in the wild forrest, and enlightned with some glimerings of Naturall knowledge; but meerely out of Nothing: Nothing pre[e]xistent in her selfe, but by power of thy Divine will and word.[32]

It is the same with Exodus: the text is a gloss on his own situation.

Thou hast delivered me, O God, from the Egypt of confidence and presumption, by interrupting my fortunes, and intercepting my hopes; And from the Egypt of despair by contemplation of thine abundant treasures, and my portion therein; from the Egypt of lust, by confining my affections; and from the monstrous and unnaturall Egypt of painfull and wearisome idleness, by the necessities of domestick and familiar cares and duties.[33]

As thou hast enlightned and enlarged me to contemplate thy greatness, so, O God, descend thou and stoop down to see my infirmities and the Egypt in which I live; and (If thy good pleasure be such) hasten mine *Exodus* and deliverance, for I desire to be dissolved, and be with thee.[34]

A reduction to nothing, the flight from Egypt, the prayerful vigil before rebirth: it is the pattern of both the *Essays* and the much later "Nocturnall upon S. Lucies Day." Each work is a commentary on the other. It is not the theme that is so different in the *Essays*, but the structure. Instead of the solitary watch of a nocturne, there is an aura of invited participation. The format is that of a court sermon, reminiscent of Lancelot Andrewes in particular and anticipatory of Donne's own "metaphysical" *partitio* in sermonizing:

Before we consider each stone of this threshold, which are 1. The *time*, *In the begin[n]ing*: 2. The *person*, *God*: 3. The *Action*, *He created*: And 4. the *Work*, *Heaven and Earth*; we will speak of two or three other things, so many words. Of the *Whole Book*; of the *Author* of those first 5 Books; And of this first book.

(*Essays in Divinity*)[35]

Behold there came Wise Men, from the East to Hierusalem; Saying, Where is the King of the Jewes, that is borne? For, we have seene His starre in the East, and are come to worship Him.

There be, in these two Verses, two principall Points, (as was observed, when time was,) 1. The Persons, that arrived at Hierusalem. And their Errand. 2. The Persons, in the former Verse; whereof hath been treated heretofore. Their Errand, in the latter: wherewith we are now to deale.

Their Errand we may best learne from them selves, out of their Dicentes etc. Which (in a word) is, To worship Him. Their Errand, our Errand, and the Errand of this Day.

This Text may seem to come a little too soone, before the time, and should have staied till the day, it was spoken on, rather then on this day. But, if you marke them well, there are (in the Verse) foure Words, that be Verba Diei hujus, proper and peculiar to this very Day. 1. For first, Natus est is most proper to this Day of all daies, the Day of his Nativitie. 2. Secondly, Vidimus Stellam: For, this Day, it was first seen; appeared first. 3. Thirdly, Venimus. For, this Day, they set forth, began their journey. 4. And last, Adorare Eum. For when He brought His onely begotten Sonne into the World, He gave in charge, Let all the Angells of God worship Him: and when the Angells to do it, no time more proper for Us to do it, as then. So these foure appropriate it to this Day, and none but this.

(Lancelot Andrewes, "A Sermon Preached Before the Kings Majestie, At White-Hall, on Wednesday, the XXV. of December, A.D. MDCXXII. Being Christmasse Day")

And therefore, as God hath opened himselfe to us, both wayes, let us open both eares to him, and from one Text receive both Doctrines.

You may apprehend the parts easily, and as easily comprehend them; they are few, and plaine, and of things agreed by all: But two; Those, these; Gods dischardge, and Mans Dis-

chardge . . . And in these *few* branches, of these *two* parts, I
shall exercise your *Devotion, and holy patience*, at this time.
First then, for the first branch of the first part. . . .
("A Sermon, Preached to the Kings Majestie at Whitehall,
24. Febr. 1625. By Iohn Donne Deane of Saint Pauls,
London")[36]

The lovely prayers of the *Essays*, in which the personal note is
so strong, are made to appear as public prayers, such as would
be recited after the Creed in church service; but Donne
sometimes is unmindful that these are common prayer and
lapses into singularity: his lament that he has no confidence
in the world and that "we have found by many lamentable
experiences, that we never perform our promises to thee"[37]
comes very close to straining the generic bond between celebrant and congregation. But it is the prayers that have exerted
the greatest appeal; even Edmund Gosse, who misunderstood
the *Essays*[38] (and was even antagonistic to them), admired
the prayers. Their personal immediacy and, simultaneously,
their universal scope achieve exactly what Donne intends. He
is less successful when he submerges his own voice amidst the
company of commentators who populate the *Essays*. This
muting of the *I* by stepping into the ranks of the authorities
aims at the same end as the prayers, and Donne uses the same
device in the *Biathanatos*. It is a much less happy alternative,
for it is easily confused with pedantry. But it was not encyclo-
pedism to which Donne was tending, but partnership; and
partnership in prayer, as Donne found out, was more satisfy-
ing both aesthetically and psychologically than partnership in
debate.

The dialectical note of the *Essays* suggests a pre-1610 date.
After *Pseudo-Martyr* and *Ignatius His Conclave*, Donne does
not argue, he illustrates and illuminates, and his sermons are
remarkably free of the disputative rancor that mars much of

the best of seventeenth-century homiletics. The *Essays in Divinity* belongs in that complex limbo where Donne creates a rhetoric that involves both himself and others in what he calls the march from Egypt to Jerusalem.[39]

The *La Corona* sonnets are in many ways similar to the *Essays in Divinity*, not in substance but in strategy. They too are a spiritualization of a theme in the secular poetry; like the *Essays*, these seven sonnets reveal Donne thrusting his most personal concerns into a larger frame of reference, and experimenting with a participatory rhetoric. In the *Essays*, the sermon form is the tentative bridge between himself and humanity, and in the *La Corona* sequence it is the public recitation of the Rosary. The immersion of private concern into communal concern, and a groping for some touch with others, is the logic behind the personalization of Genesis-Exodus and the sermon format of the *Essays*. The hypothesized audience of the *Essays* functions like the third figure of "The Exstasie," but in reverse: the poem invites a reclaimed world into Donne's privacy, while the *Essays* provide a fantasy congregation that Donne can join. The inviolability of which he was so proud in the earliest poems and the barricades of the later poems in the *Songs and Sonnets* have all begun to drop. But *Essays* as a whole (the prayers excepted) shows Donne as not yet a very clubbable man: he badgers his imaginary audience very much as he so often badgers the woman in his love poetry. The difficulties Donne had in joining the society of the spirit are also evident in the *La Corona* sonnets. As in the *Essays*, Donne has problems in translating himself into a community.

For it was a very conventional and a highly communal rite that Donne chose, i.e., the Mysteries of the Rosary, the Catholic devotion which recited the intertwining lives of Christ and the Blessed Virgin from the Annunciation through the Coronation of the Virgin as Queen of Heaven. Of the

fifteen stages in the Rosary, Donne attends to thirteen, omit-
ting the Assumption of the Virgin and her Coronation.
Donne's veneration of the Virgin was considerable, but there
were two points on which he diverged from Roman Catholic
veneration. He could not accept her as mediatrix, and he could
not accept the idea of an Immaculate Conception (Mary's
imputed freedom from original sin). Of the first, Donne
remarked in the *Essays in Divinity:*

> God forbid that I should discredit or diminish the great
> works that he hath done at the tombs of his Martyrs, or at
> the pious and devout commemoration of the sanctity and
> compassion of his most Blessed Mother. But to set her up a
> Banke almost in every good Town, and make her keep a shop
> of Miracles greater then her Sons, (for is it not so, to raise a
> childe, which was born dead, and had been buried seventeen
> days, to so small end?) (for it died again as soon as it was
> carried from her sight) is fearfull and dangerous to admit.[40]

Of the second, the doctrine of the Immaculate Conception,
Donne averred in *The Second Anniversary:*

> Up up, my drowsie soule, where thy new eare
> Shall in the Angels song no discord heare;
> Where thou shalt see the blessed Mother-maid
> Joy in not being that, which men have said.
> Where shee'is exalted more for being good,
> Then for her interest, of mother-hood.
>
> (ll. 339–344)[41]

"That, which men have said" is the claim for the Virgin's
Immaculate Conception, which Donne rejects, as he also does
in ll. 37–45 of "A Litanie."[42] The absence of the last two of
the "Glorious Mysteries" is understandable in Donne's sonnet sequence.

That Donne should have chosen the Rosary as his vehicle at a date when he certainly no longer considered himself a Roman Catholic can perhaps be explained by the particular affection that Donne had for St. Bernard. The immediate model for the *La Corona* may have been such a sevenfold meditative Rosary as was presented by the Jesuit Sabin Chambers in his 1619 *The Garden of our B. Lady. Or A devout manner, how to serve her in her Rosary,*[43] but the ultimate model for such devotion to the Virgin is St. Bernard.

Sometime after 1595 Donne, in a letter to Wotton,[44] mentions his reading of Dante; in the fourth satire (ll. 157–159) he alluded to the *Divine Comedy*, wherein, of course, St. Bernard ushers Dante into Paradise. Donne would have been familiar with St. Bernard as the symbol of contemplation, the one who takes the place of Beatrice and along with St. Lucy epitomizes the vision of eternity (*Paradiso*, canto XXXI). Bernard was distinguished by his devotion to the Virgin, and we recall how, when Dante looked for the fled Beatrice, it was St. Bernard who directed his gaze toward the enthroned Virgin, his face glowing with love: it was he who catalogued the attendant saints for Dante and then, in the thirty-third canto, uttered the magnificent hymn to the Queen of Heaven. The appositeness of St. Bernard to Donne's own search for paradise, his growing meditativeness, the tradition of Bernard's devotion to the Virgin, and the belief that it was he who inaugurated the Rosary as a form of prayer are reason enough for Donne's choice of this particular structure for his sonnets. Certainly Donne expressed high regard for St. Bernard: he seems to refer to his exposition of and sermons on the Song of Songs in the *Essays;*[45] and he analogizes himself and the Saint:

> Though these [the *Essays* themselves] lack thus much of Sermons, that they have no Auditory, yet as Saint *Bernard* did

almost glory, that Okes and Beeches were his Masters, I shall
be content that Okes and Beeches be my schollers, and wit-
nesses of my solitary Meditations.[46]

There are 130 references to St. Bernard in Donne's sermons,
and one of the earliest of Donne's homages to him is the
choice of the Rosary as a poetic structure.

It was not, unfortunately, an ideal structure in Donne's
hands. There was too much of the *given* in it, not enough
scope for Donne to stretch his own contemplation to its limit.
As the unfamiliar sermon and disputation form restricted him
in the *Essays in Divinity*, so the conventions of the Rosary pin
him down too tightly. Donne needed the more expansive
Ignatian meditation of the *Holy Sonnets*, or the free contemplation of the *Devotions Upon Emergent Occasions*, or the
flexibility of classical oration of many of the sermons; he
needed a more spacious structure than the Rosary could
provide. The *La Corona* sequence has the same understandable flaw that the *Essays in Divinity* have: there is still no
control over the medium.

But if the structure of *La Corona* fails to realize the whole
strength of Donne's intention, the concept of these poems is
no less profound; and it is tragic that the theme is arrested in
its development by the enclosing form. The *La Corona* comes
very close to being the Christian response to *The Progresse of
the Soule*, an answer to the paradoxicality of existence that
has bedeviled him since 1601.

A solution of paradox it hardly seems at first; rather, one of
the most paradoxical of all Donne's works, fairly exploding
with oxymorons and ambivalences of every sort: "changing
unchang'd Antient of dayes," "This first last end," "Immen-
sity cloysterd," "Measuring selfe-life to'a span," "the last and
everlasting day," and perhaps most arresting, since Donne has
already used it,

That All, which alwayes is All every where,
Which cannot sinne, and yet all sinnes must beare,
Which cannot die, yet cannot chuse but die, . . .
(*La Corona*, "The Annunciation,"
ll. 2–4[47]; cf. *Progresse of the
Soule*, ll. 74–76)

Once again, the congruity of Donne's work is arresting, for the problem of how to name the divinity is a central topic of the *Essays in Divinity*, and God's nomenclature continued to fascinate Donne throughout his career. In 1617 he instructed the royal household that the most suitable divine name for the administrators to be mindful of is not Jehovah, meaning infinite majesty; not Adonai, absolute power; and not Tzebaoth, force; but only "God, his name of Government."[48] Preaching to the Countess of Bedford in 1620, Donne mused that in his tribulation Job called God *Shaddai*, which means omnipotent but also means calamity: God's name may be in anything.[49] In a moving sermon at St. Paul's in 1626, Donne distinguished the three names of God: Elohim, Adonai, and Jehovah; and after demonstrating that both *Elohim* and *Adonai* mean *power*, he continued:

> So then two of Gods three Names are Names of absolute power, to imprint, and re-imprint an assurance in us, that hee can absolutely deliver us, and fully revenge us, if he will. But then, his third Name, and that Name which hee chooses to himselfe, and in the signification of which Name, hee employes *Moses*, for the reliefe of his people under Pharoah, that Name *Iehovah*, is not a Name of Power, but onely of Essence, of Being, of Subsistence, and yet in the vertue of that Name, God relieved his people.[50]

Clearly, the name of God was not an indifferent matter; specific attributes of God would be summoned depending on the name chosen. "In my afflictions," Donne prayed in 1626, "let him, at his good pleasure, reserve his *Elohim*, and his *Adonai*," and instead "vouchsafe to visit mee in that Name . . . as that I may live, and move, and have my beeing in him."[51]

In the *Essays in Divinity*, Donne fixed on the topic that "names are to instruct us, and express natures and essences."[52] With St. Thomas and Reuchlin,[53] he inclines to the inexpressible tetragrammaton as the only title which is fair to the mystery of God, and he concludes, "*If thou seek me, thou shalt finde me. I have adventured in his Name, upon his Name*."[54] Donne quotes with approval from Reuchlin's De Verbo Mirifico; in doing so he rebuts the Jewish tradition against the Messiahship of Christ, identifying Christ with the tetragrammaton, and suggesting that through the tetragrammatonic Christ "We are made partakers of the godly nature."[55]

> . . . as there is a secret property by which we are changed into God . . . so God hath a certain name, to which he hath annexed certain conditions, which being observed, he hath bound himself to be present. This is the Name, which the Jews stubbornly deny ever to have been attributed to the Messias in the Scriptures. This is the name, which they say none could utter, but the priests, and the knowledg of it perished with the Temple.[56]

The secret property by which "we are made partakers of the godly nature" is Christ, or, as Donne later expressed it in St. Paul's, "the Name of *Christ* . . . first contemplates Man, and the Humane nature, which onely could die, And then hath relation to God, and the Divine nature. So that Jesus is God, and Man in Him; And Christ is Man, and God in Him."[57] Christ is the *Verbum*, which cannot be expressed; he is paradox itself. And it is through Christ that we become

partakers of godly nature. For Donne, as for Pascal, Christ is
the ultimate paradox who resolves all paradox.[58] What we
witness in the La Corona sequence, as in this element of the
Essays, is a major transformation of the meaning of paradox
for Donne. Paradox is not the dismembered unity of The
Progresse of the Soule; it is significant of the divine essence.
Paradox is not something to flee as the language of exile from
Eden or of Cain's nightmare; it is the sound of redemption. It
would be no exaggeration to say that all of Donne's religious
expression from this point on is a refining of the central
concept of La Corona. The seminal insight into the paradoxicality of Christ is extended later to the specific paradoxes of
the Passion, of divine love, and to the most complete paradox,
the Incarnation. In "Loves Infiniteness," Donne had apprehended human love not by denying but by accepting its
discordances; in La Corona he glimpses divine love not by
destroying but by rejoicing in paradox.

"Loves Infiniteness" and La Corona are among the most
insightful of Donne's poems on the nature of secular and
sacred love, and the ambience of both poems is correspon-
dent. In technique, too, the poems are similar. The organization of "Loves Infiniteness" is one of Donne's most complex
metrical experiments, and the complexity has a distinct metaphoric value. The same can be said of La Corona. Donne
achieves a unity that presides over the seven sonnets by, first
of all, contriving to have the first and last line of the entire
sequence be the same, and each concluding line of one sonnet
be the opening line of the following sonnet. This is quite
obvious; and it was a device used by other poets, secular and
sacred, before Donne.[59] What may escape attention is that
this device (the corona effect) in converting the whole sequence into a circle establishes an endless recurrence, the first
line being last and the last first. The sequence is a sacred
parody of Revelation 21:6, "I am Alpha and Omega, the
beginning and the end." Secondly, the impression of La

Corona as a crown, an endless rosary, and as a circle at whose center is Christ, is reinforced by Donne's metrics: the sestet in the first, third, and fifth sonnets is composed of a closed quatrain and a couplet (cddc ee); the sestet in the second, fourth, and sixth is an open quatrain and a couplet (cdcd ee). Thus a pattern of alternation and recurrence is established, and the sestet of the last sonnet repeats the pattern of the sixth, so that its alternate is the rhyme scheme of the first sonnet. As we end the rhyme in the last sonnet, we are returned once again to the first sonnet. Even-numbered sonnets are, metrically, a response to odd-numbered sonnets; and the response to the last is the first. The metrics of the poem recapitulate the alpha-omega symbolism of the whole sequence. Certainly, in spite of whatever impediments there are in the constrictive tradition of the Rosary, La Corona contains a perception central to Donne's development. A presiding unity that was from the beginning and will be at the end: this is Seth's knowledge, the antidote to Cain's schism, and the architecture of La Corona. Donne has begun to counterbalance The Progresse of the Soule.

Ambiguity, in La Corona, is being metamorphosed into mystery, and Donne begins here to consider paradox not as Adamic stigma but as the essential language of salvation. Donne was altogether too human never to be frightened by the enigmas of history and the puzzles of living—his mood in the sermons of 1627, the year in which he lost his daughter Lucy, Magdalene Herbert, the Countess of Bedford, and Henry Goodyer, is only one demonstration of many that he could lose his balance when destiny worked itself out at his expense. But from 1607 on, Donne is more and more contemptuous of rhetorical paradox, and more sympathetic to religious paradox. Aside from the Holy Sonnets, where he sets a somewhat different task for himself, his religious poetry is all a reveling in sacred mystery and sacred illogic.

In "The Crosse,"[60] Donne rejoices that man cannot escape

from the oxymoron of the Passion, at once scandal and
salvation; indeed, the human fabric embraces and reflects the
mystery of the cross:

> Who can deny mee power, and liberty
> To stretch mine armes, and mine owne Crosse to be?
>
> (ll. 17–18)
>
> And as thy braine through bony walls doth vent
> By sutures, which a Crosses forme present,
> So when thy braine workes, ere thou utter it,
> Crosse and correct concupiscence of witt.
>
> (ll. 55–58)

As he will muse in a sermon in later years, "Other mens
crosses are not mine, other mens merits cannot save me. Nor
is any cross mine owne, which is not mine by a good title; If I
be not Possessor *bonae fidei*, If I came not well by that
crosse,"[61] so too here: "Be covetous of Crosses, let none fall"
("The Crosse," l. 59). The paradox of an alchemical Christ,
who transmutes base metals to gold, death to life, allows
Donne to soften the bad temper of "Busie old foole, unruly
Sunne" of 1602–1605 to the gentler

> Sleep sleep old Sun, thou canst not have repast
> As yet, the wound thou took'st on friday last;
> Sleepe then, and rest; The world may beare thy stay,
> A better Sun rose before thee to day, . . .
>
> ("Resurrection, imperfect," ll. 1–4[62])

In "Upon the Annunciation and Passion falling upon one
day. 1608," Donne watches the sequence of history, which
had so appalled him in *The Progresse of the Soule*, collapse in
liturgical time, where beginnings and endings exist simultaneously:

> This Church, by letting these daies joyne, hath shown
> Death and conception in mankinde is one:

Or 'twas in him the same humility,
That he would be a man, and leave to be:
Or as creation he had made, as God,
With the last judgement, but one period,
His imitating Spouse would joync in one
Manhoods extremes: He shall come, he is gone.

(ll. 33-40[63])

The unhesitating immersion of himself into the ironies of sacred experience ("we are made partakers of the godly nature"; "So the Name Iesus seemes to taste of more Mystery, and more Incomprehensiblenesse"[64]) is an important element of all the later religious poetry, from "Goodfriday, 1613. Riding Westward" to the last hymns.

It is in this context that *Biathanatos* is best read. There's little agreement as to Donne's intention in writing on "That Paradoxe, or Thesis, That Self-homicide is not so naturally Sin, that it may never be otherwise." Certainly *Biathanatos* has affinities with the *Paradoxes and Problems* of the earlier years; there may even have been no appreciable lapse between those short equivocations, which Donne could conceivably have continued to write after the turn of the century, and the earliest possible date for *Biathanatos*, 1606.[65] He showed the same curious solicitude for this essay as he did for his paradoxes, as the letters to Sir Edward Herbert and Robert Ker attest, in which Donne urges that the book be neither published nor burned.[66] He wanted no doubt on the issue that this was not a grave and serious piece of work: he requested of Ker that he "let any that your discretion admits to the sight of it, know the date of it; and that it is a Book written by *Jack Donne*, and not by D[r.] *Donne*."[67] But in spite of Donne's insistence on its youthful *esprit*, *Biathanatos* still provokes debate over the issue of Donne's seriousness. On the one side it has been described as a most important point in his career:

"*Biathanatos* reveals a crucial point in the progress of the soul which converted Jack Donne into Dr. Donne, for it marks the end of his naturalistic journey."[68] On the other side, it has been assessed as a consummate mockery, "a classic mock-oration in praise of what is absolutely the lowest thing in morality."[69] Even the middle position, that *Biathanatos* is essentially a satire but at the same time a serious grappling with his own inclination to suicide, has been defended: "[*Biathanatos*] is a somewhat half-hearted, somewhat unsuccessful satire on scholastic and casuistical reasoning. . . . Too satirical to be seriously convincing and too clumsily written to be convincing satire, *Biathanatos* may actually be its author's way of protecting himself against his own fascination with the subject of suicide."[70]

It seems to me equally likely that *Biathanatos* is a mockery through and through, a burlesque not only of the "vanity, or ostentation, or digression" in that "multiplicity of not necessary citations" affected by "scholastique and artificiall men," but of his own "sickely inclination" to suicide, which showed itself as early as the satires and surfaced often (as, for example, in the night pieces, "The Funerall" and "The Relique"). In the sermons Donne will deal with, not literal suicide, but Pauline suicide: the murder of the old Adam and spiritual regeneration.[71] He will very shortly lacerate literal suicides in the *Pseudo-Martyr*, and deal exclusively with Pauline suicide in the *Holy Sonnets*. There is nothing after *Biathanatos* that would suggest that Donne was ever again seriously attracted to the notion that "I have the keyes of my prison in mine owne hand, and no remedy presents it selfe so soone to my heart, as mine owne sword."[72] But while Donne characteristically insists that charity be extended to those who do commit suicide,[73] not once in *Biathanatos* does he ever advance a general defense of suicide. As there can be no binding dogma about the evil of suicide, so there can be none about its good: "And as Aquinas saies, The lower you goe towards particulars, the more you depart from the necessities of being bound to it,"[74] and "I abstained purposely from extending this discourse to particular rules, or instances, both because I dare not professe myself a Maister in so curious a science, and because the limits are obscure, and steepy, and slippery, and narrow, and every errour deadly, except where a competent diligence being fore-used, a mistaking in our conscience may provide an excuse."[75] The whole treatise is a movement from the enormous philosophic compartments of the Law of Nature, the Law of Reason, and the Law of God to the absolute solipsism of individual act, where universal laws cannot follow, and can neither condemn nor condone. The huge wheels of the three laws turn and grind, but in the end never touch the grain of singular activity. The comedy of *Biathanatos* is in building an awesome machine that doesn't work.

For it is a comedy, of the sort Donne had already practiced in the "Epithalamion made at Lincolnes Inne," and in which Lear's Fool might act, a bitter antic jest against the foolishness of men, accomplished by turning their own ceremonies back against them. Shakespeare's Fool continually invites King Lear to change places with him, so that all Lear's ceremonialism, which led to his tragic mistake, is seen as the motley of a madman. "Yes, indeed: thou wouldst make a good fool," Lear is told (I, v); and the Fool makes a good Lear in the way that he re-enacts the beginning of the tragedy of division:

Fool. Give me an egg, nuncle, and I'll give thee two crowns.
Lear. What two crowns shall they be?
Fool. Why, after I have cut the egg i' the middle, and eat up the meat, the two crowns of the egg. When thou clovest thy crown i' the middle, and gavest away both

> parts, thou borest thy ass on thy back o'er the dirt;
> thou hadst little wit in thy bald crown, when thou
> gavest thy golden one away.
>
> (I, iv)

The Fool, here, goes through the same ceremony that Lear had gone through, but in a burlesqued version that identifies the folly of the act. *Biathanatos* is a ceremony of human paradox, but in a burlesqued version that identifies the folly of human paradox. Its primary subject is not suicide (that is only the *casus belli*), but a vain preoccupation with enigmas and intellectual puzzles. In "Loves Alchymie" and "Farewell to Love," Donne had written palinodes to his secular love poetry; *Biathanatos* is the palinode to his dealing with secular dilemmas. It is just as sharp a break with human equivocation, by showing the absurdities of equivocation, as "Farewell to Love" is with the heats and passions of human love.

The nominal topic is death, and the vehicle is the parodied debate. The form of *Biathanatos* recalls the tradition of the Lord of Misrule, the topsy-turvy master of revels who subverts the usual patterns of behavior for the sake of shedding new light on old issues:[76] just the sort of thing Donne had in mind with the early "Epithalamion." Underneath the incredibly complicated and imposing facade, with its Parts, Distinctions, and Sections so involved that it becomes a parody of Scholastic argumentation, nearly every flaw in logical debate is perpetrated.[77] For instance, Aristotle distinguished ten spurious enthymemes, or fallacies in argumentation:[78] (1) conclusions without sufficient evidence, (2) argument from connotation, (3) confusion of parts and the whole, (4) indignant language, (5) argument from single instances, (6) confusion of accidental and essential, (7) false consequence, (8) *post hoc, ergo propter hoc*, (9) failure to mention time and circumstance, and (10) confusion of absolute probability with unlikely probability. Each of these errors is embedded in *Biathanatos*.

1. "We may safely infer, that nothing which we call sinne is so against nature, but that it may be sometimes agreeable to nature." (This "inference," in Part I, Distinction I, Section 7, as a matter of fact is preceded by no material from which such a conclusion can be drawn.)

2. "For as in Cramps which are contortions of the Sinewes . . . we may procure to our selfe a fever to thaw them . . . so in all rebellions and disobediences of our flesh, we may minister to our selves such corrections and remedies, as the Magistrate might, if the fact were evident." (Part 3, Distinction 3, Section 3: Donne's "proof" is simply a prejudicial analogy in which the grim connotations of *cramp* and *fever* are carried over into the body public as well as into the singular rebellion. Private man, commonweal, infirmity, and rebellion are made to seem coincident by connotative argument.)

3. The inclination to sin is transmitted by germination; but the generation of the species is natural; therefore "all actuall sinne issuing from thence, all sinne is naturall." (Part 1, Distinction 1, Section 7. Donne uses the fallacy of "the undistributed middle," where *nature* is used in his second premise as a particular reference [the natural urge to propagate] but in the conclusion as a generic reference [the universal law of nature]).

4. "If any Divine shall thinke the cause, or persons injured herein, and esteeme me so much worth the reducing to the other opinion, as to apply an answer hereunto, with the same Charitie which provoked me, and which, I thanke God hath accompanied me from the beginning, I beseech him, to take thus much advantage from me and my instruction, that he will doe it without bitternesse."

(Part 3, Distinction 1, Section 1. Donne anticipates his objectors, and spikes their guns beforehand by protestations of his fine motives in defending suicide.)

5. "*Herennius* the *Sicilian*, could endure to beat out his own braines against a post . . . *Homer* which had written a thousand things, which no man else understood, is said to have hanged himselfe, because he understood not the Fishermans riddle . . . Poore *Terence* because he lost his 108 translated Comedies, drown'd himselfe . . . *Hippionas* the Poet rimed *Bubalus* the Painter to death with his Iambiques." (Part 1, Distinction 2, Section 3. In this section Donne utilizes what Aristotle refers to as "argument from single signs," isolated instances that appear to be inductive proof but are only catalogues.)

6. "[Samson's] fact of selfe-killing is celebrated by the Church to everlasting memory, as the act of a Martyr." (Part 3, Distinction 5, Section 4. Samson's death, of course, was a secondary consequence of his destruction of the temple: a deliberate confusion on Donne's part of accidental and essential.)

7. "How much did S. And[rew] contibute [sic] to his own Crucifying? How much Saint Laurence to his broyling, when he called to the Tyrant, This side is enough, turne the other, and then eate?" (Part 2, Distinction 6, Section 7. The endurance and Thomas More-like levity, Donne implies, was a participation in execution, hence suicide. It is parodied, not logical, consequence.)

8. "And to ease the Reader, and to continue my first resolution of not descending into many particulars, I will onely present one Rule, but so pregnant, that from it many may be derived, by which not onely a man may, but must doe the whole and intire action of killing himselfe . . . if the Priest after Consecration come to the knowledge that the Wine is poysoned, [*Ne calix vitae vertatur in mortem,*[70]]

Yet if hee know this by Confession, from his assistant, or any other, and cannot by an diversion, nor disguise, escape the discovering, that this was confessed to him, without drinking it, if it bee poyson, he must drinke it." (Part 2, Distinction 6, Section 8. Acceptance of suicide is not the cause of the priest's death; that is subsequent to the real cause, i.e., honoring the seal of confession.)

9. "Beza, A man as eminent and illustrious, in the full glory and Noone of Learning, as others were in the dawning, and Morning, when any, the least sparkle was notorious, confesseth of himself, that only for the anguish of a Scurffe, which over-ranne his head, he had once drown'd himselfe from the Millers bridge in *Paris*, if his Uncle by chance had not then come that way." (*Preface*. Donne intimates that Beza's action was taken during his wise maturity; but the time and circumstances were otherwise, for this was an occurrence of Beza's childhood.[80])

10. "[Judas'] act of killing himselfe, is not added to his faults in any place of Scriptures; no not in those two Psalmes of particular accusations, and bitter imprecations against him, as they are ordinarily taken to be Prophetically purposed and directed." (Part 3, Distinction 5, Section 7. This "argument" from negative evidence advances the improbable supposition that since Judas' suicide is not specifically mentioned in the scriptural accusations, it can be assumed it was not a heinous act.)

This feast of misrepresentation is offered with pedantic unction, the debater insisting that he will proceed "without any disguising, or curious and libellous concealing"[81] but nonetheless swinging off into parentheses and divisions which nearly succeed in hiding the issue at hand:

Of all these three Laws, of Nature, of Reason, and of God, every precept which is permanent, and binds alwayes, is so

compos'd and elemented and complexion'd, that to distinguish and separate them is a Chymick work: And either it
doth only seeme to be done, or is done by the torture and
vexation of schoole-limbicks, which are exquisite and violent
distinctions. For that part of Gods law which bindes alwayes,
bound before it was written, and so it is but *dictamen recte
rationis*: and that is the Law of nature. And therefore *Isidore*
as it is related into the (a) Canons, dividing all Law into
divine and humane, addeth [Divine consists of nature, Humane of custome] Yet though these three be almost all one;
yet because one thing may be commanded in divers waies, and
by divers authorities, as the common Law, a Statute, and a
Decree of an arbitrary Court, may bind me to do the same
thing, it is necessary that we weigh the obligation of every
one of these Laws which are in the Definition.[82]

There is a consummate irony in the way the debater, at the
opening of his third part, "Of the Law of God," bumbles
about with a symbol that should elucidate but instead obfus-
cates. The metaphor is the same crisp one that Dryden will
use at the opening of his *Religio Laici*:

> Dim as the borrow'd beams of Moon and Stars
> To *lonely, weary, wandring* Travellers,
> Is *Reason* to the *Soul*: And as on high,
> Those rowling Fires *discover* but the Sky
> Not light us *here*; So *Reason's* glimmering Ray
> Was lent, not to *assure* our *doubtfull* way,
> But *guide* us upward to a *better Day*.[83]

The foolish debater of *Biathanatos* handles it thus:

> That light which issues from the Moone, doth best represent
> and expresse that which in our selves we call the light of Na-
> ture; for as that in the Moone is permanent and ever there,
> and yet it is so unequall, various, pale, and languishing, So is

our light of Nature changeable. For being at the first kindling
at full, it wayned presently, and by departing further and
further from God, declined by generall sinne, to almost a
totall Eclipse: till God comming neerer to us, first by the
Law, and then by Grace, enlightned and repayred it againe,
conveniently to his ends. And then those Artificall Lights,
which our selves make for our use and service here, as Fires,
Tapers and such resemble the light of Reason, as wee have in
our Second part accepted that Word. For though the light
of these Fires and Tapers be not so naturall, as the Moone,
yet because they are more domestique, and obedient to us,
wee distinguish particular objects better by them, then by the
Moone; So by the Arguments, and Deductions, and Conclusions, which our selves beget and produce, as being more
serviceable and under us, because they are our creatures; particular cases are made more cleare and evident to us; for these
we can be bold withall, and put them to any office, and examine, and prove their truth, or likelihood, and make them
answere as wee will aske; whereas the light of Nature, with a
solemne and supercilious Majestie, will speake but once, and
give no Reason, nor endure Examination.[84]

The images of moon, taper, and sun as emblems of nature,
reason, and God have been so qualified, applied, withdrawn,
and excepted that their value is pretty well worried out of
them.

In the conclusion of *Biathanatos*, Donne assembles a long
series of similitudes drawn from the field of medicine: he
begins by citing Paracelsus' anger against Galenic physicians
whose ministrations are worse than the disease they treat,
goes on to Hippocrates, returns to Paracelsus, refers to the
King's touch, and borrows a simile from Cassianus that "[a
lie] hath the nature of *Ellebore*, wholsome in desperate
diseases, but otherwise poison."[85] He then continues the

comparison and applies it to *Biathanatos* itself: "a ly might have the nature of medicine and be admitted in many cases . . . by the same reason am I excusable in this Paradox."[86] The final image of the treatise is of the author as physician and liar, who has offered a lie as a remedy. It is an entirely appropriate similitude. Donne, in *Biathanatos*, has prescribed a purge for what he calls "a Civill Warre of contradiction."[87] His final word is "*Qui non concoxit, dormiat,*" most simply translated as, "That one may rest who doesn't consider well." But *concoquo* has the meaning too of "promoting digestion," with a cathartic. *Biathanatos* is a Paracelsian cure, the treatment of a disease not by using drugs whose properties are contrary to the malady (as did the Galenists), but by using charms and tinctures that have a sympathy with the illness. One of the verse letters to the Countess of Bedford outlines such sympathetic medicine:

> Statesmen purge vice with vice, and may corrode
> The bad with bad, a spider with a toad:
> For so, ill thralls not them, but they tame ill
> And make her do much good against her will.[88]

Biathanatos is an extended lie, a destruction of the conundrum of existence by means of a massive conundrum. Donne's own image of *Biathanatos*, with which he prefaces his treatise, is that it is like the pool of Bethesda (John, 5:1–9).[89] An afflicted man wishes to cure his infirmity by entering the troubled waters but is drawn aside by Christ and told to "Rise, take up thy bed, and walk." The troubled pool of *Biathanatos*, a microcosm of the vexed, fallacious, eristic world, is one cure for the ambivalence of existence, a giant dose of hellebore; and Christ is another. As *La Corona* welcomes sacred paradox as a cure, *Biathanatos* in a Götterdämmerung of profane paradox bids the world's perplexities farewell. Probably written close in time, the two works form a diptych of acceptance and rejection, sacred mystery versus secular confusion.

"A Litanie" deserves more attention than is usually given it. Probably written in 1608, it is filled with protestations of melancholy and dejection and so has been chiefly considered as part of the literal biography of Donne and a portrait of the painful years at Mitcham. In a letter to Goodyer, Donne made it clear that "A Litanie" was written against a background of "much pain," and that "Since my imprisonment in my bed, I have made a meditation in verse, which I call a Litany."[90] So much is obvious, but such an interpretation neglects the more important light that the poem sheds on Donne's interior history. There are more affinities between "A Litanie" and the other works of 1607–1612 than the usual phenomenological criticism has pointed out.

In the first place, we can observe Donne still hunting after the right form of contemplation, and experimenting with the structures provided by his old religion. He has used the Rosary in *La Corona*, soon he will employ the Ignatian meditation, and still later, in the "Nocturnall upon S. Lucies Day," the Roman breviary. Here, it is a version of the Catholic litany, a form of public prayer that had been sanctioned (with modifications) by Thomas Cranmer in 1544, but had not been part of the English liturgy since 1545.[91] In the second place, "A Litanie" is very much a part of Donne's attempt to overcome his own loneliness and to create a communion with others, at least to imagine a corporateness that he had earlier disdained. In the *Essays in Divinity*, he had conjured up an audience; in *Biathanatos* he entered the arena of Scholastic debate, albeit in motley; *La Corona* is public and communal prayer. What Donne had to learn was that he was most involved when he was most alone, that his own spiritual state became universal only when it, in utter solitude, completely realized and expended itself. He approaches this realization in the *Holy*

Sonnets, and achieves it in the *Anniversaries*, but from *La Corona* to the *Holy Sonnets* he's plagued with the need for a physically realized presence of others. Donne was always stimulated by an audience, and in a sense he always demanded one. An auditory challenged him, it provoked him, and when he lacked a congregation, he invented one. But there are distinctions that must be made. Both the *La Corona* and "A Litanie" imagine a community at prayer, Donne amongst them, and neither is entirely successful. Most of the sermons, on the other hand, show a strong awareness of the audience, and Donne often achieves spectacular success as a contemplator in company. In the *Devotions Upon Emergent Occasions*, Donne is entirely alone, and yet evokes the spirit of congruence with mankind.

After so many years of barring others, of withdrawing into his own ego, Donne found it difficult to achieve human contact. The great task of the years between 1607 and 1612 was to discover a way to project himself into a kinship with others, to see all humanity as an extension of himself. He had to appreciate that when he totally communicated with himself, he touched mankind. The epiphanic realization of *self* and the identity of *self* with *mankind* are the climax of Donne's art and of the process that extends through his whole life. In "A Litanie" Donne strains to define himself and to complete his definition within a congregation. But the congregation never becomes more than a phantom.

The letter to Goodyer already cited clarifies the double nature of the poem: it is a "meditation" occasioned by his own disconsolateness; and at the same time it is that sort of prayer which Pope Nicholas V had commanded for public service, and "mine is for lesser Chappels, which are my friends."[92] For all the intimacy of the poem, Donne maintains the traditional plurality of litany responses: "Good Lord, deliver us," "Lord heare us." Even though he does vary the more conventional and unchanging *Audi nos* and *Libera nos* of the Roman

Catholic litany, a version of this plurality occurs in fifteen of the twenty-eight stanzas. The topics of these fifteen stanzas are all close to Donne's literal condition: the persistent allure of the world, attractive but frustrating intellectualism, alternate fits of pride and melancholy, the seductiveness of wit— these are all part of the public records of Donne's life. The petitions to "deliver us" don't surmount the individuality of these anxieties. The imagined chorus of petitioners has no body of its own, and remains as insubstantial as the ghostly audience of the Essays in Divinity.

But if the summoning up of a participating humanity is incomplete, the movement toward a self-identification is not. St. Paul's description of himself in Galatians as a man who died and then was reborn in God might well have been Donne's model for these years and for this poem. Beginning with "A Litanie" and continuing through the Anniversaries, an important myth evolves in Donne's poetry. It is the myth of the image of the Trinity, clouded in man but recoverable in meditation.[93] Probably Neoplatonic in origin, it is a concept that was developed by St. Augustine in both the Confessions and, in much greater detail, in his disquisition on the Trinity, was further refined by St. Bernard, and was given brief but lucid treatment by St. Bonaventure in his treatise on The Journey of the Mind to God. Given Donne's early and continuing attraction to Augustine and Bernard, it's not surprising that he should have availed himself of the concept, which envisions the Trinity as being reflected in the faculties of reason, imagination, and will; that reflection being blurred as the result of original sin; but that entire image being recoverable through meditation and the God-directed exercise of all the faculties. It is an amazingly rich idea, equally productive of poetry and spiritual effort, perfectly geared to Renaissance faculty psychology, and evidently fascinating to Donne, since it appears recurrently from now on in his writings. As Augustine's three-cycled history struck him as true to his own sense of the exterior world, so now Augustine's trinity of the spirit is accepted as relevant to his sense of the interior world.

"A Litanie"[94] is dominated by a variation on the crucial image of *Biathanatos*, i.e., a Paracelsian cure effected by sympathetic medicine. The malady is spiritual dryness, the cure an infusion of the lost trinity in man, and the physician is Christ. The image begins and ends "A Litanie." The opening invocation is to God the Father to "come/And re-create mee, now growne ruinous" (ll. 3–4). Playing on the identification of *Adam* with the Hebrew *adom*, "red," Donne laments that he has become

> by dejection, clay,
> And by selfe-murder, red.
> From this red earth, O Father, purge away
> All vicious tinctures, that new fashioned
> I may rise up from death, before I'm dead.
>
> (ll. 5–9)

This self-murder looks not only to Donne's own symbolic extinctions, recurrent in his poetry, but to the whole race: in turning his will against God's, Adam maimed himself and all posterity. Donne's opening image has the same basis as Henry Vaughan's "Ascension-Hymn":

> Dust and clay
> Mans antient wear!
> Here you must stay,
> But I elsewhere;
> Souls sojourn here, but may not rest;
> Who will ascend, must be undrest . . .

> Man of old
> Within the line
> Of *Eden* could

> Like the Sun shine
> All naked, innocent and bright,
> And intimate with Heav'n, as light;
>
> But since he
> That brightness soil'd
> His garments be
> All dark and spoil'd,
> And here are left as nothing worth,
> Till the Refiners fire breaks forth.[95]

While Donne, in the course of his poem, invokes the whole Trinity, and adopts the whole pantheon of Christianity as exemplars, he most characteristically appeals to Christ. After the roll call of the Virgin, angels, patriarchs, prophets, apostles, martyrs, confessors, virgins, and doctors, Donne surveys the evidence of his crippled condition, and images of debility abound. He is maimed (stanza XV), wounded (XVI), convulsive (XIX), the victim of plague, wars, and flood (XXII), apoplectic (XXIV), deaf (XXV), a veritable hospital of sickness. Christ, by having taken on human nature in the Incarnation, is subject to the same infirm conditions; but he is also a physician:

> Sonne of God, heare us, and since thou
> By taking our blood, owest it us againe,
>   Gaine to thy selfe, or us allow;
> And let not both us and thy selfe be slaine;
>   O lambe of God, which tookst our sinne
>   Which could not stick to thee,
> O let it not returne to us againe,
> But Patient and Physition being free,
> As sinne is nothing, let it no where be.
>
>   (ll. 244–252)

Like the alchemical Christ of "Resurrection, imperfect," this physician-Christ can transmute base metal to gold, death to life. The poem begins with a purge and ends with a cure.

The means and the end of the divine cure are the same, the Trinity. The primal health is man's resemblance to God, who is triune; Christ, defined at the Council of Nicaea (325 A.D.) as entire coparticipant in the divine nature, is at once the eternal and the historical God-Man who, like Father and Spirit, is One and Three at the same time. Donne is perfectly orthodox on this point: he invokes the Trinity as "you distinguish'd undistinct" (l. 32) and accepts the mystery of consubsisting unity and trinity.

> O Blessed glorious Trinity,
> Bones to Philosophy, but milke to faith,
>   Which, as wise serpents, diversly
> Most slipperinesse, yet most entanglings hath, . . .
> (ll. 28–31)

The recovery of the trinity within himself becomes the major impulse of the poem. The structure is triadic: Donne stifles the usual four-part movement of a traditional litany (Invocations, Deprecations, Obsecrations, and Intercessions) and instead combines Invocations and Obsecrations (stanzas I–XIII); a bridge passage (XIV) that introduces both the deprecatory "deliver us" and the supplicatory "hear us" follows; then the Deprecations (XV–XXII); and finally the Supplications (XXIII–XXVIII). Within this three-part structure, there is an effort to create a trinity interiorly. Donne isolates the distinctive offices of the Trinity and prays that all three offices will be duplicated in himself:

> As you distinguish'd undistinct
> By power, love, knowledge bee,
> Give mee a such selfe different instinct,

Of these let all me elemented bee,
Of power, to love, to know, you unnumbred three.

(ll. 32–36)

Donne's "power," "love," "knowledge" are tantamount to St. Augustine's *velle, esse, nosse* of the *Confessions*; his emphasis on a "selfe different instinct" repeats Augustine's demand that the faculties must be directed, not selfishly, but toward God;[96] and his desire to be "elemented," with all three becoming immersed in one another, is purely Augustinian:

> Now this triad of memory, understanding, and will, are not three lives, but one; nor three minds, but one . . . life, mind, essence, are always things existing absolutely in themselves. Therefore the three activities named are one, inasmuch as they constitute one life, one mind, one essence.[97]

For all the Catholic overtones of the poem, Donne comes closer to Protestant doctrine in "A Litanie" than he has ever yet; the presiding figure of Christ the physician, who must accomplish finally what man can only aim at, is far more Lutheran than Roman Catholic. Donne can create a litany, fashion a trinity, identify the trinitarian aspects of human psychology, but beyond that he cannot go. The Catholic doctrine of man cooperating in grace is not included in the beseeching commands of "A Litanie." Donne knew whereof he spoke when he called the poem "rectified devotion,"[98] for "A Litanie" is a Catholic structure permeated by a Protestant sense of total dependence on Christ. Man must strive to recover the lost image of the Trinity, but he dare not trust his own efforts:

> Pray ceaslesly,' and thou hearken too,
> (Since to be gratious
> Our taske is treble, to pray, beare, and doe)

> Heare this prayer Lord, O Lord deliver us
> From trusting in those prayers, though powr'd out thus.
>
> (ll. 122–126)

The outlines of Donne's later theology, a dilemma he will face in the *Holy Sonnets*, and another stage in his progressive evolution all appear in "A Litanie"; and still again we recognize that the poetry is an essential route for that evolution.

> Those heavenly Poëts which did see
> Thy will, and it expresse
> In rythmique feet, in common pray for mee,
> That I by them excuse not my excesse
> In seeking secrets, or Poëtiquenesse.
>
> (ll. 68–72)

Several aspects of "A Litanie" re-present themselves in *Pseudo-Martyr*, probably the least read of all Donne's writings but the one that had the most immediate effect on his material status. A compendium of his readings in theological controversy that he had begun in the 1590's and pushed forward while assisting Thomas Morton, *Pseudo-Martyr* was considered sufficient evidence for the University of Oxford to grant Donne a Master of Arts degree on April 17, 1610. Donne was lauded as *optime de republica et ecclesia meriti*, well-deserving of praise by both church and state.[99] But it is not the public aspects of *Pseudo-Martyr* that are manifestly important—more to the point is the way in which it extends the terms of Donne's self-definition. This splendidly argued brief in defense of the Oath of Allegiance, and its largely irenic approach to the problem of nonconformity by the Catholic recusants, has been most often linked with *Biathanatos*, the one condemning and the other defending certain instances of suicide. But if *Biathanatos* and *Pseudo-Martyr* belong together, it is for quite a different reason: neither work is really about suicide at all. The topic of

Biathanatos is not primarily death, but the frailties of human reason and the implausibilities of logic. Suicide is the hypothetical ground on which Donne conducts his mock debate, but it is not the central proposition. In *Pseudo-Martyr*, suicide is a consequence of folly, not the point at issue. In both these prose works, suicide is an item of evidence, not the thesis. *Biathanatos* is a satiric anatomizing of the springs of human behavior, with a defense of suicide being presented as a striking example of fallacious argument proving whatever it wants to prove. *Pseudo-Martyr* is a serious inquisition into the sources of spiritual misbehavior, with false martyrdom being shown as the most egregious consequence of error. *Pseudo-Martyr* is more akin in positive aspects to "A Litanie" than it is to *Biathanatos*.

One of the major preoccupations of "A Litanie" is despair, the awful sense of having fallen irretrievably out of the reaches of God's grace. Such despondency settled often on Donne, in the religious poetry and in the sermons; and he viewed it not only as a mental state but as an especially fearful temptation. In "A Litanie," he describes himself as "now growne ruinous:/ My heart is by dejection, clay,/ And by selfe-murder, red" (ll. 4–6). The Charybdis that matches the Scylla of despair is, for the Christian, presumption, the *hubris* of the publican in the temple; and this, too, occupies the mind of the later Donne. This is the real theme of *Pseudo-Martyr*, the great sin of presumption. It is the equation between presumption and what Donne considered false Catholic theology, and the personal and civic results of such an equation, that animates this work. *Pseudo-Martyr* was certainly an outstanding contribution to Anglican apologetics, but it was also a definition of private and personal ideals. Donne may have been recompensed by the Oxford degree, but there is nothing venal in *Pseudo-Martyr*: it is a conscientious defense of major articles in Donne's faith.

As in "A Litanie," Donne's mind is on trinities. He evidently intended a triadic organization for *Pseudo-Martyr*. Chapters I–III deal with real and false martyrdom; chapters IV–XII are concerned with the problem of spiritual and civil obedience; and chapters XIII–XIV were to have treated the extremely controversial topics of (a) the strict limits of the Oath of Allegiance and (b) the right of the monarch to re-deliver his subjects to Papal jurisdiction. The first had been Thomas More's problem, and the second was to be James II's; and the prudent Sir Edward Coke, among others, persuaded Donne that there were too many edges on both topics. Donne did not pursue the issues, but let them stand as chapter headings only.

In his third chapter, Donne avows there are three reasons for the falsity of Roman Catholic concepts of martyrdom: pseudo martyrdom is encouraged (1) by Catholic contempt of the civil magistracy, (2) "by dignifying and over-valewing our merits and satisfactions, and teaching that the treasure of the Church, is by this expence of our blood increased,"[100] (3) by the doctrine of purgatory, which maliciously hedges on the efficacy of the Atonement.

He avers there are only three reasons to provoke martyrdom, none of which can be unhesitatingly claimed by the recusants: to seal in blood a moral truth, to maintain the integrity of the universal Christian faith, or to preserve the liberties of the Church.[101] The tripartite nature of Donne's inventiveness is clear in the way he assembles and organizes his materials.

The absolute taproot of these materials is the same doctrine of works that operates in "A Litanie," and which became a keystone of Donne's theology; that is, the absolute primacy of Christ in the Atonement, the free and undeserved infusion of grace through Christ, and man's inability to merit grace through any of his works. The whole matrix of *Pseudo-*

Martyr is connected to this doctrine, it is the genus from which everything derives. God cannot be bribed into redeeming man, not even by martyrdom; Molinistic theories of regicide, which urge men to be the agents of God's providence, are of no more avail than any human activity in the drama of redemption; rebellion against manifest and established order sinfully presumes that man has a power to dictate the terms of his own redemption. Donne is at his sarcastic best when he describes Roman Catholic presumption relegating Christ to the status of participant in sacred ritual. He scathingly observes that "in solemne processions, *the Image of Christ must looke backward, if a Cardinall follow*; and God himselfe in the Host, must give them place: for at the Coronation of the pope, when they provide twelve horses for the *Pope*, and one gentle one for the Host, the dignity of place being measured by the nearenesse to the *Popes* person; the Cardinals place is, to ride betweene the Host and the *Pope*."[102]

The notion that man can, by good works, or by the intermediacy of the Church, store up merits for himself moves Donne alternately to mockery and indignation. On the question of indulgences, the Tetzelian rock on which Luther's Catholicism broke, Donne comments, "And therefore *Martin* 5. had a just and proportionall respect to the nature of this ware, when he appointed a yearly *Faire*, and yearely *Indulgence*, both of three moneths continuance, to be kept together at *Loretta*; and that the *Papists* and *Merchants* should open and shut up shoppe together."[103] The belief in purgatory, harmonious enough with the theory of indulgences, since both accept man as able to satisfy the temporal punishment due to sin, the latter through dispensation and the former through torment, gets off no more lightly. Donne, in delightful comic understatement, relates the anecdote:

> At one Masse, at the Commemoration of the Dead, a *Friar saw soules flie from Purgatorie as thicke as sparks from a furnace:* and this Masse he celebrated every day, and so did infinite others. If then that Friar made a true *relation of the state of Purgatorie in his time, That of 5000 which died in the world since his comming thether, there came but three to that place,* there is no great use of heaping so much treasure, for that imployment, since by these computations, neither the Number can bee great, nor the stay long.[104]

But along with the comedy comes the extremely serious allegation that indulgences and purgatory, especially as promulgated by the Counter Reformation and the Jesuits, are the primary instigators of the pseudo martyrs.

> For though it be hard for any man to goe further on the left hand, then the Councell of *Trent* hath done, in these two doctrines of *Merite* and Purgatrry [sic], and every Catholique be bound to that Councell, yet as in most other Doctrines, so in these also, *Pelargus* hath noted the *Iesuites* to have gone beyond others, and therefore more then others, they incite, in these points, to a false Martyrdome.[105]

As in the forthcoming *Ignatius His Conclave*, the Jesuits are severely mauled in *Pseudo-Martyr*; but it is not Donne's intention to engage in polemics. Rather, his object is peace. He professes "My easines, to affoord a sweete and gentle Interpretation, to all professors of Christian Religion, if they shake not the Foundation."[106] Dryden of the *Religio Laici* could have accepted Donne's vision of a state at rest, an orderly and submissive theology supporting an orderly political system; and Donne's Catholic activists are strangely like Dryden's restless zealots. The goal is peace, and if the Anglicanism of Donne's program looks ahead to Caroline theology, his major argument looks back to Richard Hooker. The ritual hierarchies of the *Laws of Ecclesiastical Polity* echo through Donne's appeal that "God hath *Immediately* imprinted in mans Nature and Reason, to be subiect to a power immediately infus'd from him; and that he hath enlightened our Nature and Reason, to digest and prepare such a forme [i.e., a hierarchy of power]."[107]

The Roman Catholic interpretation of the efficacy of works encourages the interruption of the infused patterns of Nature and Reason even as it "dooth . . . diminish CHRISTS Passion."[108] The alternative to the potentially disruptive Catholic doctrine is not quietism in any shape or form, but the Lutheran doctrine of "fructifying" faith. Specifically alluding to Luther, Donne outlines what he accepts on principle:

> Yet there is more Devotion in our Doctrine of good works, then in that of the Romane Church, because we teach as much necessitie of them, as they doe, and yet tye no reward to them. And we acknowledge, that GOD doth not onely make out faith, to fructifie and produce good workes as fruits thereof, but sometimes beginnes at our workes: and in a mans hart morally enclined to doe good, doth build up faith.[109]

For Donne, the ethical and political consequences of such a belief were clear: as faith must precede works in theology, so, analogously, allegiance to constituted authority must precede individual action. Chapters VIII and IX of *Pseudo-Martyr* concentrate on the question of the conflict between individual conscience and acceptance of authority, and Donne comes down firmly on the side of acceptance. Recusant intractability in the face of the Oath of Allegiance, and the attendant courting of execution, is a political offspring of a theological parent, unfortunately ignorant of a true understanding of faith and works. The seventeenth-century tendency to view religion and politics as enmeshed and complementary is evident in *Pseudo-Martyr*, and indeed defines much of its character. But typical though it may be in general outline, it is unmistakably Donnian. The closely pressed argument, the range of testimony, the density of organization, and the acidity of the satire all carry his mark. Furthermore, in the "Advertisement to the Reader" that prefaces the treatise, Donne continues to vitalize a motif recurrent between 1608 and 1610, i.e., transmutation. In "Resurrection, imperfect" Christ was imaged as the prototype of all spiritual transformation, alchemist and elixir at once:

> Hee was all gold when he lay downe, but rose
> All tincture, and doth not alone dispose
> Leaden and iron wills to good, but is
> Of power to make even sinfull flesh like his.
>   (ll. 13–16)

Biathanatos climaxes with a Paracelsian cure, a medicinal expunging of error; Christ in "A Litanie" is the administering physician whose own bloodletting restores the balance of spiritual humors. The way that Donne's imagination plays so often now with the idea of metamorphosis, purgation, spiritual health is still another indication of how conscious he was of a change within himself. Even in this public and controversial work of *Pseudo-Martyr*, the image of restored health appears. Somewhat in anticipation of "Show me deare Christ," with its feminizing of the true Church, Donne strikingly presents Catholicism as a lovely woman, who Mithridates-like has drunk poison; unravaged herself, she destroys whoever embraces her. The English statutes of conformity and the reformed doctrines of grace and obedience are purges which will drive the poison out and return the deathly woman to health.[110]

Pseudo-Martyr and sixteen of the holy sonnets were probably composed almost at the same time.[111] In the first half of

1609, Donne very likely completed the first six of the sonnets (*Divine Meditations:* "As due by many titles," "Oh my blacke Soule," "This is my playes last scene," "At the round earths imagin'd corners," "If poysonous mineralls," and "Death be not proud"). The following six (*Divine Meditations:* "Spit in my face," "Why are wee by all creatures waited on?" "What if this present were the worlds last night?" "Batter my heart," "Wilt thou love God," and "Father, part of his double interest"), inasmuch as they are so closely related in subject and mood, must be very close in time; and it seems most plausible that the four penitential sonnets ("Thou hast made me," "I am a little world," "O might those sighes," and "If faithfull soules") were written later than the first twelve, but before 1610, i.e., in the second half of 1609, making them exactly contemporary with *Pseudo-Martyr.*

These four sonnets, unlike the first twelve, rely hardly at all on the meditative patterns observable in most of the sonnets, and presumably follow rather than precede the opening twelve.[112] As to the probable terminus: from 1610 to 1612, Donne was greatly involved with the Drurys, with his travels to the Continent in Sir Robert's entourage, and with the composition and publication of the two *Anniversary* poems; so that while there was nothing actively to prevent his continuing the sonnet series later than 1609, neither would there have been much encouragement. There's a breaking point even for such energy as Donne had.

In general, then, *Pseudo-Martyr* and sixteen of the holy sonnets were moving toward articulation at the same time. It's a sobering and impressive spectacle, this range that Donne exhibits. On the one hand, he's anticipating, preparing, and finally completing a massively documented, carefully argued public defense of royal policy; and at the same time he is

engaging in the most personal and rigorous of spiritual meditations—*vita activa* and *vita contemplativa* in equilibrium.
There are no signs that Donne arbitrarily compartmentalized
his two lives: *Pseudo-Martyr* and the sonnets enrich one
another.

A substantive distinction must be made, to be sure. *Pseudo-
Martyr* is academic debate, delivered with assurance, and
aggressively unified; the sonnets are meditative, filled with
misgivings, and fluctuating in their form and intention.
Pseudo-Martyr deals with a single major issue, and subordinates all of its material to that issue, while the sonnets are
protean, appearing now as spiritual exercise, now as history—
compulsion seeking a form.

The morphology of the sonnets is a problem that is by no
means solved. It has been demonstrated that the tradition of
St. Ignatius' *Spiritual Exercises* is at work in these poems;[113]
but the extent to which Donne used the structure of the
Jesuit meditation has been variously assessed.[114] One point is
very clear: in none of the sonnets is the entire Ignatian
pattern at work, and there is a decreasing emphasis on that
pattern as the sonnets succeed one another. The entire plan
of the Ignatian meditation has been summarized by Professor
Gardner:

> The meditation is a very old religious exercise. Its essence is
> an attempt to stimulate devotion by the use of the imagina-
> tion. The method of meditation was systematized in the six-
> teenth century by St. Ignatius Loyola, whose *Exercitia Spiri-
> tualia* was printed with Papal approval in 1548. A meditation
> on the Ignatian pattern, employing the 'three powers of the
> soul', consists of a brief preparatory prayer, two 'preludes', a
> varying number of points, and a colloquy. The preparatory
> prayer is 'to ask God our Lord for grace that all my intentions,
> actions and operations may be ordered purely to the service

and praise of His divine Majesty'. The first prelude is what is called the *compositio loci:* the seeing 'with the eyes of the imagination' either a place 'such as the Temple or the mountain where Jesus Christ is found', or, if the meditation is of an invisible thing such as sin, a situation: 'that my soul is imprisoned in this corruptible body, and my whole compound self in this vale [of misery] as in exile amongst brute beasts'. The second prelude is a petition 'according to the subject matter'; thus, if the meditation is of the Passion, the petition will be for 'sorrow, tears, and fellowship with Christ in his sufferings'; if the meditation is of sin, the petition will be for 'shame'. The meditation proper follows, divided into points, usually three or five. Lastly, the memory, the storehouse of images, having been engaged in the preludes, and the reason in the points, the third power of the soul, the will, is employed in the colloquy, which is a free outpouring of the devotion aroused.[115]

This very full plan is divided amongst the earliest sonnets, with the first corresponding to the preparatory prayer, the next three to the preludes and the colloquy. But the fifth and sixth sonnets of the first group are only remotely aligned with the meditative form.[116] The second set of six sonnets makes no attempt to complete the whole framework of the meditation, while the last four sonnets can only by straining be approached as meditations proper.[117] Furthermore, it was usual for meditations to have been written in sets of seven;[118] Donne, in the introductory poem to Dorset, excused himself for sending his friend only six poems:

> But though the ingendring force from whence they came
> > Bee strong enough, and nature doe admit
> > Seaven to be borne at once, I send as yet
> But six, they say, the seaventh hath still some maime; . . .
> > ("To E. of D. with six holy Sonnets," ll. 5–8[119])

It's a curious situation, Donne obviously attracted to the meditation, and then drawing back from a full commitment to it. That he should have been attracted is not at all surprising. He was drawn to the meditative structure not because it was prestigious or available or disciplinary, but because it suited his purposes exactly. There's nothing new in Donne's treating a poem as a meditation; in a very real sense, he's always done so. The later love poetry is every bit as persistent, as focused, and as self-exploratory as the divine poetry. But from *Biathanatos* onward. Donne's anxieties became less diffuse, and he demanded more specific answers to questions of existence. As his sophistication in theological matters grew, Donne's mind turned more and more frequently to a limited glossary of experience, and he attempted to define his own goals in restrictive terms. This is not to say that the free-ranging Donne is replaced by a doctrinally inhibited Donne; only that in the first decade of the century Donne asked questions from a different standpoint, and awaited different answers: the spirit of demand remains. The prime topic of the years from 1602 to 1610 is redemption, and *au fond* all his thoughts are centered here. Christ as redeemer and as archetype of redeemed man, the trinitarian image within man as a sign of redemption, the limits of man's cooperating with his own redemption: these are the themes of the poetry, of the *Essays in Divinity*, of *Pseudo-Martyr*. Donne considered the Ignatian meditation for the simple reason that the form offered him a paradigm, a structure of questions and answers that was true to his own experience. Controlled meditation demands a direct confrontation between man and God; it assumes an expenditure of the trinity of faculties—memory, imagination, and will; this expenditure symbolizes the re-creation of the Trinity in man; its object is spiritual rebirth. These are all anticipated by the Donne of the years before the sonnets. The personal involvement in Genesis and Exodus in the *Essays in Divinity*, the triadic structure of "A Litanie," the fascination with restorative medicine and transmuting alchemy in *Biathanatos* and "Resurrection, imperfect": all the component parts of the perfectly achieved meditation are fragmentarily afloat by 1609, and they needed only a catalyst to bring them together. But it doesn't happen in the sonnets, and the inherent promise of the achieved meditation is unfulfilled. It took the seemingly unimportant occasion of Elizabeth Drury's death to fuse all the elements. For reasons that escape full comprehension, her death was truly epiphanic for Donne, and in the *Anniversaries* we witness a complete and entire meditative act. The sonnets are a movement in that direction, but the movement is aborted.

Why did Donne hesitate to accept all the demands of the Ignatian meditation, and—the more important but complementary question—why did he not fulfill the implications of meditation, the re-creation of the self through the autoexercise of the trinity within? From a strictly formal point of view we can say that Donne, as usual, refused to follow any source slavishly, and his artistic independence rebelled against complete reliance on the Ignatian structure. It is also true that the confinement of the sonnet militates against the voluminousness of an entire meditation. But these are only partial, though compelling, answers to the deeper question: why do the sonnets not achieve that purgative and re-creative aim of meditation? Why do the later sonnets withdraw almost entirely from the meditative pattern? The intention of the Ignatian meditation is spiritual transformation: the blurred image of the trinity within is like an atrophied limb that, with exercise, will be returned to its primal health. The muscular direction of memory, imagination, and will toward God will reawaken that trinity. The ostensible goal of meditation is a kind of alchemy, a metamorphosis of dead matter into divinity-touched life. But there is no trace in the sonnets that Donne believes himself capable of such a transformation, no purposeful exercising of the trinity of faculties. Instead, there is a constant reiteration of the opposite, his own inability to accomplish any such regeneration and his utter dependence on Christ. When he does use the alchemical symbolism, it is referred not to himself or to his contemplations, but to Dorset, to whom he sent the first sonnets:

> I choose your judgement, which the same degree
>   Doth with her sister, your invention, hold,
> As fire these drossie Rymes to purifie,
>   Or as Elixar, to change them to gold;
> You are that Alchimist which alwaies had
> Wit, whose one spark could make good things of bad.
>   ("To E. of D. with six holy Sonnets," ll. 9–14)

The contemporaneity of *Pseudo-Martyr* and the vehemence therein with which Donne rejects the Catholic doctrine of merits and works is a fact that must be recalled. There, the utter frailty of human participation in redemption is tested in the field of politics; in the sonnets the same frailty is examined on its own theological ground. The issue is still presumption: balanced on the edge of despair over his own spiritual condition, Donne will not presume to participate in a remaking of himself in the image of God. That is, he will not be so contradictory as to defend one doctrine in *Pseudo-Martyr* and act, through meditation, on quite a contrary doctrine in the sonnets. The image that so frequently comes through from the sonnets is not that of a penitent cooperating in his own creation, but that of an actor in a hideous travesty of Petrarchan passion. Donne's voice at times becomes the plaintive voice of the unfilled woman, compliant, desirous, and frightened; God becomes the male lover, intransigent, elusive, and cruel. This is particularly true of the tenth sonnet, and is an ingredient of the penitential sonnets.

I'm not implying that the tradition of the meditation was displaced by the tradition of Solomon's song, whereby the language of *eros* was converted to the uses of *agape*. John of the Cross wrote love poetry to Christ, and so did George Herbert; and a comparison of Donne's Christ with St. John's *Amado* or Herbert's "my dearest Lord" reveals how alien Donne's sonnets are to the amatory tradition of religious poetry. A consistent language of love is as absent from these sonnets as is a consistent use of the spiritual meditation.

There is, though, still another feature of the sonnets, a point of view which does operate consistently through at least the first six of the sonnets, and which had caught up Donne's imagination for several years. This is the Augustinian view of history, first drawn upon in *The Progresse of the Soule* and operating as an undercurrent of Donne's thought ever since. The first six of the holy sonnets continue St. Augustine's history of the world, as *The Progresse of the Soule* began it and the *Anniversaries* complete it.

The first six of Donne's sonnets are eschatological, that is, concerned with the last things: death, judgment, heaven, and hell.[120] They are intensely personal, and it is precisely the personal note that has obscured the fact that they are also universal. That is, they are not only eschatological but apocalyptic, dealing both with the individual's end and mankind's end as well. Within these six sonnets is the progression of all history, from Eden to the Final Judgment. Like Thomas Browne, who thought of himself as born in Paradise and buried in England, miscarried by Eve before she conceived Cain, Donne is always aware of the endless recoverability of sacred history within human history, the grim re-enactment of the Fall, exile, and death in each single man's life, and the promise that the tragic monotony of that cycle will be ended by Christ. Donne's sonnet sequence begins with the recollection that God's image was implanted in man, but then effaced by sin:

> I am thy sonne, made with thy selfe to shine,
> Thy servant, whose paines thou hast still repaid,
> Thy sheepe, thine Image, and till I betray'd
> My selfe, a temple of thy Spirit divine;
> Why doth the devill then usurpe in mee?
> Why doth he steale, nay ravish that's thy right?
>
> (I, ll. 5–10[121])

As in all the sonnets, resanctification can be accomplished only by God, not by man's works:

> Except thou rise and for thine owne worke fight,
> Oh I shall soone despaire, . . .
>
> (I, ll. 11–12)

The second sonnet introduces the image of the pilgrim, the soul outside the gates of Eden, bearing Adam's curse:

> Thou art like a pilgrim, which abroad hath done
> Treason, and durst not turne to whence hee is fled,
> Or like a thiefe, which till deaths doome be read,
> Wisheth himselfe delivered from prison; . . .
>
> (II, ll. 3–6)

The reprobate soul is Adam all over again, and Donne, as in "A Litanie" and in several later sermons, makes capital of the etymology of *Adam*, "red earth": all men's souls are black in mourning and red in their recapitulation of Adam; Christ must provide the whiteness of sanctity and as the new Adam provide the redness of his own blood:

> Oh make thy selfe with holy mourning blacke,
> And red with blushing, as thou art with sinne;
> Or wash thee in Christs blood, which hath this might
> That being red, it dyes red soules to white.
>
> (II, ll. 11–14)

The destiny of universal Adam, the exile beyond the gates, is death, "My pilgrimages last mile" (III, l. 2). First will come the particular judgment, when each single man will face God,[122] and then the general judgment, when all mankind will be judged: this is the subject matter of sonnets three and four, the sequence of judgments. Still again, in the third sonnet, sinful man must rely entirely on the free gift of saving grace: as he had in the elegy "To his Mistris Going to Bed," Donne insists on *imputed* righteousness (the Protestant doctrine) and not on *infused* righteousness (the Catholic doctrine). God will not be bribed nor will he give guarantees; we cannot expect that grace will have been poured into us as a reward for good behavior, we can only blindly trust that the grace has been awarded.

> Impute me righteous, thus purg'd of evill,
> For thus I leave the world, the flesh, and devill.
> (III, ll. 13–14)

The fourth sonnet speculates on the second and general judgment in the octave, while the sestet shudderingly withdraws from that judgment until such time as Christ's abundant grace has led to repentance. The fifth sonnet envisions the most direful results of the Last Judgment, and is a plea that Christ's Passion and death revoke deserved damnation:

> O God, Oh! of thine onely worthy blood,
> And my teares, make a heavenly Lethean flood,
> And drowne in it my sinnes blacke memorie.
> That thou remember them, some claime as debt,
> I thinke it mercy, if thou wilt forget.
> (V, ll. 10–14)

The sixth sonnet is sharply different in tone and attitude from those that precede it. Instead of the emphasis on loss, despair, and guilt, this is a triumphant variation of St. Paul's "O death, where is thy sting? O grave, where is thy victory?" (I Corinthians 15:55). The sonnet is a surprising reversal of all the fears that control the first five sonnets. And yet, not surprising at all: sonnets I–V survey the whole course of human time from the Fall to Final Judgment, with Donne constantly stressing that his own life is a microcosm of time; and, as in *The Progresse of the Soule*, history is a spectacle of primeval tragedy being everlastingly repeated. But in the fifth sonnet, time comes to an end, history is completed; and the sixth sonnet is a celebration based on the triumphant text of St. Paul to the Corinthians (I, 15:26), "The last enemy that shall be destroyed, is death" (a text on which Donne later delivered one of his finest sermons[123]). The exultant tone of "Death be not proud" looks ahead to the surge of joy that comes in *The Second Anniversary*, where the escape from human time is accomplished.[124]

What we witness in these six sonnets is a collusion of individual history, universal history, and sacred history, time present, time past, and time future. The prototype of Donne's insight, of each man being a recapitulation of all men, is probably to be found in two of St. Augustine's works, *The City of God* (specifically chapters 1–7 of Book XX) and *De Quantitate Animae* (chapters 33–35). In the first, St. Augustine describes history as being fulfilled in seven stages, and in the second he describes the redemptive route of the human soul as consisting of seven stages. Donne allows the two systems to collapse into one another, so that universal history and individual history march together.

In *The City of God*, St. Augustine, in speaking of God's judgment on men, first distinguishes and then coalesces the first and second resurrections. The first resurrection is the transition from death to life in this world; the second is the summoning to judgment of all men at the end of time.

> As, then, there are two regenerations, of which I have already made mention—the one according to faith, and which takes place in the present life by means of baptism; the other ac-

cording to the flesh, and which shall be accomplished in its
incorruption and immortality by means of the great and final
judgment—so there are also two resurrections—the one the
first and spiritual resurrection, which has place in this life,
and preserves us from coming into the second death; the other
the second, which does not occur now, but in the end of the
world, and which is of the body, not of the soul, and which
by the last judgment shall dismiss some into the second death,
others into that life which has no death.[125]

While the resurrections are distinct, they are also patterns of
each other. Drawing as Donne will do on the Apocalypse, or
Revelation of St. John the Divine, St. Augustine recounts
how the six days that went into the creation of the world are
symbolically re-enacted, but in reverse, through history; and as
the first six days were followed by the Sabbath, so the last six
days will also be followed by a Sabbath that shall have no
ending, "the endless rest of all the saints."[126] The "days" of
the anticreation were, for St. Augustine (as well as for
Donne), equal to six thousand years. For Augustine the
arithmetic of time is determined by the text of Peter 3:8,
"One day is with the Lord as a thousand years, and a thousand years as one day"; consequently, "these things happen in
the six thousand of years or sixth millennium, the latter part
of which is now passing."[127] Donne's equation is the same:
"Of [the] last houre we have heard three quarters strike,
more then fifteen hundred of this last two thousand spent."[128]

When Donne later preached on the text of I Corinthians
15:26, he caught up all these motifs. The sermon is on the
two resurrections and their congruence, as in St. Augustine:

> You must dye this death, this death of the righteous, the
> death to sin, before this *last enemy, Death,* shalbe destroyed
> in you, and you made partakers of everlasting life in soule and
> body too.[129]

Donne's topic is the same as Augustine's time past, present, and future: "We had a Resurrection in prophecy; we have a Resurrection in the present working of Gods Spirit; we shall have a Resurrection in the finall consummation."[130] Like Augustine, Donne takes the Revelation of St. John as his basis for distinguishing two resurrections.[131]

The structure of this sermon is most interesting: it is made up of seven parts, so that the sermon itself becomes a hiero-glyph of Augustine's anticreation, the undoing of creation in six steps followed by an eternal seventh day. "And in these seven steps we shall passe apace."[132] The *septem vestigia* through which Donne took his audience end with the ever-lasting peace with God: "This is the last abolition of this enemy, Death; for after this, the bodies of the Saints he cannot touch, the bodies of the damned he cannot kill. . . . This is that blessed and glorious State, of which . . . those two Reverend Fathers [i.e., Tertullian and Irenaeus?[133]] to whom it belongs, shall come to speake."[134]

To summarize: in St. Augustine's *City of God*, in Donne's later sermon on a text of St. Paul, and in the first sequence of the *Holy Sonnets*, there are six stages of anticreation, a process of demolition that is both individual and universal. Whereas there is a seventh stage, a plateau of eternal blessed-ness in both the *City of God* and the sermon preached at Whitehall, there is no seventh sonnet in this sequence. In-stead, there are ten more sonnets, all asserting the barriers that stand between Donne and the eternal Sabbath. There ought to be a seventh, not because seven was a usual number for meditations, but because seven is Redemption; and if "the seaventh hath still some maime," it is because Donne is not at all willing to presume that his own redemption has been achieved. The sequence of six sonnets is a fragment, but a deliberate fragment, to be completed when the old Adam within has been destroyed; and Donne was too severe and too honest and above all too reluctant to presume on God's mercy to write himself into a seventh and beatifying sonnet. Purposely unfinished though it is, this six-sonnet sequence is a great advance in Donne's identification of himself with all mankind, as he attempted to do in the *Essays in Divinity*, *La Corona*, and "A Litanie." Here, he is successful; the strains of the personal meditation and the involvement in universal history operate in perfect unison.

The following six sonnets are not a sequence in any strict sense of the word. It would have been supernumerary for Donne to have continued the design of sacred history that pulls the first six sonnets into a dramatic unity. The seventh scene, the Parousia, needs still to be acted, but otherwise the drama is complete. The next set of six sonnets is not locked into any narrative framework as are the first six. But at the same time, there are close affiliations between the two sets. The meditative pattern, though considerably muted, continues to operate: these six may be read as colloquies, similar to the last third of an Ignatian meditation.[135] There is, furthermore, a cohesion in this second group: sonnets VII–IX ("Spit in my face yee Jews," "Why are wee by all creatures waited on?" and "What if this present were the worlds last night?") concentrate on God's love for man, and X–XII ("Batter my heart," "Wilt thou love God," and "Father, part of his double interest") reverse the movement and emphasize the love man owes to God.[136] Even more importantly, this second group of sonnets further explains why Donne could not write a seventh sonnet. There is, first of all, a limit to human expression. St. Paul's assertion that the man "caught up into paradise . . . heard unspeakable words, which it is not lawful for a man to utter" (II Corinthians 12:4) was extended still further by Donne in the sermon at Whitehall already referred to. The *septimum vestigium*, the event following on the destruction of death, outruns even angelic

expression, so that "in going about to expresse it, the lips of
an Angell would be uncircumsised lips, and the tongue of an
Archangell would stammer."[137] The second resurrection is
ineffable, the first resurrection is unfathomable, a mystery of
divine love. This is the subject of the second group of sonnets,
the dimensions of love. Human art, human speech, and
human endeavor cannot produce a seventh sonnet, a beatific
vision, nor a redemption. This is an apprehension that has
been in all of Donne's writings under one guise or another
since 1601, *The Progresse of the Soule*, the belief in the
flawed condition of humanity; and this is the motif of the
deliberately incomplete heptalogy of the first sonnet group.
The seventh stage, the absolute *consummatum est*, can be
achieved only through and within divine love. *Per ipsum et
cum ipso et in ipso.*

A parallel might be drawn to Dante's progress in the
Paradiso. There, it will be recalled, Dante begins his seven-
stage journey at the Garden of Eden and ascends swiftly
through the first six spheres (lunar, Mercury, Venus, solar,
Mars, and Jupiter, cantos I–XX). Before him lies the seventh
sphere (Saturn), the withdrawal from the world and the
vision of God, and beyond that the Church Triumphant.
Dante's seventh stage is the preamble to Beatific Vision, and
the seventh sphere of Saturn represents contemplation, the
antechamber of complete spiritual vision.

It would not be inappropriate to call Donne's sonnets
VII–XII Saturnine, in Dante's sense of the word: renunciation of the world, acceptance of God's will, surrender to
divine love, all in anticipation of entering the company of the
redeemed. These are all Dante's themes in the sixth and
seventh stages of *Paradiso* (cantos XVIII–XXI), and these
are the themes of these six sonnets.

The first three sonnets of this second group all consider
divine love as it was and continues to be manifested in

Christ's Passion; and as in *La Corona*, Donne primarily stresses the absolute paradoxicality of Christ. The Atonement is an affront to human reason. Whereas the second three sonnets (the forcing of man's love for God) are laced with exclamation points, the first three are filled with questions, rhetorical, explicit, and implicit. God's is a "strange love": glorified, he is still crucified daily; unlike Jacob, who clothed himself roughly to supplant Esau's estate, Christ clothed himself *in carne* to return a lost estate (sonnet VII). That weak and sinful man should be able to dominate a powerful and sinless world of creatures is puzzle enough, but the greater puzzle is God's having chosen weak man to be redeemed (sonnet VIII). Even the laws of perception and beauty as they operate in the profane world are contradicted by the mystery of divine love: the horror of the Crucifixion becomes beauteous, and as beauty signals pity in a fleshly mistress, so the oxymoronic beauty of the dying Christ "assures a pitious mind" (sonnet IX). The surfeit of questions beyond the stretch of rational explanation is, as in *La Corona*, tantamount to a rejection of human reason. As Dante is urged, before entering into the empyrean, to check his human judgment and assent to God's will,

> Perchè il ben nostro in questo ben s'affina,
> Che quel che vole Iddio e noi volemo
> (*Paradiso*, canto XX, ll. 137–138)

so Donne in these three sonnets once again tests and decries the limits of reason. The subsequent three sonnets identify the enveloping will of God with love, an identification that reaches its climax in the superb twelfth sonnet, "Father, part of his double interest."

The tenth sonnet, "Batter my heart," is perhaps the best known of Donne's religious poetry. The language of erotic love is so forcefully used to describe man's relation to God that it can be overlooked that the amatory depiction of the man-God relationship is atypical of the sonnets as a whole. These are not love poems; Donne wrote great love poetry because he could imagine or re-enact the experience of human love; but it is an exactly opposite sense which underlies his religious poetry. Divine love outstrips human reason and imagination. The tenth sonnet, powerful as it may be, is uncharacteristic and is, in some ways, a reversion to an earlier manner. Donne's quest to realize himself led him, at times (for instance, in "Aire and Angels"), to adopt an attitude of passivity or to envision an emptying of himself by symbolic annihilation, so that he might be filled. In doing so, he fleetingly resembles the antithesis of his obvious maleness. In most of the love poetry, the passivity of the woman is the means whereby the lover can demonstrate his power and accomplish his will; almost surreptitiously, late in the secular period, Donne assumes a mood of compliant negation. "Batter my heart" returns to that mood, and for the same purpose, even though the temper is sacred rather than secular. Now it is God's power and will that is to be demonstrated through Donne's metamorphosis into a woman. The equation between acceptance and the image of a woman will be a major element in the *Anniversaries*; "Batter my heart" lies between the hesitant equation in the late love poetry and its full development in the great work of 1610–1612.[138]

From "A Litanie" on to this moment in Donne's poetry, there's been a tension between Donne's anxiety to recapture the image of the Trinity within himself and his sense of inadequacy to do so: St. Augustine's doctrine conflicting with the reformed doctrine of imputed grace, *De Trinitate* against *Pseudo-Martyr*. Not until Donne was convinced that he had entirely demolished the old Adam would he presume to rescue the interior trinity. This he will do in the *Anniversaries*; but in the meantime "Batter my heart" is a lament that he has not yet achieved submission, that the metamorphosis into an accepting woman is not complete, and that the

Trinity must smash its way in. The power of the Father, the Pentecostal wind and tongue of fire of the Spirit, and the redemptive act of the Son ("knocke, breathe, shine, and seeke to mend") all will have to be expended to the utmost ("breake, blowe, burn and make me new"). Instead of being a temple of the indwelling Spirit ("Know ye not that your body is the temple of the Holy Ghost which is in you, which ye have of God, and ye are not your own?" I Corinthians 6:19), he is a beleaguered citadel, "an usurpt towne, to'another due." The distrust of reason, so ubiquitous in Donne, reappears as a prime cause of resistance:

> I, like an usurpt towne, to'another due,
> Labour to'admit you, but Oh, to no end,
> Reason your viceroy in mee, mee should defend,
> But is captiv'd, and proves weake or untrue, . . .
>   (ll. 5–8)

But before redemption, certain transmutations must occur. The *Agnus Dei*, lamb of God, must become *Aries Dei*, ram of God (an image already used in *La Corona*: "O strong Ramme, which has batter'd heaven for mee,/ Mild lambe, which with thy blood, hast mark'd the path," "Ascension," ll. 9–10); and his own maleness must be transmuted to womanliness. The sonnet ends with a riot of paradox, God becoming a liberating captor, who makes chaste those he ravishes:

> Take mee to you, imprison mee, for I
> Except you'enthrall me, never shall be free,
> Nor ever chast, except you ravish mee.
>   (ll. 12–14)

The lines are a compressed version of *La Corona*'s central assertion, an embracing of divine paradox that overcomes human fallibility.

The eleventh sonnet follows logically: the bridge between

"Batter my heart" and "Wilt thou love God" is the text of St.
Paul already quoted, I Corinthians 6:19. The temple of the
heart, translated by sin into a citadel in the tenth sonnet,
reappears as a temple now that the siege is over. "God the
Spirit, by Angels waited on/ In heaven, doth make his
Temple in thy brest" (ll. 3–4). The transition having been
made, Donne reverts to metaphors of legalism, something he
has rarely done since "Loves Infiniteness," and doing so
prepares for the movement into the last sonnet of this group.
Donne follows the allusion to I Corinthians with a second
Pauline text, this time from Romans 8:15–17, which he
compresses into the lines:

> [God] Hath deign'd to chuse thee by adoption,
> Coheire to' his glory,' and Sabbaths endlesse rest; . . .
>
> (ll. 7–8)

The legal tone of the inheritance image is picked up through
reference to English law on the recovery of stolen goods:

> And as a robb'd man, which by search doth finde
> His stolne stuffe sold, must lose or buy'it againe:
> The Sonne of glory came downe, and was slaine,
> Us whom he'had made, and Satan stolne, to unbinde.
>
> (ll. 9–12)

Donne elects to choose the version of the Atonement which is
based on the idea of ransom, rather than the Atonement as
recapitulation (Christ is the second Adam, whose death must
involve mankind even as did the first Adam's), as satisfaction
(God's honor having been stained by Adam's defection, the
honor must be recovered through Christ's sacrifice), or as
penal-substitutionary (Christ paid the debt that man owes to
God).[139] Christ's Incarnation, Passion, and death pays the
ransom for man's soul to Satan the thief.

The twelfth sonnet now picks up this legal tenor, and the

poem is drenched with the language of the law courts: "joynture," "Wills," "Legacie," "invest," "statutes," "lawes abridgement." The Biblical texts from which Donne draws are redolent of the law:

<blockquote>
he
Hath made two Wills, . . .
(ll. 6–7)
</blockquote>

[Christ] is the mediator of the new testament, that by means of his death, for the redemption of the transgressions that were under the first testament, they which are called might receive the promise of eternal inheritance.

<blockquote>
(St. Paul, Hebrews 9:15)
</blockquote>

<blockquote>
None doth, but all-healing grace and Spirit,
Revive againe what law and letter kill.
(ll. 11–12)
</blockquote>

<blockquote>
The letter killeth, but the spirit giveth life.
(St. Paul, II Corinthians 3:6)
</blockquote>

<blockquote>
thy last command
Is all but love; . . .
(ll. 13–14)
</blockquote>

A new commandment I give unto you, That ye love one another; as I have loved you, that ye also love one another.

<blockquote>
(John 13:34)
</blockquote>

The movement from St. Paul, the author of the law-preoccupied epistles to the Galatians and Hebrews, to St. John, "the disciple whom Jesus loved" (John 21:20) is significant: it parallels the development of Donne's central idea. That is, between the tenth and twelfth sonnets Donne moves from citadel to temple to court of law; from recovered wealth to inheritance to "Will" as testamentary instrument; and, in the twelfth sonnet, from "Will" as testament to "Will" as purpose and purpose as love. At the apex of a whole series of witty transformations stands love. This shying away fom "will" as decree and the association of "will" with love is perhaps the most essential fact of Donne's theology as it is formed over the years. It is the mainspring of his greatest sermons, and it is the nexus between Jack Donne and Dean Donne. He became as great a divine as he was a love poet, because in both lives he dealt with the same thing.

The four penitential sonnets leave a much stronger impression of a uniquely lonely and concerned Donne than do any of the preceding meditations. Whereas, in the first two groups, Donne is a part of universal destiny, sharing with all men a history and a promise, the last four sonnets nearly silence such objective frameworks as Augustine, Paul, John, or Ignatius can provide. While Donne will relax the doctrine of imputed grace in the *Anniversaries*, the mood of his meditations remains in full force here: he is completely at the mercy of God, and will not be so proud as to imagine that he can in any way cooperate with saving grace. "Not one houre I can my selfe sustaine" is the major refrain now; God must "like Adamant draw mine iron heart." "I am a little world made cunningly," and Donne uses with great effect the commonplace of microcosm-macrocosm. So long as the macrocosmic elements are located in man, they are perverse, mutable, and frustrated; it is only when the elements are commanded by God that they become purposeful. Donne imagines himself, in the second sonnet of this third group, "a little world" (microcosm) "made cunningly/ Of Elements" (earth, water, fire, air). But the stable earth and space have been expanded from an eight- to a nine-, ten-, and eleven-sphere system by Ptolemy, Alphonsus of Castile, and Clavius respectively.[140] The element of water had to be transformed from the waters over which the Spirit of God moved in Genesis to the punishing waters of the Deluge. The element of fire will be a second scourge (Genesis 9:11–16; II Peter 3:6–7). However stable the elements may have been *in origine*, God's justice requires that they be changed, put to a punitive purpose as soon as they become involved with sinful man. Donne tries a metamorphosis of his own, a conversion of the Deluge into baptism:

> Powre new seas in mine eyes, that so I might
> Drowne my world with my weeping earnestly,
> Or wash it, if it must be drown'd no more: . . .
> (Penitential Sonnet 2, ll. 7–9)

But his own attempts at conversion fail, and he must trust in the activity of the Lord. The conclusion of the sonnet records a rapid series of conversions, all effected by God—a sharp contrast to the abortive attempts of Donne to convert the fearful elements into benign symbols of his own repentance:

> Let their flames retire,
> And burne me ô Lord, with a fiery zeale
> Of thee and thy house, which doth in eating heale.
> (ll. 12–14)

The fire of lust and envy can be converted to zeal (Psalm 69:9) and still further to a token of purification. The powerful alchemy of the Deity can effect conversions; the crippled will of Donne cannot. The sonnet is a close-textured contrast between the several meanings of conversion (stability to instability, macrocosm to microcosm, literal element to spiritual symbol, emblems of punishment to emblems of repentance), with the conversions failing in the human dimension but succeeding in the divine dimension.

The note of repentance is exceptionally strong in the last two sonnets, stronger perhaps than in any of the meditations that precede them. They make a suitable climax to the spiritual effort contained in this body of poetry, and assuredly say something of Donne's earnestness. Admittedly, the question of sincerity in poetry is a slippery issue, not helped by the Sidnean idea that poets are great liars. But it seems improbable that the sensitivity of Donne would not have appropriately responded to the inevitable climax of such effort, even supposing he began the cycle of meditation (as he certainly did not) with cynicism or indifference. The power of the sonnets is not something that can be casually put aside, even by the reader who happens not to share Donne's frame of reference; and if a reader might be moved to a sympathetic acceptance, no matter how short-lived and no matter how quickly dissipated once the reading is concluded, how much more so the intelligence creating the sonnets? There are more reasons for accepting Donne's protest of his grief in the penultimate sonnet ("O might those sighes and teares returne againe") and his surrendering his naked soul to the omniscient stare of God in the last sonnet ("If faithfull soules be alike glorifi'd") than there are for rejecting the protest and surrender. The man in the sonnets, at least, concludes his sixteen meditations in a mood of felt repentance.

Donne's letters affirm this image of a man wholly absorbed in an examination of his spiritual state. His mood at Mitcham was certainly depressed, as the pathetic letter to Goodyer in 1608 attests—a letter whose reference to "kindle[d] meditations" perhaps shows Donne on the eve of the sixteen sonnets, needing to fight his way out of personal misery.

> I write not to you out of my poor Library, where to cast mine eye upon good Authors kindles or refreshes sometimes meditations not unfit to communicate to near friends; nor from the high way, where I am contracted, and inverted into my self; which are my two ordinary forges of Letters to you. But

I write from the fire side in my Parler, and in the noise of
three gamesome children; and by the side of her, whom because I have transplanted into a wretched fortune, I must
labour to disguise that from her by all such honest devices, as
giving her my company, and discourse, therefore I steal from
her, all the time which I give this Letter, and it is therefore
that I take so short a list, and gallop so fast over it. I have not
been out of my house since I received your pacquet. As I
have much quenched my senses, and disused my body from
pleasure, and so tried how I can indure to be mine owne
grave, so I try now how I can suffer a prison.[141]

There is a letter, which Donne's son as editor opined
(probably wrongly)[142] was written also to Goodyer, that
could well be assigned to this same period, wherein Donne
asserts that a realization of his spiritual condition is a cure in
itself: not an inadequate description of a meditation at all.

If I knew that I were ill, I were well; for we consist of three
parts, a Soul, and Body, and Minde: which I call those
thoughts and affections and passions, which neither soul nor
body hath alone, but have been begotten by their communica-
tion, as Musique results out of our breath and a Cornet. And
of all these the diseases are cures, if they be known. Of our
souls sicknesses, which are sinnes, the knowledge is, to ac-
knowledge, and that is her Physique, in which we are not
dieted by drams and scruples, for we cannot take too much.[143]

A long letter to Goodyer emphasizes Donne's need for
meditation, and at the same time broaches a problem that will
much vex him: that is, the respective claims of sacerdotal and
secular faith. It is a theme of the poem to Tillman, an issue of
several sermons. It will be dramatized in Donne's decision in
1612 to enter orders and then his renouncing of that decision
and spending two years looking for a role to play in the active

world. The religious life encourages meditation and a contemplative awareness of God; but Luther had insisted, in his 1532 sermon on Matthew 6:24–34, that a secular life, too, can be a continuing demonstration of faith. For a time, Donne was attracted to Luther's sanctification of the secular life, but as with everything else he had to be absolutely sure of every side of the case. By the time he had concluded the sonnets and the *Anniversary* poems, all Donne's instinct directed him to a life in the ministry. But characteristically Donne had first to be totally convinced that the world was not a better theatre for him to bear witness in, and ordination was delayed. The important two-year pause between his informing Rochester "[I am] resolved to make my profession Divinity"[144] and telling Goodyer "I will make an end with the world"[145] will be considered in its place. In the meantime, just before beginning the sonnets, Donne shows himself aware of the choices he will have to confront. The most germane passages of this 1608 letter to Goodyer are lengthy, but worth quoting in full:

> The primitive Monkes were excusable in their retirings and enclosures of themselves: for even of them every one cultivated his own garden and orchard, that is, his soul and body, by meditation, and manufactures; and they ought the world no more since they consumed none of her sweetnesse, nor begot others to burden her. But for me, if I were able to husband all my time so thriftily, as not onely not to wound my soul in any minute by actuall sinne, but not to rob and cousen her by giving any part to pleasure or businesse, but bestow it all upon her in meditation, yet even in that I should wound her more, and contract another guiltinesse: As the Eagle were very unnaturall if because she is able to do it, she should pearch a whole day upon a tree, staring in contemplation of the majestie and glory of the Sun, and let her young

Eglets starve in the nest . . . I would not that death should take me asleep. I would not have him meerly seise me, and onely declare me to be dead, but win me, and overcome me. When I must shipwrack, I would do it in a Sea, where mine impotencie might have some excuse; not in a sullen weedy lake, where I could not have so much as exercise for my swimming. Therefore I would fain do something; but that I cannot tell what, is no wonder. For to chuse, is to do: but to be no part of any body, is to be nothing. At most, the greatest persons, are but great wens, and excrescences; men of wit and delightful conversation, but as moalls for ornament, except they be so incorporated into the body of the world, that they contribute something to the sustenation of the whole.[146]

Donne's entering the religious life is too often portrayed as a last desperate maneuver, a renunciation of a world that had already renounced him. But there was no weariness behind Donne's decision; it was the accepted consequence of the state of mind achieved in the sonnets and perfected in the Anniversaries. The poems of these middle years of 1605–1609 were not withdrawals, but vigils.

CHAPTER IV

The *Anniversaries*

1610–1612

D ONNE'S VIGIL ends with the Anniversary poems. An *Anatomy of the World and Of the Progresse of the Soule* constitute the apogee of his interior life, the irreversible moment toward which everything before moves and from which everything after flows. Donne's life was, up to this point, a series of pseudo climaxes, turning points whose completeness is belied by the emergence of still other crises and other climaxes. There are enough peripeties and denouements in Donne to lend dramatic structure to several lives. A new kind of awareness is signaled in the 1601 *Progresse of the Soule*, a major re-evaluation of himself is portrayed in the prose works of 1607–1610, and the early religious poetry marks off a whole new terrain to be explored. It is nothing less than amazing to realize how often Donne created axial situations for himself, and then raced beyond them. But all the critical stages of his own progress, the nuclei of perceptions and insights, came to fruition in the *Anniversaries*. The quest ordained in the third satire is completed in these poems: the soul's rest and the mind's endeavor are finally realized.

As a matter of fact, a great many things are completed in the *Anniversaries*. The fragmented history of *The Progresse of the Soule* is mended here, the evanescent woman of the love

poetry is captured here, and the incomplete cycle of meditation in the *Holy Sonnets* is finished here. A very great number
of Donne's earlier themes are brought into harmonious collaboration in the *Anniversaries*. The mortally wounded Adam
of *The Progresse of the Soule* reappears:

> Man all at once was there by woman slaine,
> And one by one we'are here slain o'er againe
> By them. . . .
>> (*The Progresse of the Soule*, ll. 91–93)

> One woman at one blow, then kill'd us all,
> And singly, one by one, they kill us now.
> > (*Anatomy of the World*, ll. 106–107)[1]

The senescent sun of "The Sunne Rising" and "A Lecture
upon the Shadow" intrudes in the *Anatomy* ("seeming weary
with his reeling thus,/ He meanes to sleep, being now falne
nearer us," ll. 273–274). The recollections of Dante that are
observable in the fourth satire and in *Ignatius His Conclave*
appear again,[2] and St. Bernard, who plays a role in the *Essays
in Divinity* and *La Corona*, is involved in the background of
the poem,[3] as are St. Augustine's trinitarianism and the
Augustinian seven stages of redemption. The Ignatian meditation informs the structure of the *Anniversaries* even more
entirely than in the meditative sonnets, and with a fuller
acceptance by Donne of the spiritual effort envisioned by
Ignatius.

To paraphrase one of Donne's own images: the *Anniversaries* like adamant have drawn random pieces of iron from his
previous work. But these poems are no *omnium-gatherum*, a
receptacle for shreds and patches from other writings. The
contrary is true: these are among the most cunningly assembled of all his poetry, the strongly focused vision of a poet
who hardly knew how to be diffuse. It seems to me that a

central question must be asked of the *Anniversaries:* what was the catalyst that pulled all the separate intuitions together? Why should the kaleidoscopic fragments of Donne's imagination suddenly be fixed in the numinous symbol of a mysterious "She" who draws into herself the substance of Donne's earlier thought?

We need to bear in mind Donne's continual excitement over the way events collapse into one another, revealing in a sudden flash a pervasive unity in the world. The work of his maturity is filled with wonder over the marvelous congruences that of a sudden show different places, objects, and times rushing together, charismatically asserting a pattern that underlies all experience. His was an imagination that could delight in the Annunciation and the Passion falling on one day:

> Th'Abridgment of Christs story, which makes one
> (As in plaine Maps, the furthest West is East)
> Of th'Angels Ave,' and *Consummatum est.*[4]

He could find both Adams met in him, and think that Christ's Cross and Adam's Tree stood in one place, beginnings and endings occurring in an identical space time.[5] He could conceive of man's life as a real and entire recapitulation of all history: "I was built up scarce 50. yeares ago, in my Mothers womb, and I was cast down, almost 6000. years agoe, in *Adams* loynes; I was *borne* in the last Age of the world, and *dyed* in the first."[6]

Donne is quintessentially a poet in the way he perceived such mysterious juxtapositions, mandalas in experience. These epiphanies were, for Donne, manifestations of a significance that gives the lie to the profane illusion of directionless and inchoate existence. Donne was no monist, but he did believe that there were moments when creation surrendered its origi-

nal design to human view. It is Seth's wisdom; and such
moments (which become more and more frequent in the
middle years) are not to be thought of as peripheral or as
arbitrarily designed by Donne. They are a central condition of
his poetry and his greatest prose, a starting point rather than a
way station. And he does not invent them; he recognizes them
as atypical but very real facts of experience.

It was, I believe, just such an unsolicited manifestation that
set the *Anniversaries* in motion. On December 13, 1610, the
Feast of St. Lucy, the first reports of Elizabeth Drury's death
were abroad.[7] For an imagination not alert to such announce-
ments of a pattern working itself out in human affairs, this
would be a coincidence, nothing more. For Donne, the death
of a virginal fourteen-year-old on this liturgical festival and
almost on the eve of her marriage was an indisputable declaration, a demand being made on him. He sensed a plan
underlying the jumble of history, and to comprehend it fully
he needed to articulate it in his poetry. The simple coincidence became the charged symbolic core around which
Donne's major ideas and intuitions arranged themselves: a
solar system whose center involves Lucy, the patroness of
light.

At no time in his life was Donne's synthesizing power so
imaginatively operative as at this moment. On this December
13, 1610, and in the days of composition that followed,
Donne's creative energies must have been reaching back,
absorbing, assimilating, until he had perfected one of the
most complex and richest symbolic statements in English
poetry. We can only sequentially and willfully attempt to
retrace what was an instinctive poetic response; and it would
be vain to imagine that we can entirely elucidate the causes
and the full scope of the symbolic ordering that goes on
within the *Anniversaries*. Like all great poems, they finally
frustrate the invasions of rational analysis. But, fragmentary

though our reconstruction must be, we can see the traces of the developing symbol.

First, the poems are not eulogies in the usual sense of the word. To relate them to the encomiastic tradition, along with Donne's elegies to Cranfield, Lord Harington, or Lady Markham, ignores the difference between the public character of such "Epicedes and Obsequies" and the essentially private character of the *Anniversaries*. That they are meditations has been amply demonstrated by Professor Martz.[8] We may go beyond Professor Martz; they are meditations in a much deeper, more fully realized way than are the meditative sonnets, accepting as they do all the implications of the meditative structure. *The First Anniversary*, which is earthbound,[9] is a pentad, a five-part statement, with each part divided into three units (meditation, eulogy, refrain and moral).[10] This is in keeping with the typical Jesuit exercises which "normally involve a series of five exercises daily for a period of about a month, each meditation being precisely divided into points, usually into three points."[11] But five also represented for Donne incompleteness, an entity needing to be joined to something else to achieve perfection. So he used it in the *Essays in Divinity:*

> From Sarai's name He took a letter which expressed the number ten, and reposed one which made but five; so that she contributed that five which man wanted before, to show a mutual indigence and support;[12]

and so he will use it in "The Primrose."[13] *The Second Anniversary* completes and fulfills *The First Anniversary*, showing as it does "The Progres of the Soule" into eternity. Eternity was represented by Donne as *seven*, as we can see in the *Holy Sonnets* and in the sermon at Whitehall on March 8, 1621/2; and *The Second Anniversary* is a heptad, a seven-part whole.

The repose of Donne, the assurance of redemption, inheres in the whole tenor of *The Second Anniversary*, and it is a long-awaited transformation. A significant doctrinal shift occurs in these poems: in *Pseudo-Martyr* and in the meditative sonnets, Donne took the most arduous Protestant stance on the question of man's cooperating in God's plan for redemption. The ultimate object of meditation, the full exercise of man's faculties as a way of requickening the trinitarian image of God within, is never achieved in the sonnets, for it seemed to Donne to be a presumptive defiance of his own fallen nature. But in the *Anniversaries*, the triple spiritual effort is fully operative:

> It becomes apparent that the tripartite structure of the *Anniversaries* is identical with the central symbol that rises from it. Put into Aristotelean terms, it is the same as the relationship between efficient and final cause. The symbol is the principle because of which the poem moves toward the production of its effect. It is the form. But at the same time, seen from a slightly different perspective, the symbol is also the process itself that produces the effect. It is both the object and the wit. More concretely, if through the process of the poem—the threefold act of memory, understanding, and will—we arrive at the right valuation of this world and the next, we will have achieved within ourselves the Image of God that was lost.[14]

Once in the pulpit, Donne's teachings on cooperative grace, free will, and man's role in the redemptive process stand somewhere between Geneva and Rome.[15] While still dependent on bestowed and undeserved grace, man may will to be redeemed, and accept God's prevenient grace. This less anxious doctrine of man's estate is first assumed in the *Anniversaries*.

In other words, the very completeness of the meditative act in these poems suggests the private quality; the subject and the auditory are not Elizabeth and Sir Robert Drury, but John Donne. As the subject of *The Progresse of the Soule* was finally, I believe, to have been Donne himself, so the real subject of the *Anniversaries* is Donne. I cannot think that it was Donne's first intention to present the *Anniversaries* to Sir Robert. Like the sonnets, they were originally conceived of as private meditations, the pursuit, through poetry and prayer, of self-understanding. For some reason, Donne changed his mind, and allowed *The First Anniversary* to be published in 1611, the first poem to be so printed in his lifetime and an uncharacteristic surrender of his privacy. Having set the course, Donne then permitted the publication, in 1612, of both *Anniversaries, Of the Progres of the Soule* having been completed in France sometime before March, 1612. He immediately regretted the publication, as his letters from France show, and he was deeply disturbed by the adverse criticism of his work.[16] He should have trusted what I believe were his first instincts. He did write an elegy for Elizabeth Drury, and this he might with impunity have put into the public domain; but the *Anniversaries* are not really about Elizabeth, and Donne encouraged the misinterpretation by allowing the poems to be printed. It seems clear to me that while the *Anniversaries* are not *about* Elizabeth Drury, they were certainly provoked by the December 13 death of Elizabeth. The full titles of the poems are *An Anatomie of the World. Wherein, By Occasion of the Untimely death of Mistris Elizabeth Drury, the frailty and the decay of this whole World is represented* and *Of the Progres of the Soule. Wherein, By occasion of the Religious death of Mistris Elizabeth Drury, the incommodities of the Soule in this life, and her exaltation in the next, are contemplated* (underscoring mine). The only poem about Elizabeth is "A Funerall Elegie," which was printed along with *The First Anniversary* in 1611, and then in the 1612 edition. It is true that in 1610 "Drury was in need of a poet, Donne of a patron,"[17] but the grace-offering was not, in Donne's original plan, *An Anatomy of the World*, but the 106 lines of "A Funerall Elegie."

Not a great deal of attention has been paid to the elegy, nor is there much reason that there should have been. It is hardly more distinguished than the other competent epicedes that Donne wrote under pressure or need or command. E. K. Chambers' notion that the elegy was written first and then expanded into the *Anniversaries* has been credibly challenged,[18] and it's probable that Donne turned aside from his major and private work to indite this conventional lament for the real Elizabeth. For "A Funerall Elegie" is a pastiche of bits of the symbolism of *The First Anniversary* and stereotyped funereal themes, all pressed into the service of much-needed patronage. No tomb is rich enough to hold the precious girl; even less so (in a reversal of the Horatian *monumentum perennius*) can his verse contain her, particularly since her death has crippled all things of this world. She was the music that harmonized the world, but it may be she has entered into a greater harmony through death. So delicate that she seemed heavenly while she lived, she has preserved her delicacy by dying. Not even fifteen years of age, she was so exemplary in virtue that she can be a pattern for the living. This is adroit, but it is in a different range of poetry from the *Anniversaries*.

The death that is lamented in "A Funerall Elegie" is, then, the literal death of Elizabeth Drury: stubborn details that describe only her are obvious ("Much promis'd, much perform'd, at not fifteene," l. 86). But the death of the *Anniversaries* themselves is not hers. On December 13, 1610, the center for which Donne had been looking for ten years was offered in a girl's death, and his intellectual and emotional life leapt into symmetry. Donne dated his own death in 1601: writing to Wotton from France, early in 1612, Donne spoke of his "Metaphoricall death," and remarked:

> If at last, I must confesse, that I dyed ten years ago . . . yet it wil please me a little to have had a long funerall, and to have kept my self so long above ground without putrefaction.[19]

His marriage, the collapse of his fortunes, and especially the grim vision of the first *Progresse of the Soule* were Donne's first death. The later poetry is at times a counterinsurgence against death:

> All other things, to their destruction draw,
> Only our love hath no decay; . . .
> ("The Anniversarie," ll. 6–7)

> Love, all alike, no season knowes, nor clyme,
> Nor houres, dayes, months, which are the rags of time.
> ("The Sunne Rising," ll. 9–10)

> We dye and rise the same, and prove
> Mysterious by this love.
> ("The Canonization," ll. 26–27)

The self-abnegation that characterizes true love ritualizes and makes benign the death that permeates the world:

> When love, with one another so
> Interinanimates two soules,
> That abler soule, which thence doth flow,
> Defects of lonelinesse controules.
> ("The Exstasie," ll. 41–44)

If our two loves be one, or, thou and I
Love so alike, that none doe slacken, none can die.
> ("The Good-morrow," ll. 20–21)

But even love may be marked by death:

Love is a growing, or full constant light;
And his first minute, after noone, is night,
> ("A Lecture upon the Shadow," ll. 25–26)

and woman may play the Judas, throwing man back into his own loneliness:

Perchance as torches which must ready bee,
Men light and put out, so thou deal'st with mee,
Thou cam'st to kindle, goest to come; Then I
Will dreame that hope againe, but else would die.
> ("The Dreame," ll. 27–30)

Love may even become death itself:

Little think'st thou
That it will freeze anon, and that I shall
To morrow finde thee falne, or not at all.
> ("The Blossome," ll. 6–8)

(. . . each such Act, they say,
Diminisheth the length of life a day)
> ("Farewell to Love," ll. 24–25)

Love promises to control defects of loneliness and achieves nothing but a perverse alchemy, not the desired "abler soule" of "The Exstasie," but the "pregnant pot" of "Loves Alchymie." The whole complex question of self-discovery and self-annihilation, the snarled metaphysical puzzle of Being and not-Being, is explored in the later love poetry, and eventually Donne is driven back into his own isolation. The proud privacy of the *Satires*, the insistent selfishness of the *Elegies*, the rambunctious singularity of the early love poetry merges into the defiant duets, the "abler interinanimated" souls, of the post-1601 period. But the expectation that submerging the lonely alienated *I* into a protective *I-Thou* pact will be re-creative: this proves delusive. It is as if between "The Ex-stasie" and "Loves Alchymie" Donne tried to secularize St. John's text, "Except a corn of wheat fall into the ground and die, it abideth alone; but if it die, it bringeth forth much fruit" (John 12:24), and hoped through the images of a mutual selflessness in love to find a shield against the disorder of existence as he envisioned it in *The Progresse of the Soule*. The seductive appeal of a literal death is tied to a lie in *Biathanatos*, forcefully rejected in *Pseudo-Martyr*. In the *Essays in Divinity*, *La Corona*, and "A Litanie," Donne approaches another way of surrendering his own loneliness to a corporate sanctuary, but only fitfully succeeds in conjuring up a communion with others (an imaginary congregation at prayer). Then, in the first six of the holy sonnets, Donne achieves a fusion between his own spiritual career and universal history. The universal-narrative, personal-dramatic movement of those sonnets reveals a central myth: the recapitulation of patterned destiny in each individual life. But Donne did not complete the pattern in the sonnets. He pulled back from the seventh and final stage of the myth and, prior to the penitential sonnets, remained convinced of his inability to re-enact in himself the entire drama of resurrection. The title of one of his poems, "Resurrection, imperfect," is an ironic commentary on those sonnets. What should have been a group of seven sonnets is a group of six; as did Augustine, Donne saw redemption as seven successive stages, but instead of the redemptory *seven*, Donne's sonnets reflect the apocalyptic *six*: "And all that dwell upon the earth shall worship him, whose names are not written in the book of life of the Lamb slain from the foundation of the world. . . . Here is wisdom. Let him that hath understanding count the number of the beast: for it is the number of a man; and his number is Six hundred threescore and six" (Revelation 13:8, 18).

The mythic structure of a human life was demonstrated to Donne in the coincidence of Elizabeth Drury's death and St. Lucy's festival. The disconnected episodes of St. Lucy's martyrdom, Elizabeth's death, his own metaphorical death in 1601, and his own meditated resolutions arranged themselves in concentric circles around a central and illuminated focal point. In the *Anniversaries*, Donne describes a hierophany, a structured image of an eternal archetype working itself out in human affairs. The poet who worked brilliantly with the symbolism of light in the later love poetry, of whose extant sermons sixteen are on the Gospel of St. John (a number exceeded only by those sermons on the Psalms and on St. Paul's epistles[20]), and whose epitaph identifies the watched-for Christ with the light from the east has created in the *Anniversaries* one of the most cogent and detailed studies of the symbolism of *light* in order to capture for himself, once and for all, the experience of a total unity in the world. The St. John of the Gospel of light and the epistle of love is ubiquitous in both poems.

The First Anniversary introduces a plethora, apparently, of departed virgins. Joseph Hall, in his accompanying tribute "To the Praise of the Dead, and the Anatomy," seems to have been undismayed by the problem of who the woman is in Donne's poem; he accepted the idea that she is Elizabeth Drury:

> Sing on, thou Virgin soule, whose losseful gaine
> Thy love-sicke Parents have bewayl'd in vaine; . . .
> ("To the Praise of the Dead, and the Anatomy,"
> ll. 45–46)

Hall's identification simply will not do.[21] The woman in the first poem is a queen, not recently dead, whose death provoked both joy and mourning (ll. 7, 20); she is an exemplar, a prototype of all spiritual wholeness (ll. 1–6, 16–18); she was both speech and memory (ll. 28, 30), dead not just now but many months (l. 39). She reappears as a glimmering light (l. 70); she was prophesied by the ancients (l. 175), repaired the damage wrought by Eve (l. 180). She antedated all order in the world (ll. 223–236) and is synonymous with harmony, symmetry, and peace (ll. 306–322). She was sight and color (ll. 351–368), music and rebirth (ll. 446–451). Whoever she is, she is not Elizabeth Drury; or, rather, Elizabeth Drury is involved in her, even as Queen Elizabeth, the Virgin Mary, and all lovely women are involved in her. She is so inclusive a symbol that she is that vision repeated in all passing loveliness, Yeats's "ghostly paradigm of things" ("Among School Children," l. 42), the archetypal woman who has been symbolized in the cabala's Shekinah, the Neoplatonic Paradisal Woman, as the eternal consort of God in Proverbs, the Augustinian *Sapientia*.[22] She is one of the dreams of the human race—absolute beauty, absolute peace, absolute fulfillment. She is also truly archetypal, in the sense that the awareness of her is infinitely plastic:[23] she is not a precise image, but a precondition of imagery, and she can be embodied in endless doctrinal structures. A "dynamic nucleus" rather than a formed symbol, "ready to actualize itself and manifest itself as a symbol,"[24] she can be incarnated endlessly, and thus can be apprehended in a dizzying array of garments. She appeared to Donne as St. Lucy, and beginning as Lucy she expanded into the universal symbol that caught up Donne, time, and eternity in one great cluster.

That St. Lucy was the energizing source of Donne's symbolism is clear from the situational references in *The First Anniversary*. Behind the whole procession of those incarnate versions of the mysterious *femina* is Donne's reiteration that the setting of the poem is St. Lucy's Day, the winter's depth, the shortest day and longest night, the commemorative day of St. Lucy's martyrdom. He alludes to the woman's continuing example on this short-lived day, December 13:[25]

> For there's a kind of world remaining still,
> Thou shee which did inanimate and fill
> The world, be gone, yet in this last long night,
> Her Ghost doth walke; that is, a glimmering light,
> A faint weake love of vertue and of good
> Reflects from her, on them which understood
> Her worth; And though she have shut in all day,
> The twi-light of her memory doth stay; . . .
>
> (ll. 67–74)

His poem is written at the collapsed end of the year and is an *anniversary* tribute, a yearly remembrance:

> Accept this tribute, and his first yeares rent,
> Who till his darke short tapers end be spent,
> As oft as thy feast sees this widowed earth,
> Will yearely celebrate thy second birth,
> That is, thy death.
>
> (ll. 447–451)

It's been usually assumed that these lines were directed to Elizabeth Drury and, incredibly, to her patronizing father; Donne would never have been so clumsy as to relegate his poetry to a literal rent payment. The woman whose "feast" is celebrated on the day of "darke short tapers" is St. Lucy, who, like Elizabeth, was scarcely fifteen years old, dead before a projected marriage, dying on December 13. The anniversary is, subordinately, Elizabeth's, more importantly St. Lucy's, and most importantly it became Donne's own.

But there is more than specific allusion to the time of the

year to connect the poem with St. Lucy. The world bears all of Lucy's wounds. Ordered by the officer of Diocletian, Paschasius, to renounce her Christianity in fourth-century Syracuse and refusing, Lucy was exposed to public prostitution, then tormented by fire. Surviving both ordeals, she was blinded (in some versions, self-blinded) and then stabbed through the throat.[26] But in her legend, it was not she who suffered, but the world that administered the torture. Thrown into a brothel, she kept her virginity; heaped with burning coals, she remained unburned; throat-pierced, she continued to prophesy and pray; blinded, she became apotheosized into the patron saint of sight and a symbol of divine illumination. In the *Golden Legend*, Lucy's reproofs to Paschasius as he orders each of her trials are that she will suffer no corruption from the brothel, no domination from the fire, and will be unsilenced by the sword. Donne's catalogue of the sickness in the world is prefaced by the lament,

> Her death did wound, and tame thee than, and than
> Thou mightst have spar'd the Sunne, or Man; . . .
>
> (ll. 25–26)

The purity of the world, unlike Lucy's, has been corrupted ("Her death hath taught us dearely, that thou art/Corrupt and mortall in thy purest part," ll. 61–62). Sight has become blear and purblind ("Sight is the noblest sense of any one,/ Yet sight hath onely color to feed on,/ And color is decayd," ll. 353–355). The world has been burnt to a cinder (l. 428) and has become nearly mute (ll. 30, 53–54, 445–446, 455, 474). Lucy, on the other hand, is a continual affront to the polluted, blind, burned, and silent world. A memory of her virtue remains and, virginal, she plays no part in the coital death of mankind (ll. 100–110). Her ordeal by fire was an alchemical purification, not an incineration (ll. 175–182). While the world feels "this consuming wound, and ages dart" and the cosmos has been "empayld" (ll. 248, 263), she is all

harmony and proportion (ll. 308–314), she is sight, color,
and song (ll. 353–364, 446). In very large terms, she is the
response to the divided soul of *The Progresse of the Soule*.
Augustine's history, it will be recalled, postulates schism that
antedates time (the rebellion of Lucifer), this schism then
being re-enacted in Eden and then through the whole fabric
of history. This was Donne's pattern in 1601, and it is his
pattern again:

> Then, as mankinde, so is the worlds whole frame
> Quite out of ioynt, almost created lame:
> For, before God had made up all the rest,
> Corruption entred, and deprav'd the best:
> It seis'd the Angels, and then first of all
> The world did in her Cradle take a fall,
> And turn'd her braines, and tooke a generall maime
> Wronging each ioynt of th'universall frame.
> The noblest part, man, felt it first; and than
> Both beasts and plants, curst in the curse of man.
>
> (ll. 191–200)

In Augustine's metahistory, the race of Abel-Seth-Enoch preserves the memory of wholeness and bears witness that the
aboriginal unity will be recovered. So does St. Lucy in
Donne's poem:

> She that should all parts to reunion bow,
> She that had all Magnetique force alone,
> To draw, and fasten sundred parts in one; . . .
>
> (ll. 220–222)

She is the typological response to the civil war between the
two cities that rampages through history:

> Shee, who if those great Doctors truely said
> That th'Arke to mans proportions was made,
> Had beene a type for that, as that might be

> A type of her in this, that contrary
> Both Elements, and Passions liv'd at peace
> In her, who caus'd all Civill warre to cease.
>
> (ll. 317–322)

Even with all the details in the poem emphasizing the December 13 anniversary and the recital of the wounds of St. Lucy, she is not at the exact center of the poem. That place is reserved for Donne's own experience of rebirth, the climax of his own progress. He views his own resurrection, not in purely personal terms, but in genuinely mythic terms, as the re-creation of a universal pattern whose outline was most clearly enunciated in the first epistle and the Gospel of St. John. St. Lucy's martyrdom, and all the hagiographic details of her legend, evidently struck Donne as a type of the rebirth motif in St. John and as an analogue of his own experience. That Elizabeth Drury should have died on the feast of the longest night, that St. Lucy on this same day should have fulfilled St. John's message, that his own career might find its symbolic counterpart in the Elizabeth–St. Lucy–St. John complex, all operating in a timeless simultaneity: these are the generators of the poem.

In the first epistle of St. John, the same one on which Donne drew for the last of his meditative sonnets ("Father, part of his double interest"), Christ gave another command-ment to his followers: "Again, a new commandment I write unto you . . . because the darkness is past, and the true light now shineth" (I John 2:8). This new commandment, which belongs to the generation of light, is love, and the absence of love is darkness (I John 2:8–11). After the identification of love and light, John's epistle continues:

> Love not the world, neither the things that are in the world. If any man love the world, the love of the Father is not in him. For all that is in the world, the lust of the flesh, and the lust of the eyes, and the pride of life, is not of the Father, but

is of the world. And the world passeth away, and the lust
thereof: but he that doth the will of God abideth forever
(I John 2:15–17).

The parallels between the epistle and the life of Lucy are
evident, so evident that I believe Donne read her legend as a
historic fulfillment of Christ's injunction. It is not merely that
Lucy, *lux, lucis,* is equivalent to John's central image; it is that
each detail of what Donne calls "thy second birth,/ That is,
thy death" is so reflective of St. John's whole epistle. The
fifteenth verse ("love not the world") is enacted in Lucy's
giving her entire patrimony to the poor. The three temptations of the world (lust of the eyes, flesh, and pride of life)
are epitomized in her blinding, the assaults on her virginity,
and the inquisitorial court of Paschasius. The sixteenth verse
(the world passes, but the righteous abide) is recapitulated in
Lucy's apotheosis ("Her Ghost doth walke; that is, a glimmering light"). St. Lucy endured her own darkness, as did
Nicodemus in the third chapter of St. John's Gospel, to
whom Jesus came at night and proclaimed, "Ye must be born
again" (John 2:1–7). The rebirth at night, and a host of
implications that Donne saw in the idea, provided him later
on with a sweeping *propositio:*

> Here is the compass, that the essential Word of God, the
> Son of God, *Christ Jesus,* went: He was God, *humbled in the
> flesh;* he was Man, *received into glory.* Here is the compasse
> that the written Word of God, went, the Bible; that begun
> in *Moses,* in darknesse, in the *Chaos;* and it ends in Saint
> *John,* in clearnesse, in a Revelation. Here is the compass of all
> time, as time was distributed in the Creation, *Vespere &
> mane;* darknesse, and then light: the Evening and the Morn-
> ing made the Day.
>
> ("A Lent-Sermon Preached before the King, at White-Hall,
> February 16, 1620")[27]

The progress from dark to light is the movement from the first to the second *Anniversary*. Donne's contempt for the "sicke world" (l. 23) alternates with his reflection on the *light* that has been "shut in all day" (l. 73) on this feast day, and the contemplation of that light provides him with

> the matter and the stuffe of this,
> Her vertue, and the forme our practise is.
>
> (ll. 77–78)

Lucy is a double reflection, first of St. John's epistle of light and rebirth, and secondly of Donne himself, the "forme" of his "practise." "Thy feast" (l. 449) becomes a remembrance of "thy second birth" (l. 450), which at the same time becomes his own "second birth." It would seem that Donne, quite literally, accepted December 13 as his own anniversary or *natalia*, a day that means birthday, commemorative festival, restoration to one's birthright, and recollection of martyrdom.[28] The things that lead me to believe this are a letter to Goodyer, the subject of several of his sermons, and, most importantly, "A Nocturnall upon S. Lucies Day, being the shortest day."

Donne had the maddening habit of only rarely dating his letters, though he often located the place from which he was writing his letters ("Strand, S. Peters," "From Micham," "Drury house") or even gave specific hours ("at nine," "at 4," "friday morning").[29] In the collection *Letters to Severall Persons of Honour*, for instance, out of 129 letters, only 39 are dated at all; 19 of these are incompletely dated, lacking either the year or the month. But when Donne wrote to Goodyer with his final decision, "by the end of next terme, I will make an end with the world, by Gods grace," that is, his decision to take Holy Orders, he dated the letter: December 13.[30]

Once in orders, when Donne's preaching assignments fell on or close to this anniversary date, he spoke on texts that mirrored his own experience of conversion. In 1617, he preached on December 14 on the subject of worldly love being converted to love of God.[31] Sometime in December of 1618, he delivered a sermon on the symbolic rebirth of baptism.[32] On December 12, 1626, in a funeral sermon, he dwelt on the two resurrections, the first in time and the second at the end of time.[33] One of his prebend sermons of 1627, perhaps delivered in December, describes the passage through the fire and darkness of mortification to the knowledge of God.[34] That so few of Donne's sermons have survived frustrates our knowledge at how faithful Donne was to his own *natalia,* but I suspect he was ever mindful of it.

But it is the "Nocturnall upon S. Lucies Day"[35] that is most representative of Donne's accepting December 13 as the specific occasion of his rebirth. While there is a remote possibility that Donne wrote the poem as early as 1606 during a serious illness of his wife Ann (but the poem specifically refers to the woman's death, and Ann did not die at that time) or in 1612 during the Countess of Bedford's illness (but the poem bespeaks an intimacy that is foreign to all of his verses on the Countess), it is practically certain that "A Nocturnall" belongs to Ann and is Donne's elegy for her. It is, and considerably more besides.[36]

In this lovely and lonely elegy, Donne pays Ann the highest tribute he could have paid: he puts her at the heart of his poetry. Her death recalls to him the collapsed world of *The First Anniversary,* loathsome in deformity there, "Dead and enterr'd" here (l. 8). Without her, he has been converted into his own angry man of "Loves Alchymie": as in that bitter poem, love's alchemy is perverse and has produced "A quintessence even from nothingnesse" ("Nocturnall," l. 15). Ann is metamorphosed into the fantasy woman of the later love poetry, the weeper of the valedictions, the private kingdom of "The Good-morrow" and "The Anniversarie":

> Oft a flood
> Have wee two wept, and so
> Drownd the whole world, us two; oft did we grow
> To be two Chaosses, when we did show
> Care to ought else; and often absences
> Withdrew our soules, and made us carcasses.
>
> ("Nocturnall," ll. 22–27)

Her death has brought about what he had flirted with in "Aire and Angels," complete extinction:

> But I am by her death, (which word wrongs her)
> Of the first nothing, the Elixer grown; . . .
>
> ("Nocturnall," ll. 28–29)

Grieving, Donne names Ann the genius of his love poetry. When he took Holy Orders in 1615, he anticipated making an offer of his poetry as the most suitable abnegation of the world;[37] this gift he makes to his wife is offered in the same spirit, the presentation of his creativity.

The poem, however, continues beyond lament into vision; and Ann becomes the spirit of rebirth following upon annihilation. Borrowing qualities from St. Lucy, she becomes the promise of light. Apparently drawing on the Roman breviary, Donne presents his wife as a manifestation of St. Lucy, identifies his own dejection with this anniversary of martyrdom, and forecasts a resurrection and reuniting. The figure addressed in the closing lines is both Ann and St. Lucy:

> Since shee enjoyes her long nights festivall,
> Let mee prepare towards her, and let mee call
> This houre her Vigill, and her Eve, since this
> Both the yeares, and the dayes deep midnight is.
>
> (ll. 42–45)

Donne's title and certain details point to the nocturns of the matins service as contained in the traditional Roman breviary.

Donne had known and used Catholic devotional books long
before this, of course: *La Corona* and the *Holy Sonnets* are
evidence enough. Furthermore, at some time after 1605
Donne owned a copy of the Divine Office, which contains,
among other things, the rubric of the breviary.[38] The breviary
divides the matins or night vigils into three nocturns, which in
turn contain *lectiones* or instructions. The first group of *lectiones* is scriptural, the second historical, the third homiletic.
In the "lectures" of St. Lucy's nocturns, the refrain is constant: Lucy in scorning the world ought to become our
exemplar. In the homily of the last nocturn, the "watcher" is
advised in the breviary to develop the *lectio* in the manner of
Gregory's homilies: the contrast between the flame of Lucy's
torment and the flame of love is commended as proper
meditation.

In his poem, Donne contrasts the heat of the world with
the coolness of the night, the time of the vigil for St. Lucy.
His sun, his love for Ann, cannot renew (in the second
nocturn, beginning at midnight, the breviary prayer is *rogavi
. . . ut ignis iste non dominetur mei*). Carnal lovers will
experience the flame of passion:

> You lovers, for whose sake, the lesser Sunne
> At this time to the Goat is runne
> To fetch new lust, and give it you,
> Enjoy your summer all; . . .
>
> (ll. 38–41)

Ann, however, is now free from such heats, "she enjoyes her
long nights festivall" (in the first nocturn, St. Lucy is addressed, *tuae festivitate gaudemus*). In one of the "lectures"
of the second nocturn, St. Lucy is venerated in the words
Quia jucundum Deo . . . habitaculum praeparasti, "you
have prepared a joyful dwelling place for the Lord"; now, of
Ann, Donne says, "Let mee prepare towards her" (l. 43). By

the end of the poem, Ann and St. Lucy have become practically indistinguishable.

The curious fact is that while Ann's office is made to be the same as St. Lucy's, *their* anniversaries are not the same. Ann Donne died in August;[39] Donne certainly did not compose the poem then, for if he had, the central conceit of the poem would have made no sense. Donne wrote the poem on his *natalia*, on December 13, 1617, four months after his wife's death, powerfully interpreting Ann as a hierophant, a concelebrator of the rebirth he had experienced seven years before. "A Nocturnall upon S. Lucies Day" keeps the promise that Donne made at the conclusion of *The First Anniversary*, this time a promise kept with Ann:

> As oft as thy feast sees this widowed earth,
> [I] Will yearely celebrate thy second birth,
> That is, thy death.
>   (*The First Anniversary*, ll. 449–451)

What Donne had strained for in the sonnets, a sense of temporal and personal resurrection, is nearly achieved in *The First Anniversary*. What needs still to be finished is the total identification of himself with St. Lucy and St. John's epistle, the equation between his own longest night and the anniversary of December 13, the passage from dark to light. All these things occur in *The Second Anniversary*. By 1611 (Donne began *The Second Anniversary*, while still in France, on December 13: the promise kept) Donne's vision is entire: he has sensed his own communal involvement in a perpetual drama of rebirth occurring throughout history. The corroding history of *The Progresse of the Soule* has been opposed by a dimension of light that was from the beginning, that united fourth-century Syracuse and seventeenth-century England, and that knows no time at all.

St. Lucy as the specific virgin-martyr and a *type* of rebirth is not merely repeated in *The Second Anniversary;* her symbolic values are still further expanded to the point where she is not so much an exemplar as she is a microcosm of resurrection. The emphasis in *The Second Anniversary* is not on the long night of decision and death, but on the day of rebirth. As she was a compass, a guide through the world, in *The First Anniversary* (ll. 223–226), Lucy in this second poem shares an emblem with Seth as Donne described him in the earlier *Progresse of the Soule:* she is an astronomer, a guide through celestial geography (ll. 78–80, 294–295). This poem does not re-experience Nicodemus' night, but looks ahead through the icon of St. Lucy to the promised light of St. John's epistle:

> Thinke, then, My soule, that death is but a Groome,
> Which brings a Taper to the outward roome,
> Whence thou spiest first a little glimmering light,
> And after brings it nearer to thy sight: . . .
>
> (ll. 85–88)

Lucy's function in *The Second Anniversary* is very like her function in *The Divine Comedy:* she is first a guide out of the Dark Wood, through Inferno and Purgatory, and then the representative of the total light that rests at the end of the progress.[40]

As before, Donne clearly indicates that his poem is a celebration of the feast of December 13 ("my Muse/ . . . [whose] chast Ambition is,/ Yearely to bring forth such a child as this," ll. 34–36), and he is insistent in his use of St. Lucy's emblems. That a death to the world is but a prelude to reawakening in the spirit is specifically identified with the celebration:

> Thinke that they bury thee, and thinke that rite
> Laies thee to sleepe but a saint Lucies night.
>
> (ll. 119–120)

Writing in France, he exempts Lucy from his derision of Catholic hagiolatry:

> Here in a place, where mis-devotion frames
> A thousand praiers to saints, whose very names
> The ancient Church knew not, Heaven knowes not yet,
> And where, what lawes of poetry admit,
> Lawes of religion, have at least the same,
> Immortal Maid, I might invoque thy name.
> Could any Saint provoke that appetite,
> Thou here shouldst make mee a french convertite.
>
> (ll. 511–518)

St. Lucy's particular attributes, and especially her allegiance to *light*, account for a most considerable part of the poem's imagery. Her virginity and her title as an undefiled temple of the Spirit (a theme on which the *Golden Legend* dwells at length, and which appears in the *tua virginitate habitaculum* of the breviary, and in the metaphor of Donne's eleventh holy sonnet) appear in ll. 33–36 and 459–462. Her endurance at her trial and her refusal either to condemn or submit to her torturers are alluded to in ll. 361–375, while her traditional icons are manifest: the trial by fire (l. 76), the sword-thrust through the throat (ll. 90–93, 102–103), her most important symbol, eyes and light (ll. 78–80, 200), and even a symbol traditionally associated with St. Lucy, but not used by Donne in *The First Anniversary*, a book,[41] emblematic of wisdom (ll. 315–320).

But this is not a poem in praise of St. Lucy, and certainly Donne has not abjured the Protestant "rectified devotion" behind a poem like "A Litanie," a devotion where martyrology is decidedly at the outer edges of an evangelical faith. Donne intends all his celebrations of St. Lucy to be read typologically: she is the ideal form of Christian redemption through the Word of the Gospels (particularly the Gospel of

St. John). Donne is quite clear on this point: Lucy is the embodiment of a sacred theme and a model of the redeemed spirit. She "could not lacke, what ere this world could give,/ Because shee was the forme, that made it live" (ll. 71–72). She is not simply to be venerated, but imitated; in realizing how she typifies the Light, we participate in that Light.

> Onely who have enioyed
> The sight of God, in fulnesse, can thinke it;
> For it is both the obiect, and the wit.
>
> (ll. 440–442)

Lux, which is Love and Wisdom ("And the light shineth in darkness; and the darkness comprehended it not," John 1:5), is what we recognize in Lucy, and only through Love and Wisdom can man see rightly at all.

> Thou shouldest for life, and death, a patterne bee,
> And that the world should notice have of this,
> The purpose, and th'Autority is his;
> Thou art the Proclamation; and I ame
> The Trumpet, at whose voice the people came.
>
> (ll. 524–528)

This sense of Lucy, not as the *Verbum* herself, but as a proclaimed pattern, an incarnate demonstration of the meaning of St. John's Gospel of light and epistle of love, moves not only through the imagery of the poem, but also through its structure. The seven-stage alternation between meditation on the world and eulogy of the vanished virgin pointed out by Professor Martz[42] gains in impact when we realize that the virgin is Lucy, and that the contempt for the world and juxtaposed celebrations of her glory are compressed versions of her legendary scorning of the three temptations. The first passage of *contemptus mundi* (ll. 45–64) compares the world to old clothes, cast off a year ago (i.e., the contemning

of the world in *The First Anniversary*), while the eulogy and
the refrain (ll. 65–84) respond with recollections of Lucy's
eyes, which look beyond "fragmentary rubbidge." The second
meditation (ll. 85–120) summons up an awareness of death,
voiceless, feverish, and surrounded by ministers of Pride and
Lust ("For all that is in the world, the lust of the flesh, and
the lust of the eyes, and the pride of life"), and is answered
(ll. 121–156) with remembrances of uncorrupted beauty.
The cramped and foul body, "A Province Pack'd up in two
yards of skinne" (ll. 157–178), is contrasted with the soul
quick-threading its way through the spheres to eternity (ll. 183–
212), and such flight is epitomized in the vanished virgin's
delicacy and brightness (ll. 220–250). The silly pedantry
of the world (ll. 291–320) is replaced by St. Lucy with her
book (ll. 291–320). The corruption infecting all the affairs
of men (ll. 321–338) is renounced for the beadroll of
a litany, ending with the virgin martyrs: of the four great
virgins of the Latin church (SS. Cecilia, Agatha, Agnes, and
Lucy), Lucy is the one representing wisdom, and Donne
wittily describes the last virgin as bestowing academic honors
on the other three:

> Up to those Virgins, who thought that almost
> They made ioyntenants with the Holy Ghost,
> If they to any should his Temple give.
> Up, up, for in that squadron there doth live
> Shee, who hath carried thether, new degrees
> (As to their number) to their dignitees.
>
> (ll. 353–358)

The impermanence of earthly beauty and of everything that
man secularly worships (ll. 383–434) is put aside for the
permanence of God, to whom Lucy gave her virginity and her
life (ll. 435–470). The vicissitudes of life (ll. 471–486) are
balanced against the stability of eternity and of Lucy, who by

now has been transformed into her own iconographic book (ll. 487–510). The seven stages of redemption that Donne later expounds in the sermon at Whitehall in March, 1621/ 22, are traced out here within the framework of rejection of the world and the search for paradise, typified by St. Lucy's legend. And the final image for Lucy is one that Donne will apply to all mankind in the *Devotions*: she is a book authored by God and translated by death into a better language; she is both book and light to read by, both the object and the wit.

This is the most important of three such seven-stage progresses that occur within the poem. There is also a miniature progress in ll. 185–218, and another in ll. 339–358. In the first, the freed soul races through the middle regions of air, passes through the debatable region of fire, and then moves through the spheres like "so many beades/ Strung on one string." The lunar region, then Venus, Mercury, the Sun, Mars, Jupiter, and Saturn fall quickly behind, until the firmament is pierced. Except for the fact that Donne reverses the positions of Venus and Mercury, this is the same journey that Dante takes in the *Paradiso* (cantos III, V, VIII, X, XIV, XVIII, and XXI), impelled by the influence of St. Lucy (*Inferno*, canto II; *Purgatorio*, canto IX; *Paradiso*, canto XXII). Among the company at the end of Dante's progress is St. John, blindingly symbolic of love (canto XXV), while at the end of Donne's small swift progress is also the Light:

> For when our soule enioyes this her third birth,
> (Creation gave her one, a second, grace,)
> Heaven is as neare, and present to her face,
> As colours are, and obiects, in a roome
> Where darknesse was before, when Tapers come.
>
> (ll. 214–218)

In the second of the small progresses within the larger progress of the whole poem, Donne envisions the soul as joining the Church Triumphant, which he describes in seven parts: the Virgin Mary, Patriarchs, Prophets, Apostles, Martyrs, Virgins, and Doctors (ll. 339–358). This is not the same pantheon as that of "A Litanie," in which the category of Confessors intruded between Martyrs and Virgins. Donne has been accused of impropriety in introducing the Confessors at all into that earlier poem: he was joining the emblematic whiteness of virgins' purity and confessors' robes as a contrast to the red blood of the martyrs, a conceit for which there is no liturgical precedent.[43] In any case, Donne here follows not Cranmer's Litany, which did not recognize Doctors, but the Roman Litany, which does. He evidently wanted the reinforcement of Lucy's association with wisdom that "Doctors" could give him, and by keeping them and rejecting "Confessors" he could reduplicate the heptad motif of his entire poem.

There is a quite spectacular geometry of profound experience between Donne's two progresses of the soul. In 1601, he experienced a metaphorical death; ten years later he is celebrating his own rebirth. The poem of 1601 is a fragment, dealing with a fragmented reality; the poem of 1611 is distinguished by its coherence, order, and totality. The earlier Progresse recounts the disruption of God's design in the world; the later Progres celebrates the fulfillment of that design. The first poem describes bestiality; the second poem is an affirmation of divine love. The Progresse of the Soule was intended to track down the ancestry of Cain and the City of Man, and Of the Progres of the Soule reaffirms Seth's generation and the City of God. The earlier poem is a bitter recital of the disunity that flows from rebellion; the later poem is a contemplation of the serenity that follows upon sacrifice and acceptance. Progresse is a poem of darkness; Progres, of light. The whole sequence of events and the whole cycle of poetry since 1601 peak in the Anniversary poems. Donne's own progress is finished in these poems of December 13, and from this point on there is none of that metaphysical ache for a vision of unity in experience that we recognize in the earlier Donne. Doubts, hesitations, and frustrations still scar his career, but they are all transitory, veneer and not substance. Nor are there are significant developments in his beliefs and insights; what he became by 1611 is what he essentially remained. Donne completes himself by a submersion into a great design controlled by love, enunciated in the Gospels, recurrent through history, forcing itself on his imagination through the winter death of a young girl. The ramifications of his discovery remain to be explored in the great sermons, the *Devotions*, and the few poems yet to be written, but the real progress [44] of John Donne is ended.[45]

JOHN DONNE'S LIFE: 1615-1631

IT WAS SHORTLY after his ordination that Donne was appointed Chaplain-in-Ordinary to His Majesty, King James I; and thus began his distinguished connection with the royal family at Whitehall, where many of his finest sermons were delivered, first to King James and then, from 1625, to King Charles I. The seventeenth century can boast of its preachers; and even among the most eloquent, such as Lancelot Andrewes before him and Jeremy Taylor after him, Donne is perhaps the greatest. But he was never a court preacher only: his first parish appointment was to Keyston, in Huntingdonshire, and later he was named rector of the parish of Sevenoaks in Kent. Donne did not reside in either of those parishes: he preached occasionally, but his base was London, and according to custom he left the actual administration to curates.

In the autumn of 1616 he was named Reader in Divinity to the students at Lincoln's Inn, and a circle was closed. Twenty-two years before he had been a normally rambunctious bencher himself; now he was required to preach fifty times a year to one of the most demanding of congregations, sophisticated young men on the alert to spot any hypocrisy on the part of an alumnus whose own student days had not been distinguished by piety. Over the next five years (Donne reluctantly left the Readership in 1621), close bonds developed between the new cleric and the students at Lincoln's Inn.

Donne suffered a severe loss in 1617, when his wife Ann died. Izaak Walton recorded that Donne preached in London shortly thereafter on the text from Jeremy's Lamentations, "Lo, I am the man that has seen affliction," and Walton wrote that "Indeed, his very words and looks testified him to be truly such a man." The sermon has been lost, but in the sonnet "Since she whom I lov'd hath paid her last debt" we can glimpse the depth of Donne's grief.

Nearly two years after his wife's death, Donne traveled abroad—as it turned out, his last voyage out of England. The Thirty Years' War had broken out in Germany, and King James dispatched what he hoped would be a peace mission, with the Viscount Doncaster as his spokesman. Donne traveled as Doncaster's chaplain; and it is evident, both from the farewell sermon that he delivered at Lincoln's Inn and the poem "A Hymne to Christ, at the Author's last going into Germany," that he did not expect to return. It was not merely the hazardous voyage that provoked such an idea: Donne had begun to suffer from the intestinal cancer that ultimately killed him. But he did return; and during the embassy he was able to visit the Princess Elizabeth, now Electress of the Palatinate in Bohemia, whose wedding hymn he had written.

In November of 1621, Donne received the post and the title in which he took greatest, and deserved, pride: he was named Dean of St. Paul's in London, the splendid medieval cathedral that was later destroyed in the Great Fire of 1666. It was in the pulpit of St. Paul's that he was to achieve his greatest success as a preacher. His first sermon was delivered on Christmas Day, and he spoke on the text from St. John, "He was not that light, but was sent to bear witness of that light." Donne's poetry abounds in images of light; his own epitaph identifies him as "one who awaits the Light." It was fitting that he should have begun his Deanship with that symbol.

Only two years after his appointment, Donne contracted a severe illness, very likely a form of that plague that ravaged

England in 1592, 1603, 1625, and again in 1665. Donne composed the *Devotions Upon Emergent Occasions*, in which he traced out the physical and spiritual tremors that racked him during his sickness. By the end of the first week in December, 1623, he was out of danger. In the spring of the following year, he acquired another benefice: he was appointed vicar of St. Dunstan's, a west London parish. Izaak Walton was his most illustrious parishioner, and the admiring first biography of Donne probably had its genesis in Walton's worshipful attentiveness to the new vicar's preaching.

His last illness began in the late summer of 1630. There had been rumors that Donne was to be advanced to a bishopric, but his declining health made any such preferment out of the question. On December 13 (a fateful date for Donne, as his *Anniversary* poems attest), he prepared his will; and on the first Friday of Lent in 1631 he delivered his last sermon, "Death's Duel." It seemed to many of his auditors that he was preaching his own funeral sermon.

The last days are best described by Walton:

> Dr. *Donne* sent for a Carver to make for him in wood the figure of an *Vrn*, giving him directions for the compass and heights of it; and to bring with it a board of the just height of his body.
>
> These being got: then without delay a choice Painter was got to be in a readiness to draw his Picture, which was taken as followeth.—Several Charcole-fires being first made in his large Study, he brought with him into that place his winding-sheet in his hand, and, having put off all his cloaths, had this sheet put on him, and so tyed with knots at his head and feet, and his hands so placed, as dead bodies are usually fitted to be shrowded and put into their Coffin, or grave. Upon this *Vrn* he thus stood with his eyes shut, and with so much of the sheet turned aside as might shew his

lean, pale, and death-like face, which was purposely turned toward the East, from whence he expected the second coming of his and our Saviour Jesus. In this posture he was drawn at his just height; and when the Picture was fully finished, he caused it to be set by his bed-side, where it continued, and became his hourly object till his death: and, was then given to his dearest friend and Executor Doctor *Henry King*, then chief Residentiary of St. *Pauls*, who caused him to be thus carved in one entire piece of white Marble, as it now stands in that Church.

The marble statue, executed by Nicholas Stone, survived the Great Fire of 1666, and the bombings of London in the Second World War. Donne stands still in Christopher Wren's St. Paul's Cathedral, with the legend inscribed *Aspicit eum cuius nomen est Oriens*, "He watches for him whose name is Light."

CHAPTER V

Aftermath

1612–1631

THREE YEARS SEPARATE *Of the Progres of the Soule* and Donne's ordination in January, 1615; but to imagine that for three years he was compromising himself would be a great mistake. Donne did not "fall, like an overripe peach, into the lap of Mother Church,"[1] as one biographer has expressed it. If ever a man entered into a religious commitment on his own terms, it was John Donne. To conceive of him as having renounced the world by 1612, then backing away from his renunciation to curry favor and advance a secular career, only wearily accepting the inevitable—this is a formidable misunderstanding of Donne's mind. The whole point of the *Anniversaries* is that redemption works itself out in the world and that the sense of Divine Presence must be a truly incarnate experience. Donne's life is like a parable of the myth of Antaeus: he drew his strength from the earth, and this is just as true of his religious life as it was of his secular life. His earliest poetry is compelling because he is so aware of all the quotidian lumber of love; the restless hands, the rumpled beds, the quicksilver sweat, the loud perfume impart an immediacy to the abstractions of desire. In the sermons, the press of this time and this place does not dissipate the sacred, but reinforces it: "though knowledge be of a spirituall nature, yet it is but as a terrestrial Spirit, conversant upon Earth."[2] Donne

was no *magnus* celebrating a mystery religion remote from profane existence; he was a *theandrist*, triply aware of the Incarnation as a dogma, as a historical event, and as the manifestation of divinity through the fabric of the world. Properly
valued, the world becomes the sacramental theatre in which
the drama of redemption is to be acted. The three years of
fumbling are not reluctance, but Donne's making sure of his
own theatre of operations. The 1608 letter to Goodyer (*v.s.* p.
194 makes the point very well: "To choose is to do," he told
Goodyer then, and between 1612 and 1615 he's examining
the grounds of choice. It was only after he was certain that
the pulpit was as good a place as the ambassador's residence at
Venice in which to bear witness that he could, on his own
December 13 anniversary, tell Goodyer that "by the end of
next terme, I will make an end with the world, by Gods
grace." Donne never undervalued the world, he never saw
it as intrinsically antagonistic to revelation. "God hath not
removed man, not with-drawne man from this Earth," he said
in 1624 at St. Paul's; "he hath not given him the Aire to flie
in, as to Birds, nor Spheares to move in, as to Sun and Moone;
he hath left him upon the Earth; and not onely to tread upon
it, as in contempt, or in meere Dominion, but to walke upon
it, in the discharge of the duties of his calling; and so to be
conversant with the Earth, is not a falling."[3]

Donne tested the possibility of a refurbished alliance with
the world on several fronts between 1610 and 1615. The idea
of returning to the law had occurred to him while he was still
in France with the Drurys: he broached the topic to George
Garrard and to Dean Morton.[4] Or perhaps a diplomatic post:
there were inquiries made about vacancies in Virginia,[5] Venice,[6] and, closer to home, in the clerkship of the Privy
Council.[7] During these same years there are important verse
epistles, too: three to the Countess of Bedford, one apiece to
the Countesses of Huntingdon and Salisbury.[8] Criticism has
not dealt kindly with these poems: they are quickly dismissed

as flattery, and venal flattery at that.[9] But why it should be
automatically assumed that there's an equation between ve-
nality and insincerity is a moot point; and it seems to me much
more important that these epistles show the residual effects of
Donne's recent spiritual experience than that in them he
seeks necessary patronage.

Donne's relationship with the Countess of Bedford grew
increasingly strained from 1612 onward. During her illness of
that year, she was attended by Dr. John Burges, a minister
and physician of such pronounced Puritan sympathies that he
was imprisoned for a short time in 1604 on account of certain
incendiary pronouncements against what he considered a dangerous royal policy of toleration for the Papists. It was probably Burges' influence, as much as anything else, that encouraged the Countess' gradual drift away from the importu-
nate John Donne.[10] In a letter to Goodyer in 1615, Donne
certainly laid the blame on Burges. Puzzled by the coolness
that she had displayed on his entrance in orders, Donne
wrote:

> Of my Lady Bedford, I must say so much as must importune
> you to burn the letter; for I would say nothing of her upon
> record, that should not testify my thankfulness for all her
> graces. But upon this motion, which I made to her by letter,
> and by Sir Thomas Roe's assistance, if any scruple should
> arise in her, she was somewhat more startling, than I looked
> for from her; she had more suspicion of my calling, a better
> memory of my past life, than I had thought her nobility could
> have admitted; of all which, though I humbly thank God, I
> can make good use, as one that needs as many remembrances
> in this kind, as not only friends but enemies can present, yet
> I am afraid they proceed in her rather from some ill impres-
> sion taken from Dr. Burges, than that they grow in herself.[11]

Earlier than this, the Countess was much on Donne's mind,
and he was concerned about her unwonted aloofness. He

wrote to "my lord G.H." (probably George Hastings, fourth Earl of Huntingdon) on the eve of his departure for France in November, 1611: "I must entreat you to continue that wherein you have most expressed your love to me, which is, to maintain me in the same room in my Lady Bedford's opinion, in which you placed me. I profess to you that I am too much bound to her for expressing every way her care of my fortune, that I am weary before she is."[12] Not content with leaving the Earl with this injunction to safeguard his reputation with the Countess, Donne wrote her directly during his voyage. He was concerned over how often he ought to remind her of his affection and expressed some uneasiness on the matter to George Garrard in July, 1612: "I can glory of nothing in this voyage but that I have afflicted my Lady Bedford with few letters. I protest earnestly to you, it troubles me more to despatch a packet into England without a letter to her than it would be to put in three. But I have been heretofore too immodest towards her, and I suffer this purgatory for it."[13] He called on his friends to support his position with the Countess: Sir Henry Wotton, in February, 1612, and George Garrard, in March, were both urged to keep the Countess mindful of him. To Garrard Donne wrote, "Sir, you do me double honor when my name passes through you to that noble lady in whose presence you are."[14] His verse letter "To the Countesse of *Bedford*. Begun in France but never perfected" shows the same anxiety, and the intention of keeping in her good graces.

> Though I be *dead*, and buried, yet I have
> (Living in you,) Court enough in my grave,
> As oft as there I thinke my selfe to bee,
> So many resurrections waken mee.
> That thankfullnesse your favours have begot
> In mee, embalmes mee, that I doe not rot.[15]

But the verse letters of this period of anxiety do nothing to relieve the strain between patroness and protégé. As a matter of fact, they take on a tone of aggressive instruction, and far from showing abject solicitation of the Countess' favors, they demonstrate Donne pressing an issue that could hardly have pleased her. Following her illness in 1612, the Countess showed an unanticipated tendency to withdraw into solitude. Once one of the most scintillating ladies of the court, she had become one of the most somber. Lady-in-waiting in the court of Elizabeth, attendant on Queen Anne of Denmark when Anne followed her husband, King James I, from Scotland,[16] "a lady not more celebrated for beauty and vivacity of wit than for her generosity to men of genius, the taste which she carried into all her pursuits, and the success with which she cultivated some of those lighter sciences that minister to taste its most refined gratification,"[17] courted and flattered by Shakespeare,[18] Ben Jonson, Samuel Daniel, Michael Drayton, George Chapman, and Lord Herbert of Cherbury:[19] this was the lady of whom John Chamberlain reported at this time "shows herself again court, though in her sickness she in a manner vowed never to come there. . . . Marry, she is somewhat reformed in her attire, and forbears painting, which, they say, makes her look somewhat strangely among so many vizards, which together with their frizzled, powdered hair, makes them look all alike, so that you can scant know one from another at the first view."[20] Donne never showed much sympathy for Puritanism,[21] and he wasn't prepared to tolerate it in the Countess no matter how anxious he was about their relationship. The Countess, following her convalescence in 1612, retreated from the world, and such a retreat was alien to Donne's deepest convictions; "holy simplicity of the soule," Donne argued in 1625, "is not a darknesse, a dimnesse, a stupidity in the understanding, contracted by living in a corner, it is not an idle retiring into a Monastery, or into a

Village, or a Country solitude,"[22] it is living in the world. His epistles to the Countess show him urging her to re-enter her proper sphere of action. To her too-enthusiastic renunciation of the world, Donne takes exception:

> Too many vertues, or too much of one
> Begets in you unjust suspition; . . .
> ("T'Have written then," ll. 77–78)[23]

A fine amphibious balance is what's needed:

> Who prayer-lesse labours, or, without this, prayes,
> Doth but one halfe, that's none; . . .
> (ll. 46–47)

Just when he wrote the New Year's epistle to the Countess ("This twilight of two yeares") is uncertain,[24] but 1614 is a possibility. Donne speaks of a "twilight" that has lasted for two years, during which time he has been "of stuffe and forme perlext" (ll. 1–3), i.e., having realized what his "form" is (The St. Lucy of the *Anniversaries* is "form," "frame," "original," "example," "figure," "proclamation"), he's still uncertain how to implement his belief. Such perplexity is projected onto the Countess: "these times shew'd mee you" (ll. 10). She is wrong to have immured herself and should ask God "how you should lay out/ His stock of 'beauty,' 'learning,' 'favour,' 'blood'" (ll. 36–37). Most importantly, she should realize that virtue ought to walk in the world, not away from it:

> good and bad have not
> One latitude in cloysters, and in Court; . . .
> (ll. 41–42)

In anticipation of Milton's sentiments in *Areopagitica* is Donne's strong line, "*Vertues* whole summe is but *know* and *dare*" ("Honour is so sublime perfection," l. 33).

The fulsome poem to the Countess of Huntingdon,[25] however, is unabashed flattery, and Donne admitted it: "If you can thinke these flatteries, they are" (l. 49). But the grounds of his flattery in his epistle to her, "Man to Gods image; Eve, to mans was made," are most interesting. The Countess is made to look like a simulacrum of Donne's own St. Lucy: she is light, resurrection, the fulfillment of a prophecy. Unlike the Countess of Bedford, this "other Countess" has contracted her rarified virtues into a real office, she has not retreated.

> Though you a wifes and mothers name retaine,
> 　'Tis not as woman, for all are not soe,
> But vertue having made you vertue, 'is faine
> 　T'adhere in these names, her and you to show, . . .
> 　　　　　　　　　　　　(ll. 29–32)

This is exactly the same refrain as his address to the Countess of Salisbury ("To the Countesse of Salisbury. August. 1614"[26]). She is not only an idea of beauty, but beauty resident in the whole book of creatures; not a little abstraction, but a massive demonstration of virtues. As the supernatural soul informs the vegetable and rational soul in man, she informs the baser world, so that when Donne thinks of fairness, greatness, goodness,

> 　　　　　now I am come
> From having found their *walkes*, to find their *home*.
> 　　　　　　　　(ll. 63–64)

We have every right to be suspicious of a man who forfeits his beliefs for favors; but there's no forfeiture going on in these poems.

Donne's chief productions during these years of testing are not such epistles, however, but the much more ambitious *Ignatius His Conclave*, the two epithalamia, and the elegies to

Prince Henry and Lord Harington. The eclogue and epithalamion written for the marriage of Somerset and Frances Howard in December, 1613, is the only work that deliberately advances a suit for preferment. All the other writings are either disinterested occasional pieces or payments for favors already received. They are all consonant with Donne's deepest convictions.

Ignatius His Conclave was both occasional piece and repayment. *Pseudo-Martyr* had been published early in 1610: it was in the King's hands by the end of January. In April, Donne was awarded the Master of Arts by Oxford, with a graceful commendation for his defense of Church and State. One month later, the murder of Henry IV in France provided ironic contrast to Donne's regard for the monarchy. Both the Sorbonne and the Parliament of Paris detected one of the causes of Henry's murder: they proscribed the work of the Spanish Jesuit Juan de Mariana entitled *De Rege*, in which it had been asserted that monarchs who resisted the authority of the papacy might be legitimately executed. *Ignatius His Conclave* is a reassertion of Donne's defense of the monarchy, a favor returned for a favor given, and a very funny skewering of the Jesuit order.

It must have been written almost contemporaneously with *The First Anniversary*, thus revealing a fine ambidexterity on Donne's part: modeling one work on St. Ignatius' meditations, at the same time he consigns the founder of the Jesuit order to a lunatic church. For *Ignatius His Conclave* could not have been written earlier than June, 1610. Donne's dedication alludes to the Sorbonne episode; and he makes references to Galileo's *Siderius Nuncius* (dated March, 1610) and Kepler's *Dissertatio cum Nuncio Sidereo* (April, 1610).[27] The first Latin edition of Donne's satire was registered on January 24, 1611, the English version on May 18, 1611. In other words, *Ignatius His Conclave* was begun just a few

months prior to *The First Anniversary*, and the two composi-
tions may even have overlapped. This helps explain the form
of the satire, the descent into the underworld; 1610 was
Donne's year for dark journeys.

The satire is generally aimed at whoever would controvert
the ideal that Donne had set up in *Pseudo-Martyr*, the reconciliation of differences in the interest of peace, or whoever
contributes to the disturbed order of *The Progresse of the
Soule*. The contenders for a place in hell are the innovators,
those who destroy unities and established designs: Mahomet,
the Papacy, Copernicus, Paracelsus, Machiavelli. There's little
personal rancor shown against any but the Papacy: Copernicus is hardly upbraided ("I had never heard ill of his life, and
therefore might wonder to find him there,"[28] and what
Copernicus believed "may very well be true"[29]), and Paracelsus is a figure of fun, hardly malevolent; in fact, all but the
Papist innovators are framed by objectivity, as though Donne
were establishing the theme of rebellion dispassionately, as a
fact to be observed. This comic detachment keeps the satire
above simple vilification, and makes the scarification of the
Jesuits, when it does occur, all the more effective.

In a dream, the Scipionic Donne watches the major claim-
ants to hellish honor (Copernicus, Paracelsus, Machiavelli)
approach the throne of Lucifer, at whose side stands Ignatius
Loyola. Quickly realizing who the real master is, all three
direct themselves to the Jesuit, who, knowing that he must
reserve places in hell for all his followers, is determined to
keep everyone else out. When a great crush of innovators
besieges Ignatius, Lucifer, in a desperate move to maintain his
own primacy, decrees that all Jesuits will be transferred to a
new hell on the moon, thereby establishing the Lunatic
Church. Just as the news of Ignatius' canonization by Pope
Paul V reaches the infernal regions, and as Ignatius flies at
Pope Boniface for usurping his place at the side of Lucifer,

the dreamer awakens and in a mocking apology foretells the downfall of the whole Jesuit order.

The shakers and disturbers of traditional order, whether cosmic, medical, political, amatory, geographic, or spiritual (Copernicus, Paracelsus, Machiavelli, Aretino, Columbus, Philip Neri), have all been outdone by the Jesuits. In contrast stands the monarchy of England, represented by Queen Elizabeth and King James: their business was ever with league and amity, not confusion and disruption. There is a bifocal quality in Donne's satire. It looks back to the defense of order in *Pseudo-Martyr* and forward to the celebration of achieved design of *The Second Anniversary*. Principally a political satire, at the same time it reflects Donne's quest for a unity that manifests itself in the world.

As *Ignatius His Conclave* has something of the nature of a debt repaid, so has Donne's lovely *Epithalamion, Or mariage Song on the Lady Elizabeth, and Count Palatine being married on St. Valentines day,* 1613. This is the first work of his that Donne presented to the princess with so tragic a history, the daughter of James I who became the "Winter Queen" whose kingdom dissolved in the Thirty Years' War.[30] It was not to be Donne's last presentation. He visited her court during the 1619 German tour with Doncaster, and preached before her and her husband; he sent her a copy of his first published sermon in 1622 and a copy of the *Devotions Upon Emergent Occasions* in 1624. Donne had an evident respect for Princess Elizabeth, and that affection shows in the *Epithalamion*.

But there is considerably more in the background of the poem than personal fondness. The guardians of the Princess, from 1603 when she took up residence with them at Combe Abbey, were John, 1st Lord Harington of Exton, and his wife, the parents of the Countess of Bedford. The King's choice of Lord Harington as the Princess' guardian was canny: the

Haringtons were descendants of the noble family of Bruce, and they were staunchly Protestant and monarchist.[31] That the Princess became associated in the popular mind with the ultra-Protestant cause, and something of a storm center in the anti-Catholic feeling of the 1610's and 1620's, was partly owing to the Puritan and nationalistic fervor of her guardians. During the Gunpowder Plot of 1605, an armed band surrounded the Harington home at Combe Abbey, with the intention of proclaiming the Princess Queen once word had been received that King James was dead. The plot aborted, of course, and Lord Harington wrote to his kinsman, Sir John Harington: "Her Highness doth often say, 'What a Queen should I have been by this means? I had rather have been with my royal father in the Parliament-house, than wear his crown on such condition.' "[32] As Elizabeth was made a pawn in the 1605 Protestant-Catholic conflict, so was she again from 1608 onward. The balance of power on the Continent was becoming focused on the Bohemian Palatinate, where in 1608 the Union of South German Protestant Princes was established as a counterbalance to the surge of Catholic influence across Europe. Crucial to the strategy of the Union's chief architect, Christian of Anhalt, was a liaison with England, the most important of the Protestant powers; and the liaison was to be achieved by the marriage of Frederick, Prince Palatine, to Elizabeth, only daughter of King James. The Catholic powers, naturally, were opposed to any such alliance, and the young Princess found herself in the middle of a diplomatic tug of war. "About the beginning of the summer of the year 1612, the general discourse was of the marriage of . . . Elizabeth; which was various, according to the different affections of the persons, as Protestants or Papists; some wishing her to be married to the King of Spain, some to the Prince of Savoy, some to the young Landgrave of Hesse-Cassel, and others to Frederick the Elector Palatine."[33] Elizabeth would not even have had to look outside her own family to be aware of the battle that was being fought over her. Her brother, Prince Henry, a rallying center for the Protestant party, urged the marriage to Frederick;[34] Queen Anne, who was at least a crypto-Catholic, did everything she could to discourage the match, which was "contrary to the graine of the catholick church, and the desires of [the Queen], who looked upon it so much below [the Princess Elizabeth], as she could not refraine to call her Goodwife Palsgrave before she had put off her wedding shooes."[35] When Prince Henry died on November 6, 1612, there were persistent rumors that he had been poisoned so that his checking of Catholic plans might be squelched once and for all.[36] Rightly or wrongly, connections were made between Prince Henry's death and Elizabeth's Protestant marriage (which had to be postponed for a suitable period of mourning).

There is significance in Henry Peacham's publication of 1613: *The Period of Mourning. Disposed into six Visions. In Memorie of the late Prince. Together With Nuptiall Hymnes, in Honour of this Happy Marriage betweene the Great Princes, Frederick Count Palatine of the Rhene, And The Most Excellent, and Aboundant President of all Vertue and Goodnes Elizabeth onely Daughter to our Sovereigne. Also the manner of the Solemnization of the Marriage at White-Hall, on the 14. of February, being Sunday, and St. Valentines day.* Eros and Thanatos in one cover, with epicedes and hymns both stressing the triumph of the Protestant cause, Peacham's work crystallizes a current suspicion. Peacham's aims appear somewhat analogous to Donne's objective in both the *Epithalamion* and his "Elegie upon the untimely death of the incomparable Prince Henry."

It has been pointed out that the tenor of the entire *Lachrymae Lachrymarum*, the collection of laments for Prince Henry published in 1613, combines medieval *contemptus mundi* and Renaissance political consciousness.[37] Grierson's charge that

Donne's contribution to the volume is nothing more than
"tasteless extravagance"[38] is countered by Professor Ruth
Wallerstein's remark: "We have to remember how far men of
that day still believed in the historical force of the great, good
man, and how much real hope England set on Prince Henry.
We must remember, too, that Donne believed implicitly in
the hierarchy of the state and in the unction of its leaders."[39]
Donne did tell Jonson that "he wrott that Epitaph on Prince
Henry *Look to me, Faith* to match Sir Ed: Herbert in
obscureness,"[40] but to regard Donne's elegy as nothing more
than an exercise represents a considerable misreading. Like
the *Holy Sonnets* and the *Anniversaries*, Donne's elegy is a
meditation, within an Augustinian framework, on man's involvement in divine intelligence.[41] Like Elizabeth Drury's,
Prince Henry's death was a beginning, not an object. The
"Elegie upon the untimely death of the incomparable Prince
Henry"[42] contemplates the effects of a challenged order
within the world, while the *Epithalamion* celebrates a return
of that order. Wholly different in tone, these two poems
belong together because, like Peacham's collection, they unite
Henry and Elizabeth in the theme of shock withstood and
pattern maintained. Politics are in the background, but it is
politics as a showcase of prevailing unity in the world.

Donne begins the elegy by stating that both his reason and
his faith have been jolted by Prince Henry's death. Reason
comprehends the natural world, faith the transcendent
(ll. 5–13); and "reason, put to'her best extension,/ Almost
meetes faith" (ll. 15–16). That such a bridge between material and transcendent truly exists was emblematized by the
Prince himself:

> And nothing ever came so neare to this,
> As contemplation of that Prince, we misse.
>
> (ll. 17–18)

Prince Henry moved in both the active and the contemplative worlds: a great statesman (ll. 25–30), and a philosopher whose goal was to reproduce on earth the peace of eternity (ll. 31–38).

Must the Prince's death now shake this belief? If we must be disabused of the sense that there is a commerce between the world and eternity, "wee/ May safelyer say, that we are dead, then hee" (ll. 79–80). But though dead, the Prince may have left behind some pattern for the living to follow, some clue as to how eternity infuses itself into the world. That pattern and clue is love, a love the Prince must have shared with a woman. To find that woman, to learn from her the doctrine of love, and so through love to re-establish the contact between the "Quotidian things" of reason (l. 7) and "Gods essence, place and providence" of faith (l. 11): this is the task left to the poet.

> Yet . . . I can reach him thus,
> As he embrac'd the fires of love, with us.
> O may I, (since I live) but see, or heare,
> That she-Intelligence which mov'd this spheare,
> I pardon Fate, my life: Who ere thou bee,
> Which hast the noble conscience, thou art shee,
> I conjure thee by all the charmes he spoke,
> By th'oathes, which onely you two never broke,
> By all the soules yee sigh'd, that if you see
> These lines, you wish, I knew your history.
>
> (ll. 87–96)

(It may even be that this woman is a resummoned Elizabeth Drury, who so recently had provided Donne with a bridge between temporality and eternity. Sir Robert had somewhat grandiose ideas that his daughter might one day be the Prince's consort and perhaps occupy the English throne,[43] and the concluding lines of Donne's elegy might be a double commemoration, to Henry and Elizabeth together.)

The escape from confusion through love, and love as the link between finite and infinite: this is a distillation of Donne's *Anniversaries* and, for that matter, the central theology of his sermons.

The *Epithalamion*[44] on Princess Elizabeth's marriage is the other side of the coin, the triumphant restoration of shaken nature through love. There is also the possibility that the *Epithalamion* is still another favor returned, to Sir Robert Drury, who had made impudent and derogatory remarks against the Palgrave and his marriage to the Princess.[45] It was "as if to offset the bad impression created by Sir Robert Drury's indiscretion in criticizing the Elector Palatine [that] Donne celebrated the Princess Elizabeth's postponed wedding, which took place on St. Valentine's Day, 1613, with the most charming of his epithalamions."[46]

But even though this might be the case, Donne's *Epithalamion* is more than a genuflection in the direction of Drury Lane. It is a splendid praise of the fact that "Nature againe restored is" (l. 100), an affirmation of life to counter the quiddities of Prince Henry's death. Frederick and Elizabeth, on this day when Bishop Valentine joins all birds in love, are the birds of eternal rebirth, two phoenixes. In joining, they will kindle great fires, from which both they and new phoenixes, their progeny, will arise (ll. 15–28). The fall of the Princess, unlike her brother's, is the little death of consummated love, and it signifies not an end, but a beginning:

> a Great Princess falls, but doth not die;
> Bee thou a new starre, that to us portends
> Ends of much wonder; And be Thou those ends.
>
> (ll. 38–40)

The egregious begging note of Donne's last epithalamion,[47] that on the infamous marriage of the Earl of Somerset and

Frances Howard, Countess of Essex,[48] is all the more noticeable for its being unique in Donne's art of these years. That he wrote it at all shows Donne hazarding everything on one throw. To address himself to Somerset was certain to alienate further the Countess of Bedford. Relations with her were, by 1613, as already noted, precarious. Donne was still mindful of her in 1614, when he confided to Goodyer that he was preparing an edition of his poems[49] and expecting to include some of his verses to her; and the Countess was not so estranged that she would not give Donne thirty pounds to pay some debts before he entered the Church.[50] But certainly "for her other way of expressing her favour to me, I must say, it is not with that cheerfulness as heretofore she hath delivered herself towards me."[51] The Countess of Bedford was in active opposition to Rochester's power at court,[52] and, indeed, it was she who first introduced George Villiers, later Duke of Buckingham, into the royal circle and encouraged Villiers' supplanting of Rochester, Earl of Somerset, as the King's favorite.[53] Rochester, from 1612 onward, was the recipient of most of Donne's appeals for a place in government,[54] and Donne confided to his friend Sir Robert Ker (the "Allophanes" of the epithalamion) that a wedding poem might move Rochester to action on his behalf.[55]

In structure, Donne's poem is the least subtle artifact he ever produced. He is "Idios," the man excluded from court; and not having been present at the Christmas wedding of the Countess and the Earl, he is giving the epithalamion proper to his friend Allophanes, all the while lamenting that "I am not then from Court" (l. 55). Unable to be among the great, he protests too much his disinterest and really uses the epithalamion as a jog to the memory of the influential:

> Reade then this nuptiall song, which was not made
>   Either the Court or mens hearts to invade,
> But since I'am dead, and buried, I could frame

No Epitaph, which might advance my fame
So much as this poore song, which testifies
I did unto that day some sacrifice.

(ll. 99–104)

After hearing the nuptial song, Allophanes does just what is
expected of him:

But let me goe
Backe to the Court, and I will lay'it upon
Such Altars, as prize your devotion.

(ll. 233–235)

Of the epithalamion itself, even Gosse (who thought
Donne hideously compromised himself in the whole affair)
considered it "one of Donne's happiest efforts in this direction—rich, ingenious, and virile."[56] Such effort notwithstand-
ing, the Somerset epithalamion is offensive, not because of
any supposed moral lapse on Donne's part, but because of a
lapse of his usual finesse. His undignified scrambling came
back to haunt him when, sometime after 1618, he wrote "To
Mr. Tilman after he had taken orders," where he regretted
the "time and paine" spent on the quest for titles and pre-
eminences, ambassadorships and dignities.[57]

Between the two epithalamia, Donne wrote "Goodfriday,
1613. Riding Westward," returning thereby to the introspective spiritual effort of the sonnets and the Anniversaries; for
the poem is once again a concentrated meditation, modeled
on the three-stage analysis of the Ignatian system.[58] Good
Friday, the culmination of Passion Week, the Lenten climax,
and the prelude to Easter, came on April 2 in 1613.[59] Behind
Donne is the feast of All Fools, April 1, the day traditionally
celebrated by sending one's friends on fools' errands; now
Donne, hurrying toward the west (literally Wales, metaphori-
cally death) when his real business is in the east (com-

memoratively Golgotha), contemplates "Christ crucified
. . . unto the Greeks foolishness" (I Corinthians 1:23). As
in *La Corona*, Donne faces the absolute paradox of Christ,
which eludes simple comprehension. The man who had
played Lord of Misrule in the "Epithalamion made at Lincolnes Inne" and in *Biathanatos* turns from the "forraigne
motions" that have sent him on his own fool's errand and
accepts the vision of the Crucifixion, much in the spirit of St.
Paul's advice, "Let no man deceive himself. If any man
among you seemeth to be wise in this world, let him become a
fool, that he may become wise" (I Corinthians 2:18); "we are
made a spectacle unto the world, and to angels, and to men.
We are fools for Christ's sake" (I Corinthians 4:9–10).

Donne's habitual attention to Lenten devotions was em-
phasized by Izaak Walton, who reported how Donne, mortally ill in Essex, made the return to London so that "upon
his old constant day, the first *Friday* in Lent,"[60] he might
deliver what came to be called "Donne's own Funeral Sermon," *Death's Duel*, preached at Whitehall, February 25,
1631. The surviving Lenten sermons show why Walton
should have made special note of this episode in Donne's life;
in their emphasis on the presential reality of Christ, these
particular sermons almost read as a gloss on "Goodfriday,
1613," which is saturated with the sense of the Real Presence.[61] In "A Lent-Sermon Preached at White-hall" on February 20, 1629, Donne identified the Christian as one who has
graduated from the grammar school of typology to the university of the *Logos*, from *exempla* to the living presence of
Christ.[62] This same sense of being present at the Crucifixion,
not separated from it by the cushion of history, is the primary
fact of "Goodfriday, 1613. Riding Westward."[63] The concordant notes of poem and sermons reveal several of the
central preoccupations of Donne's maturity. To go from his
poem to his sermons demonstrates, once again, the concinnity

of his work, the continuing but changing execution of basic designs.

Thus, for instance, we can observe Donne transforming two major themes of the poetry into a court sermon. In the poem, Donne stresses the humiliation of Christ during the Passion:

> Could I behold that endlesse height which is
> Zenith to us, and to'our Antipodes,
> Humbled below us?
>
> (ll. 23–25)

It is a humiliation that becomes a chastising and purification, the raised hand of Christ transformed from mutilated palm to divine scourge:

> I turne my backe to thee, but to receive
> Corrections, till thy mercies bid thee leave.
>
> (ll. 37–38)

The passage from humiliation to sanctification occupied Donne's mind in the Lenten sermon of February 20, 1618, too.

> As the Church celebrates an Advent, a preparation to the Incarnation of Christ, to his coming in the flesh, in humiliation: so may this humiliation of ours in the text, be an Advent, a preparation to his Resurrection, and coming in glory: And, as the whole life of Christ was a passion, so should the whole life (especially the humiliation) of a Christian, be a continual meditation upon that.[64]

The image of Christ as the supreme harmony, the tuner of all spheres ("Could I behold those hands which span the Poles,/ And tune all spheares at once, peirc'd with those holes?" ll. 21–22), is repeated in the Whitehall Lenten sermon of 1619, wherein Christ is *musicum carmen*, the love song restoring the primeval music of creation.[65] The utter

mystery of the event of Good Friday, which can be expressed
only in paradoxes, is at the heart of the poem (especially ll.
11–28) and appears in a 1621 Lenten sermon, where Donne
describes the Incarnation as "*Mysterium, opertum, &
apertum,* hid from those that are lost, but manifested to his
Saints."[66]

We've already seen how important to Donne was the
concept of the interior trinity. It was a frequent theme in his
sermons, for instance, when he preached at Lincoln's Inn:

> That plural word *nos,* which was used by God, in the making
> of Man, when God said *Faciamus, Let us, us make man, ac-
> cording to our image,* as it intimates a plurality, a concur-
> rence of all the Trinity is our making, so doth it also a
> *plurality in that image of God,* which was then imprinted in
> us; as God, one God created us, so wee have a soul, *one soul,*
> that represents, and is some image of that one God; As the
> three Persons of the *Trinity* created us, so we have, in our
> one soul, a *threefold impression* of that image, and, as Saint
> Bernard calls it, *A trinity from the Trinity,* in those three
> *faculties* of the soul, the *Understanding,* the *Will,* and the
> Memory.[67]

The motif of the restored image of God concludes the poem
("Restore thine Image, so much, by thy grace,/ That thou
may'st know mee, and I'll turne my face," ll. 41–42) and
begins the marvelous sermon preached at Whitehall on
March 8, 1622, "The Last Enemie That Shall Be Destroyed,
Is Death."[68] I've suggested that one of the major differences
between the *Holy Sonnets* and the *Anniversaries* is the way
that Donne frustrates the restoration of God's image in the
sonnets, but completes it in the *Anniversaries;* and the reason
for the difference is Donne's two attitudes toward grace. His
earliest work accepts the most stringent version of imputed
grace, the absolutely reprobate state of man, who can do

nothing to participate in the sanctifying process. But the doctrine is modified in the *Anniversaries*, to the extent that man can participate; and the reconstituting of the lost image is a crucial employment of the *Anniversaries*. Donne never surrendered the Reformed idea of the primacy of faith:

> If thou shouldst see a man pull at an Oare, till his eye-strings, and sinews, and muscles broke, and thou shouldst aske him, whither he rowed; If thou shouldest see a man runne himselfe out of breath, and shouldst aske him whither hee ranne; If thou shouldst see him dig till his backe broke, and shouldst aske him, what he sought, And any of these should answer, they could not tell, wouldst not thou thinke them mad? So are all Disciplines, all Mortifications, all whippings, all starvings, all works of Piety, and of Charity madnesse, if they have any other root then faith, any other title or dignity, then effects and fruits of a preceding reconciliation to God.[69]

But along with the primacy of faith, Donne believed in a *prevenient* grace, a preparation for faith; and he believed that man owes *all* his faculties to God: faith, for him, was no passive acquiescence.

Prevenience, re-creation of the defaced image, and human participation in redemption are all in "Goodfriday, 1613 Riding Westward." The entire poem is a recapitulation of the Trinity, a full threefold meditation in the manner of the *Anniversaries*:[70] and the conclusion of the poem combines prevenience and participation: "Restore thine Image, so much, by thy grace,/ That thou may'st know mee" is matched by "and I'll turne my face." Here, amazingly compressed, are essential components of Donne's theology. The poem's assurance that God's grace anticipates the poet's own endeavor, and that the turning of his face to God is an activity in which he can play a part, is quite unlike the anxious note of the

sonnets, and it stems from a doctrine well defined by Donne
himself in a Lenten sermon of 1627:

> We consider a *preventing* Grace in God; and that preventing
> Grace is before all; for that prevents us so, as to *Visite us when
> we sit in darknesse*. And we consider an *Antecedent-Will* in
> God, and that *Antecedent Will* is before all; for by that Will,
> God would have *all* men saved. And when we call Gods Grace
> by other names then Preventing, whether *Assisting* Grace,
> that it stand by us and sustain us, or *Concomitant* Grace, that
> it work with us, and inanimate our action, when it is doing,
> or his *Subsequent* Grace, that rectifies or corrects an action,
> when it is done; when all is done, still it is the *Preventing
> Power*, and quality of that Grace, that did all that in me: If
> I stand by his Assisting Grace, if I work with his Concomitant
> Grace, if I rectifie my errour by his Subsequent Grace, that
> that moves upon me in all these, is still the preventing power
> of that Grace.[71]

The emphasis on action, power, stress in all of Donne's comments on faith is seen in the poem's energy, the swift play of
ideas, the stretched imagination, the exercise of all the faculties; and this too springs from Donne's attitude toward man's
cooperating in redemption. "God requires the heart, the
whole man, all the faculties of that man,"[72] Donne insisted,
and that meant man's *reason* and *imagination* along with his
will to be redeemed. Blind faith, unreasoning faith, unimagi-
native faith was nonsense to Donne;[73] such faith was "an
incapable and barren stupidity," to be found "in a washy
soule, in a liquid, in a watery, and dissolute, and scattered
man."[74] Donne's ideas of what constituted faith were good
for his artistry; "Goodfriday, 1613. Riding Westward" is a
better poem for being grounded on a careful theological
distinction.

This poem, written in the midst of political confusion,

solicitations to the court, and obligations to patrons, is a meditative reaffirmation of the *Anniversaries:* Christ breaks into human history and forces recognition of his Real Presence. Except for the last three of the *Holy Sonnets* (which were provoked by specific occasions and are not of the same metaphysical scope as the investigative sixteen sonnets of 1609),[75] "Goodfriday, 1613. Riding Westward" is Donne's last private and contemplative poem. *The Second Anniversary* ended with the announcement that he would henceforth be the celebrant of an indwelling divinity:

> Thou art the Proclamation; and I ame
> The Trumpet, at whose voice the people came.

It became his definition of his ministry:

> God shall send Prophets, Trumpets, and Trumpetors, that is, preachers of his word, and not the word of men; and they shall be heard willingly too; for as they are *Tubae,* Trumpets, so they shall be *musicum carmen,* acceptable music to them that hear them.[76]

Poetry as exploration gave way to poetry as proclamation, and what remains are two public elegies ("Obsequies to the Lord Harington" and "An hymne to the Saints, and to Marquesse Hamylton"), liturgical psalmody ("The Lamentations of Jeremy"), and hymns ("A Hymne to Christ, at the Author's last going into Germany," "Hymne to God my God, in my sicknesse," and "A Hymne to God the Father," this last being set to music and sung in St. Paul's[77]). The rationale seems quite clear: in "Goodfriday, 1613. Riding Westward" Donne returned to introspective meditation as a counterbalance to his involvement with the Drurys, the court, and Somerset; he returned again to meditation in three sonnets when confronted by immediate and specific crises (his wife's death, the religious wars in Germany, an imagined spiritual apathy). But otherwise the insight of the *Anniversaries* was so total and so all-encompassing that what it demanded was not investigation but proclamation. The Church was the ideal instrument, the sermon the ideal vehicle; and when Donne wrote poetry at all, he did it in such a way that the poetry might be absorbed into liturgical ceremony, in close collaboration with the Anglican prayer service. It is really not entirely true to say, as several commentators have said,[78] that Donne was preaching to himself when he was in the pulpit. In the sermons, Donne reaches out and attempts to draw his congregation into the region he discovered in the *Anniversaries*, and even when he does privately meditate in the *Devotions Upon Emergent Occasions*, he is as much a representative of humanity as he is a solitary contemplative. Poetry, as Donne habitually understood it and used it, as a means of discovery, becomes less important now that he's been persuaded that the ultimate discovery has been made. It's not surprising that the elegy on the death of Lord Harington, the Countess of Bedford's brother (February, 1614) should resemble an overdraft upon "your noble brothers fortune,"[79] now in the possession of the Countess; or that Donne frankly told his friend Sir Robert Ker, who requested the Hamilton elegy (March, 1625), that the poem was something "which I was loathe to doe."[80] When Donne insisted that he was burying his muse in Lord Harington's grave,[81] he was in effect saying that his poetry had accomplished what he had demanded of it, it had gotten him to the top of that "huge hill,/ Cragged, and steep," (*Satire III*, ll. 79–80) and that now his office was to be the expresser of what his poetry had found.

> Christ is *verbum*, The word; not A word, but The word: The minister is *Vox*, voyce; not A voyce, but The voyce, the voyce of that word, and no other; and so, he is a pleasing voyce, because he pleases him that sent him, in a faithfull

executing of his Commission, and speaking according to his dictate; and pleasing to them to whom he is sent, by bringing the Gospel of Peace and Reparation to all wounded, and scattered, and contrite Spirits.[82]

Donne's resolve, made just over a month before his ordination, to publish his poetry flustered Sir Edmund Gosse. Of that projected but unachieved intention Gosse remarked, "Donne's friends, one cannot doubt, would dissuade him from taking the moment of his ordination to publish a collection of worldly verses which he had never been able to make up his mind as a layman to print."[83] But Donne certainly knew what he was doing when he told Goodyer that "I apprehend some incongruities in the resolution, and I know that I shall suffer from many interpretations; but I am at an end of much considering that, and if I were as startling in that kind as ever I was, yet in this particular I am under an unescapable necessity."[84] Read in their proper sequence, Donne's poems constitute an *Unplain Man's Pathway to Heaven*, an intimate and step-by-step progress toward an intense experience of conversion. From the *Satires* through the *Anniversaries*, the bits of experience have converged into a complete design, and Donne quite rightly viewed such a full portrait as a suitable pre-ordination disclosure. Donne insisted that he was "under an unescapable necessity" of so publishing his poems. Though there is nothing in the Anglican ordination ceremony that would have required such a concrete *vale*, still the episcopal exhortation and examination of candidates stresses renunciation and sacrifice, in the spirit of Christ's command to Levi (Matthew 9:9; Mark 2:14; Luke 5:27) to leave everything and follow, or the injunction to the young man to "sell whatever thou hast . . . and follow me" (Mark 10:21). On December 20, Donne wrote to Goodyer that "I must do this, as a valediction to the world, before I take orders";[85] I think it conceivable that Donne considered giving up his poetry in imitation of the Synoptic Gospels' accounts of Levi and Christ's demand.

Augustus Jessop guessed that Donne was ordained on St. Paul's feast day; [86] his dates were wrong, but his instincts were right. Like Luther, Donne evidently thought Paul the greatest of the apostles, and he achieved a certain identification with St. Paul. He remarked once, at Lincoln's Inn, that his spiritual appetite was best satisfied by the psalms of the Old Testament and the Pauline epistles of the New: "My meditations . . . returne oftnest to these two."[87] Izaak Walton, for one, saw St. Paul as an analogue, and his *Life of Dr. John Donne* frequently draws parallels between the two men: Donne's delay in entering into the Church repeated St. Paul's humility;[88] his preaching duplicated St. Paul's rapture of II Corinthians 12:1-5;[89] his dedication to preaching was Pauline;[90] his return to Lincoln's Inn, the scene of his youth, as chaplain was St. Paul replacing Saul of Tarsus;[91] his voyage out of England and into Germany was like Paul's leave-taking of the Ephesians.[92] Donne's own actions suggest he recognized an affinity: he discoursed more on the texts of St. Paul than on those of any other writer of the New Testament,[93] and he made a particular point of preaching on the Feast of St. Paul's Conversion. The sermon preached at St. Paul's the Sunday after the feast in 1625 gives some indication of the depth of Donne's attraction. The whole sermon is an encomium to St. Paul, who is made the object of Ecclesiastes' injunction, "Let us now praise famous men." Paul is presented as a type of all men, for his conversion "embrace[s] all, involve[s] and enwrap[s] all."[94] Paul was the man upon whom Christ laid hold; if the Roman doctrine of transubstantiation has any validity at all, it is in the mutation of Saul to Paul: "Here was a true Transubstantiation, and a new Sacrament. These few words, *Saul, Saul, why persecutest thou* me, are words of Consecration; After these words, *Saul* was no longer *Saul*, but he was Christ: *Vivit in me Christus*, sayes he, *It is not I that live*, not I that do anything, *but Christ in me*."[95] Donne has gone right to the heart of Pauline theology here. It's no simple coincidence that Donne should have drawn more on St. John and St. Paul than on any of the other New Testament writers, for in these two Donne found buttressing for his own sense of an ultimate unity in creation. While it took him nearly twenty years and the bulk of his poetry to apprehend fully that unity, the insight came, and when it did, it came in the Johannine terms of Light and One. To his new-found sense of unity, Donne added the distinctively Pauline doctrine of the absolute centricity of Christ. For Paul, Christ was the cosmic center of all things, the "pleroma." "For by him were all things created, that are in heaven, and that are in earth, visible and invisible, whether they be thrones, or dominions, or principalities, or powers: all things were created by him, and for him: And he is before all things, and by him all things consist" (Colossians 1:16–17). It's been objected that Donne's theology was a thin affair, made up of very few ideas that he deployed in different ways.[96] They are few, certainly, but they're hardly thin. The bedrock of Donne's faith was the plenitude of the Incarnation as developed in both St. John and St. Paul, and particularly the latter. No one who is familiar with Donne's long quest for a sense of unity can fail to appreciate why he should have based his theology on the Gospel of light and the epistles of the pleroma.[97] Teilhard de Chardin might have been discussing Donne when he wrote, "What is the supreme and complex reality for which the divine operation moulds us? It is revealed to us by St. Paul and St. John. It is the quantitative repletion and the qualitative consummation of all things: it is the mysterious Pleroma, in which the substantial *one* and the created *many* may fuse without confusion in a *whole* which, without adding anything essential to God, will nevertheless be a sort of triumph and generalisation of being."[98]

Everything about Donne's sermons carries this Pauline glow of the repletion and consummation of all things in Christ. His preaching was not a harangue, nor was it meditation overheard, nor indoctrination; it was a festival of love, himself and his congregation achieving what the love poetry strove after: absorption into one another, into a great quiet, and into a fulfilling unitive experience. The "every where" of the bed in "The Sunne Rising" or the "one little roome, an every where" of "The Good-morrow" occurred at Whitehall or Lincoln's Inn or St. Paul's, wherever Donne preached. As in the *Anniversaries* or "Goodfriday, 1613. Riding Westward," the events of sacred history were not consigned to the past when Donne spoke, but were resummoned, re-created at the instant he was speaking, and he asked his congregation to step into the residing and presiding mystery that remains undisturbed through all the rush of history. Donne's emphasis on the present-ness of God's word, rather than on an elucidation or allegorical interpretation, was more or less standard Anglican procedure. In contrast to the allegoric tendency of Catholic scriptural interpretation, or the instructive exegetics of the Puritans, Anglican theory rejected the Alexandrianism of the first and the contentiousness of the second, insisting on the literalness of sacred scripture and its relevance to the living situation.[99] "It is most historical and most accurate to think of Donne's sermons as spiritual or, specifically, tropological exegesis. Their central concern is the Christian soul. Donne applies the text to his auditory."[100] But whether we stress the Anglicanism, or the Augustinian cast,[101] of Donne's hermeneutics, it is his own career as a love poet that best explains the quality of his sermons. Love which dissolves time: that describes a great deal of the poetry and the preaching. But now, instead of the sun halting at "this bed [which]

thy center is, these walls, thy spheare," the sun of St. Paul's
pleromatic Christ is at the center. But it is still an act of love,
and the consequences are the same.

> The best determination of the Reall presence is to be sure,
> that thou be really present with him, by an ascending faith:
> Make sure thine own Reall presence, and doubt not of his:
> Thou art not the farther from him, by his being gone thither
> before thee.[102]

Thou art but a little world, a world but of a few spanns in
length; and yet Christ was sooner carried from east to west,
from *Jerusalem* to these parts, then thou canst carry him over
the faculties of thy Soul and Body; He hath been in a pilgrimage towards thee long, coming towards thee, perchance
50, perchance 60 years; and how far is he got into thee yet? . . .
He entred into thee, at baptism; He hath crept farther and farther into thee, in catechisms and other infusions of his doctrine into thee; He hath pierced into thee deeper by the
powerful threatenings of his Judgments, in the mouths of his
messengers; He hath made some survey over thee, in bringing
thee to call thy self to an account of some sinful actions; and
yet Christ is not come into thee; either thou makest some new
discoveries, and fallest into some new ways of sin; and art loth
that Christ should come thither yet, that he should trouble
thy conscience in that sin, till thou hadst made some con-
venient profit of it; thou hast studied and must gain, thou hast
bought and must sell, and therefore art loth to be troubled
yet; or else thou hast some land in thee, which thou thy self
hast never discover'd, some waies of sin which thou hast
never apprehended, nor considered to be sin; and thither
Christ is not come yet: He is not come into thee with that
comfort which belongs to his coming in this Text (I Tim.
1.15. This is a faithful saying, and worthy of all acceptation,
that Christ Jesus came into the world to save sinners; of which

I am the chiefest), except he have overshadowed thee all, and be in thee intirely.[103]

The sermon on St. Paul that Donne delivered in 1628 gives particular emphasis to Paul's preaching, and as preacher he was greater than all the other apostles, for he became thereby "an universall soule to the whole Church."[104] Donne's praise of Paul for eschewing "problematicall points" and concentrating on "unanimity in fundamentall Doctrines"[105] is a sensible response to any charge of doctrinal thinness in his own work. The 1629 sermon on St. Paul's conversion contains one of Donne's most effective recitals of the continuing presence of Christ in the world:

> Poore intricated soule! Riddling, perplexed, labyrinthicall soule! Thou couldest not say, that thou beleevest not in God, if there were no God; If there were no God, thou couldest not speake, thou couldest not thinke, not a word, not a thought, no not against God; Thou couldest not blaspheme the Name of God, thou couldest not sweare, if there were no God: For, all thy faculties, how ever depraved, and perverted by thee, are from him; and except thou canst seriously beleeve, that thou art nothing, thou canst not beleeve that there is no God. If I should aske thee at a Tragedy, where thou shouldest see him that had drawne blood, lie weltring, and surrounded in his owne blood, Is there a God now? If thou shouldest answer me, No, These are but Inventions, and Representations of men, and I beleeve a God never the more for this; If I should ask thee at a Sermon, where thou shouldest heare the Judgements of God formerly denounced, and executed, redenounced, and applied to present occasions, Is there a God now? If thou couldest answer me, No, These are but Inventions of State, to souple and regulate Congregations, and keep people in order, and I beleeve a God never the more for this; Bee as confident as thou canst, in company; for company is

the Atheists Sanctuary; I respit thee not till the day of Judgement, when I may see thee upon thy knees, upon thy face, begging of the hills, that they would fall downe and cover thee from the fierce wrath of God, to aske thee then, Is there a God now? I respit thee not till the day of thine own death, when thou shalt have evidence enough, that there is a God, though no other evidence, but to finde a Devill, and evidence enough, that there is a Heaven, though no other evidence, but to feele Hell; To aske thee then, Is there a God now? I respit thee but a few houres, but six houres, but till midnight. Wake then; and then darke, and alone, Heare God aske thee then, remember that I asked thee now, Is there a God? and if thou darest, say No.

And then, as there is an universall Atheist, an Atheist over all the world, that beleeves no God, so is he also an Atheist, over all the Christian world, that beleeves not Christ. That which the Apostle sayes to the *Ephesians, Absque Christo, absque Deo,* As long as you were *without Christ,* you were *without God,* is spoken (at least) to all that have heard Christ preached; not to beleeve God, so, as God hath exhibited, and manifested himselfe, in his Son Christ Jesus, is, in S. *Pauls* acceptation of that word, Atheisme: and S. *Paul,* and he that speaks in S. *Paul,* is too good a Grammarian, too great a Critique for thee to dispute against.[106]

The last of the surviving sermons on St. Paul was delivered in 1630, and in it Donne recalled the three earlier sermons he had delivered on this festival.[107] It is a curious text on which Donne chose to preach, that of Acts 23:6–7, in which Paul provoked dissension between the Sadducees and Pharisees and so avoided the judgment planned against him by the high priest Ananias. Donne wonders "whether this that Paul did, were well done,"[108] and given Donne's own irenic temper in religious matters, we can understand his wonder. But Donne's strategy is to argue, as he always does, that his auditors are themselves involved in scripture (just as in the *Essays in Divinity* he saw himself involved in Genesis and Exodus) and that "we have all *Sadduces* and *Pharisees* in our own bosomes."[109] Donne's topic thus becomes the same triad of order that operates through all his religious work, the *Anniversaries* most especially included, i.e., a universal theme, operative in sacred history and reduplicated in human action. The sermon is constructed around this triplicity. First, Donne shows that "no Example of man is sufficient to constitute a certaine and constant rule; All the actions of the holiest man are not holy."[110] As evidence he cites the examples of Abraham's proceedings with his son Isaac, Noah's drunkenness, Lot's incest, David's anger, Samson's suicide. How in purely human terms, Donne asks, are we to decide which acts were sinful and which justified? Their actions, as men, are useless as guides, as are the examples of the Patriarchs, the Fathers, and the generations of commentators.

The next part of Donne's *divisio* concerns Paul's action before the court of Ananias. He rests his defense of Paul on the grounds that in disturbing the court, Paul was no denier of authority, that "He did not calumniate nor traduce the proceedings of that Court, nor put into the people ill opinions of their superiors, by laying aspersions upon them; There are that doe so; S. *Paul* did not. But his end and purpose was onely to put off the tryall for that time, till he might be received to a more sober, and calme, and equitable hearing."[111] The second part of Donne's triad is occupied with an analysis of the specific historical act of St. Paul before the tribunal.

The third part unites all the previous matter of the sermon: if the ways of even holy men are an uncertain guide, can even the justifiable action of St. Paul before Ananias be revered? Donne finds his answer in the symbolic values he attaches to

Sadducees and Pharisees. Paul brought the court to an uproar by declaring his belief in the Resurrection, a belief shared by the Pharisees but rejected by the Sadducees. On this point Donne folds his whole organization together:

> . . . though it be not safe to conclude, S. *Paul*, or any holy man did this, therefore I may do it (which was our first part) yet in this which S. *Paul* did here, there was nothing that may not be justified in him, and imitated by us (which was our second part) Remains onely the third, which is the accomodation of this to our present times, and the appropriation thereof to our selves, and making it our own case.[112]

The dialectic of "The Exstasie" is rejoined: "Our Sadduces will have all body, our Pharisees all soule, and God hath made us of both, and given us offices proper to each."[113] The clash between Sadducees and Pharisees is a continuous process—it occurs in man, in the body politic, in religious controversy, in the sadducism of presumption and the pharisaism of despair. The only solution of the dilemma is in Christ.

> All thy life thou shalt be preserved, in an Orientall light, an Easterne light, a rising and growing light, the light of grace; and at thy death thou shalt be super-illustrated, with a Meridionall light, a South light, the light of glory. And be this enough for the explication, and application of these words, and their complication with the day; for the justifying of S. *Pauls* Strategem, in himselfe, and the exemplifying, and imitation thereof in us. Amen.[114]

This last of Donne's St. Paul's festival sermons would not be unfairly represented as an epitome of his whole hermeneutic system, which envisions metahistory, scriptural history, and personal history all reflecting the same design, with Christ at the center of that design. The organization and the imagery of Donne's sermons often reflect the complexities of his trinitarianism, which is at one and the same time the paradigm of spiritual effort, true history, and creation (God fashioned the world in trinities, reveals himself in time through trinities, and can be approached through the trinity of faculties); but this sermon of 1630 is classic in its appropriation of trinitarianism for structural control.[115]

It is just such a system of trinitarianism that accounts for much of the unity in Donne's later work. His *Devotions Upon Emergent Occasions* is a case in point:[116] Donne's own condition and the scriptural context in which he places himself are so reciprocal that it is impossible to tell which is vehicle and which is tenor. The "quotidian ague" that struck Donne down in October, 1623 ("A bacteriologist has diagnosed it as relapsing fever"[117]), was the occasion of three, and perhaps four, of his best-known works: the *Devotions*, "A Hymne to God the Father," "Hymne to God my God, in my sicknesse,"[118] and, possibly, the sonnet "Oh, to vex me, contraryes meete in one." The sonnet is a private meditation that converts the "fantastique Ague" (l. 13) of illness into spiritual irresolution and then into benign trepidation ("Those are my best dayes, when I shake with feare," l. 14). But the private nature of the sonnet is more than matched by the communal characteristics of the two hymns. They are not the solo music of his earliest nine songs, but choral music:

> Since I am comming to that Holy roome,
>   Where, with thy Quire of Saints for evermore,
> I shall be made thy Musique; As I come
>   I tune the Instrument here at the dore,
>   And what I must doe then, thinke now before.
>   ("Hymne to God my God, in my sicknesse,"
>   ll. 1–5)[119]

In "A Hymne to God the Father,"[120] the obvious punning on his name ("When thou hast done, thou hast not done," ll.

5, 11) is given over to the choristers of St. Paul's, and individuality is absorbed into liturgy. Walton paid attention to
this self-surrendering aspect of the hymm:

> I have rather mentioned this *Hymn,* for that he caus'd it to
> be set to a most grave and solemn Tune, and to be often sung
> to the *Organ* by the *Choristers* of St. *Pauls* Church, in his own
> hearing; especially at the Evening Service, and at his return
> from his Customary Devotions in that place, did occasionally
> say to a friend, *The words of this* Hymn *have restored to me
> the same thoughts of joy that possest my Soul in my sickness
> when I composed it. And, O the power of Church-musick!
> that Harmony added to this Hymn has raised the Affections
> of my heart, and quickned my graces of zeal and gratitude;
> and I Observe, that I always return from paying this publick
> duty of Prayer and Praise to God, with an unexpressible
> tranquillity of mind, and a willingness to leave the world.*[121]

The universalizing of such an immediately personal item as
death is accomplished in the *Devotions* as it is in the hymns;
Walton unconsciously used almost the same terms to describe
the prose as he did the poetry: Donne, in the *Devotions,*
"paraphrased and made publick" what began as "the most
secret thoughts that then possesst his Soul."[122] Donne
achieves this universalizing effect, not by choral harmonies,
but by a system of trinities.

We cannot and ought not deny the vaunted intimacy of
the *Devotions;* but I suspect that readers who most insist on
the intimacy pay attention only to the Meditations, and overlook the Expostulations and the Prayers. For the whole collection of twenty-three devotions is a ritualization of personal
misery, Donne's securing of a place in a transpersonal order.
Each devotion is divided into the three parts of Meditation,
Expostulation, and Prayer, a deliberate return to the medi-

tative pattern of the sonnets and the *Anniversaries*. In the Meditations, Donne begins always with his own immediate situation and then, by considering himself a microcosm, extends himself into the whole Book of Creatures so that his condition becomes a parable of creation. Following this, the Expostulations draw on scripture and absorb creation into Sacred Writ, thus giving a sacral character to secular experience. Finally, the Prayers complete the movement from secular to sacred by the fact of their being part of the liturgical order of Donne's own Teaching Church, the ordained bridge between the human condition and the divine order. Donne's prayers are not extempore: they deliberately echo the cadences of the Book of Common Prayer.[123] Stylistically, the devotions move from broken rhythms in meditation, to interrogatory abruptness in expostulation, to Ciceronian equilibrium in prayer;[124] intellectually, from anxiety to reflection to security; and conceptually, from singularity to communality. The *Devotions* epitomizes Donne himself and his theological system.

For instance, the first meditation describes the onslaught of the fever: "Variable, and therfore miserable condition of Man; this minute I was well, and am ill, this minute."[125] This variable misery is then extended to include the entire "perplex'd discomposition, riddling distemper, miserable condition of Man," who "hath these *earthquakes* in him selfe, sodaine shakings; these *lightnings*, sodaine flashes; these *thunders*, sodaine noises; these *Eclypses*, sodain offuscations, and darknings of his senses; these *Blazing stars*, sodaine fiery exhaltations; these *Rivers of blood*, sodaine red waters. . . ."[126] The expostulation then locates scriptural parallels for such melancholic afflictions in the stories of Job and the Prodigal Son, each one a lesson in God's use of affliction to manifest himself. Like Jacob, Donne thinks that "Surely the Lord is in this place, and I knew it not."[127] The prayer

apostrophizes God as the link between Israel and London, Job
and Donne, beginnings and endings:

> O Eternall, and most gracious God, who, considered in
> thy selfe, art a *Circle*, first and last, and altogether; but con-
> sidered in thy working upon us, art a *direct line*, and leadest
> us from our *beginning*, through all our wayes, to our end,
> enable me by thy grace, to looke forward to mine end, and
> to looke backward to, to the considerations of thy mercies
> afforded me from my beginning.[128]

Or the seventeenth devotion: the sound of the tolling bell
reminds Donne of the Mystic Body of which he is a part:

> Perchance hee for whom this *Bell* tolls, may be so ill, as that
> he knowes not it tolls for him; And perchance I may thinke
> my selfe so much better than I am, as that that they who are
> about mee, and see my state, may have caused it to toll for
> mee, and I know not that. The *Church* is *Catholike*, *uni-
> versall*, so are all her *Actions*; *All* that she does, belongs to *all*.
> When she *baptizes a child*, that action concernes mee; for that
> child is thereby connected to that *Head* which is my *Head*
> too, and engraffed into that *body*, whereof I am a *member*.[129]

The sounds of and preparations for death are complemented,
in the expostulation, by accounts of the last hours of Jacob,
Moses, Ezechias, and Christ, as recounted in Genesis,
Deuteronomy, Kings, and the testaments of St. Peter and St.
John, respectively. Finally the prayer coalesces the sound of
the bell, the promise of resurrection, and Christ's last words
with a climax echoing the burial service:

> . . . why thy *left hand* lay his *body* in the grave (if that bee
> thy *determination* upon him) and with thy *right hand* receive

his soule into thy Kingdome, and united *him* and *us* in one *Communion of Saints*. Amen.[130]

(Donne's imagery of the left and right hand of God is interesting, perhaps echoing phrases of the Catholic mass for the dead, *Statuens in parte dextra . . . voca me cum benedictis,* "Call me with the saints to stand at thy right hand." The transfer of the notion of *ad dextram patris* from Christ to the whole communion of saints emphasizes the *congregate* death of the entire seventeenth devotion.[131])

At the apex of the sacramental system of the *Devotions,* where Donne, the *dramatis personae* of the Old and New Testaments, and the visible Church are all co-temporal with one another, is Christ. The Incarnate Word, who was from the beginning and entered history to complete it, is the object of all but the thirteenth, fifteenth, and twenty-third prayers in the *Devotions*; and in those three prayers, Donne's petition is for God's mercy, the quality inherent in Christ's office. St. Paul's words to the Corinthians, *Omnia in ipso constant,* were interpreted by Donne in the fullest sense, in the sense of the *pleroma.*

It is the unceasing preaching of the consubsistence of all things in Christ that gives the palpable coherence to Donne's sermons, diverse and complex as they are. To consider the sermons in their totality can be unnerving; and the impressive scholarship that has been devoted to them[132] has served mainly to show how much still needs to be done.[133] It is not merely that they are so learned and so allusive; most of Donne's citations have been tracked down, and the traditions out of which he operated have been identified. The problem is that each sermon in itself is a little eschatology, a compressing of great spans of history, personal and extrapersonal, into an articulated word. For Donne placed a tremendous responsibility on himself and on all preachers, whom he called "*speculatores*, men placed upon a watch tower,"[134] entrusted with nothing less than locating by their voice the voice of God in the world. He considered the *word* more efficacious than the sacraments, noting that "when Christ had undertaken that great work of the Conversion of the world, by the Word, and Sacraments, to shew that the word was at that time the more powerfull meanes of those two (for sacraments were instituted by Christ, as subsidiary things, in a great part, for our infirmity, who stand in need of such visible and sensible assistances) Christ preached the Christian Doctrine, long before he instituted the Sacraments."[135] "God is *Logos, speech and reason*; He declares his will by his Word."[136] "This Word, manifesting itself differently in Father, Son, and Holy Ghost, utters other words. The Father, or creator, spoke at the creation the words that are incarnate in the Book of the Creatures, the world. The Holy Ghost spoke in tongues of flames to the apostles, in bestowing upon them the gift of languages; and he is also the author of the written word, the Scriptures. The Son was incarnate (Word made word) in the flesh of Christ, and uttered himself again in Scripture by means of the Holy Ghost."[137] So the preacher must duplicate the spirit moving over the waters of Genesis and by the word create order out of chaos; he must be the Pentecostal wind of the Acts of the Apostles and infuse the Word into the followers of Christ; and he must become with Christ *musicum carmen*: "God rectified all again, by putting in a new string, *semen mulieris*, the seed of the woman, the Messias . . . But if we take this instrument, when God's hand tun'd it the second time, in the promise of a *Messias*, and offer of the love and mercy of God to all that will receive it in him; then we are truly *musicum carmen*, as a love-song, when we present the love of God to you, and raise you to the love of God in Christ Jesus."[138] Donne thought of himself not as the expositor of the triune Logos, but as a functioning triune Logos himself; and in a sermon delivered on Easter Monday in 1622, he appropriated to himself the creative Word of the Father, the illuminative Word of the Spirit, and the redemptive Word of the Son: "I shall open unto you that light, which God commanded out of darkness, and that light by which *he hath shin'd in our hearts*; and this light, by which we shall have *the knowledge of the glory of God, in the face of Christ Jesus.*"[139] This is not *hubris* at all, but St. Paul: "And my speech and my preaching was not with enticing words of man's wisdom, but in demonstration of the Spirit and of power; That your faith should not stand in the wisdom of men, but in the power of God" (I Corinthians 2:4–5). Again, in a sermon (preached, appropriately enough, on Trinity Sunday), Donne coalesced Christ and Word, and did so through a triune organization:

> Christ is not defined, not designed by any name, by any word so often, as by that very word, *The Word, Sermo,* Speech; In man there are three kinds of speech; *Sermo innatus,* That inward speech, which the thought of man reflecting upon it selfe produces within, He thinks something; And then *Sermo illatus,* A speech of inference, that speech which is occasioned in him by outward things, from which he drawes conclusions, and determins; And lastly, *Sermo prolatus,* That speech by which he manifests himselfe to other men. We consider also three kindes of speech in God; and Christ is all three. There is *Sermo innatus,* His Eternall, his naturall word, wnich God produced out of himselfe, which is the generation of the second Person in the Trinity; And then there is *Sermo illatus,* His word occasioned by the fall of *Adam,* which is his Decree of sending Christ, as a Redeemer; And there is also *Sermo prolatus,* His speech of manifestation and application of Christ, which are his Scriptures. The first word is Christ, the second, the Decree, is for Christ, the

third, the Scripture, is of Christ. Let the word be Christ, so
he is God; Let the word be for Christ, for his coming hither,
so he is man; Let the word be of Christ, so the Scriptures
make this God and man ours.[140]

The Word is past, present, and future; the Word is creation,
redemption, and wisdom; and the Word is the particular
responsibility of the preacher. Each sermon of Donne's was
intended as a miniature cosmogony, a fact which ought to
terrify any commentator.

But it is not *terra incognita;* most of the great themes
realized through the poetry are in the sermons. Of first importance is the refrain of *unity,* a phantasm in the love poetry
and an experience in the *Anniversaries.* The elusive woman of
the *Songs and Sonnets* becomes the apprehended light an-
nounced by St. John and reflected in a virgin-martyr; the "any
beauty I did see,/Which I desir'd, and got, 'twas but a
dreame of thee" of "The Good-morrow" becomes the Bride
of Christ in the late sonnet "Show me deare Christ, thy
spouse, so bright and cleare."[141] The fragmented reality of the
pre-*Progresse of the Soule* or the re-experienced fragmentation
of "Loves Alchymie" is checked by the unity in God:

> So we are changed *in naturam Dei,* as S. Peter expresses it: By
> his precious promises we are made partakers of the divine na-
> ture . . . this transmutation is a glorious restoring of Gods
> image in us, and it is our conformity to him; and when either
> his temporal blessings, or his afflictions, his sun, or his fire,
> hath tried us up to that height, to a conformity to him, then
> come we to that transmutation, which admits no re-transmu-
> tation, which is a modest, but infalible assurance of a final
> perseverance, so to be joyned to the Lord, as to be one spirit
> with him; for as a spirit cannot be divided, so they who are
> thus changed into him, are so much His, so much He, as that

nothing can separate them from him; and this is the ladder, by which we may try, how far we are in the way to heaven.[142]

Almighty God ever loved unity, but he never loved *singularity*.[143]

[David] considers God totally, entirely, altogether; Not altogether, that is, confusedly; but altogether, that is, in such a Name as comprehends all his Attributes, all his Power upon the world, and all his benefits upon him. The Gentiles were not able to consider God so; not so entirely, not altogether; but broke God in pieces, and changed God into single money, and made a fragmentarie God of every Power, and Attribute in God, of every blessing from God, nay of every malediction, and judgement of God. A clap of thunder made a *Iupiter*, a tempest at sea made a *Neptune*, an earthquake made a *Pluto*; *Feare* came to be a God, and a *Fever* came to be a God; Every thing that they were in love with, or afraid of, came to be canonized, and made a God amongst them. *David* considered God as a center, into which and from which all lines flowed.[144]

From the beginning God intimated a detestation, a dislike of *singularity*; of beeing *Alone*.[145]

The alien elegist has come quite a distance.

Love was always the central experience of Donne's life; but in most of the poetry it was a restless and moving center. The voice that is heard in the love poems, early and late, is demandingly male, insulting, admonishing, but never begging. And yet, the maleness was often contradictorily passive, cherishing its own receptive emptiness, often prohibiting any real challenge to its private supremacy. Beneath the active, domineering masculinity of the love poetry was a *demi-vierge* of the spirit that alternately invited and repelled the rape of itself. And the woman of the love poetry was equally paradoxical; for all her passivity she was the antithesis of *nothing*, she was the active completion of love. The strains of this complex ambiguity—the dominating male who harbors the nervous virgin, the persuadable and passive woman who provides the incarnate strength of love—set up a resonating conflict of satyr-virgin, hermit-pilgrim, active-passive, extinction-completion within Donne that was finally resolved in his religious experience. His ascent to divine love was charted in two of his poems, the sonnet written after his wife's death and "A Hymne to Christ, at the Author's last going into Germany,"[146] in both of which Christ becomes the fulfilling lover:

> Since she whome I loved, hath paid her last debt
> To Nature, and to hers, and my good is dead,
> And her soule early into heaven ravished,
> Wholy in heavenly things my mind is sett.
> Here the admyring her my mind did whett
> To seeke thee God; so streames do shew the head, . . .
>> (ll. 1–6)

> Seale then this bill of my Divorce to All,
> On whom those fainter beames of love did fall;
> Marry those loves, which in youth scattered bee
> On Fame, Wit, Hopes (false mistresses) to thee.
>> (ll. 25–28)

Human love as a prolegomenon to divine love, even sharing the transmutative powers of divine love, was a frequent topic of Donne's sermons:

> The highest degree of [human] love, is the love of woman;
> Which love, when it is rightly placed upon one woman, is dignified by the Apostle with the highest comparison, *Husbands love your wives, as Christ loved his Church:* And God himself forbad not that this love should be great enough to change natural affection, *Relinquent patrem,* (for this, a man shall

leave his Father) yea, to change nature it self, *caro una,* two shall be one.[147]

[Marriage is] *bonum Sacramenti,* a mysticall representation of that union of two natures in Christ, and of him to us, and to his Church.[148]

The magnificent sermon "Preached at a Mariage" [the marriage of Mistress Margaret Washington at the Church of St. Clement Danes, May 30, 1621][149] launches the love of man and woman into the trinitarian structure of Donne's thought: the marriage being celebrated is a type of "first, a secular marriage in Paradise; secondly, a spirituall mariage in the Church; and thirdly, an eternall mariage in heaven."[150] The young couple's love becomes the embodiment of all time, from Eden to Eternity.

The centrality of love becomes an image of the centrality of Christ: "The union of Christ to the whole Church is not expressed by any metaphore, by any figure, so oft in the Scripture, as by this of *Mariage*";[151] "*God is Love,* and the *Holy Ghost* is amorous in his *Metaphors.*"[152]

The dream of love as a true alchemy, pursued through all the love poetry but then blasted in "Farewell to Love" and "Loves Alchymie," is achieved in Donne's Christocentric world. "Love is a Possessory Affection," he said in 1617, "it delivers over him that loves into the possession of that that he loves; it is a transmutatory Affection, it changes him that loves, into the very nature of that that he loves, and he is nothing else."[153] Such a stunning experience had been attained in "The Exstasie" and, sporadically, in the poetry of 1602–1605; it is consummated in the sermons: "And as this affection, love, doth belong to God principally, that is, rather then to any thing else, so doth it also principally another way, that is, rather then any affection else; for, *fear of God is the beginning of wisdom,* but the love of God is the consum-

mation, that is, the marriage, and union of thy soul, and thy
Saviour."[154]

Donne began as an angry man, and out of the anger came
some of the best of iconoclastic poetry; he became a fearful man, and the fear made him a greater love poet than
he would otherwise have been. The anger, fear, and love were
not dissipated in his religion, but redirected against himself
and toward God. The contempt he showed for empty institu-
tions in the satires becomes a self-contempt in the late sonnet
"Oh, to vex me, contraryes meete in one," and he resembles
there his own earlier motley humorist:

> Away thou fondling motley humorist . . .
> Shall I leave all this constant company,
> And follow headlong, wild uncertaine thee?
> ("Satyre I," ll. 1, 11–12)

> As humorous is my contritione
> As my prophane love, and as soone forgott: . . .
> "Oh, to vex me," ll. 5–6)

The difference is that there was no excuse for the fool of the
satires, but there is for the "ridlingly distemperd" Donne.

> Those are my best dayes, when I shake with feare.
> ("Oh, to vex me," l. 14)

The love of God begins in fear, and the fear of God ends in
love; and that love can never end, for God is love.

> (Sermon preached at St. Dunstan's,
> April 25, 1624[155])

> I have a sinne of feare, that when I have spunne
> My last thred, I shall perish on the shore;
> Sweare by thy selfe, that at my death thy Sunne
> Shall shine as it shines now, and heretofore;
> And having done that, Thou hast done,
> I have no more.
> ("A Hymne to God the Father," ll. 13–18)

The inconstancy and fearfulness of the fool of the satires is transposed, and becomes the fulfilling love that Donne has sought continually. The earlier fearful Donne often thought of annihilation, real or symbolic, as a release from the sickness and trembling of living:

> the thirst
> Of . . . faire death, out pusht mee first.
> (The Calme," ll. 41–42)

Whensoever any affliction assails me, mee thinks I have the keyes of my prison in mine owne hand, and no remedy presents it selfe so soone to my heart, as mine owne sword.[156]

But the appeal of *nothingness* is transformed in the later Donne:

And when upon the consideration of Gods miraculous Judgements or Mercies, I come to such a melting and pouring out of my heart, that there be no spirit, that is, none of mine own spirit left in me; when I have so exhausted, so evacuated my self, that is, all confidence in my self, that I come into the hands of my God, as pliably, as ductily, as that first clod of earth, of which he made me in *Adam*, was in his hands, in which clod of earth, there was no kinde of reluctation against Gods purpose; this is a blessed nullification of the heart. When I say to myself, as the Apostle professed of himself, *I am nothing*; and then say to God, Lord, though I be nothing, yet behold, I present thee as much as thou hadst to make the whole world of; O Thou that mad'st the whole world of nothing, make me, that am nothing in mine own eyes, a new Creature in Christ Jesus: This is a blessed nullification, a glorious annihilation of the heart. So there is also a blessed nullification thereof, in the contrition of heart, in the sense of my sins; when, as a sharp winde may have worn out a Marble Statue, or a continual spout worn out a Marble Pavement, so, my holy tears, made holy in his Blood that gives them a tincture, and my holy sighs, made holy in that Spirit that breathes them in me, have worn out my Marble Heart, that is, the Marbleness of my heart, and emptied the room of that former heart, and so given God a *Vacuity*, a new place to create a new heart in.[157]

The energy and the triumph of the love poetry carry over into the sermons, but without the optative condition of the love poems:

> Let us possesse our world, each hath one, and is one.
> > ("The Good-morrow," l. 17)
> True and false feares let us refraine,
> Let us love nobly, 'and live, . . .
> > ("The Anniversarie," ll. 27–28)
> For Godsake hold your tongue, and let me love, . . .
> > ("The Canonization," l. 1)
> Enter these armes, for since thou thoughtst it best,
> Not to dreame all my dreame, let's do the rest.
> > ("The Dreame," ll. 9–10)

In the sermons, "let" is replaced by "shall," ending in "joy":

> As my soule shall not goe towards Heaven, but goe by Heaven to Heaven, to the Heaven of Heavens, So the true joy of a good soule in this world is the very joy of Heaven; and we goe thither, not that being without joy, we might have joy infused into us, but that as Christ sayes, *Our joy might be full,* perfected, sealed with an everlastingnesse; for, as he promises, *That no man shall take our joy from us,* so neither shall Death it selfe take it away, nor so much as interrupt it, or discontinue it, But as in the face of Death, when he layes hold upon me, and in the face of the Devill, when he attempts me, I shall see the face of God, (for, every thing shall be a glasse, to reflect God upon me) so in the agonies

of Death, in the anguish of that dissolution, in the sorrowes of that valediction, in the irreversiblenesse of that transmigration, I shall have a joy, which shall no more evaporate, then my soule shall evaporate, A joy, that shall passe up, and put on a more glorious garment above, and be joy superinvested in glory. Amen.[158]

The pre-*Anniversaries* Donne was not betrayed by the post-*Anniversaries* Donne. The poetry, the engagement with life, the deep experience of themes crucial to man's awareness of himself were never surrendered, but fastened down. Donne was ever an explorer; his poems are replete with sea voyages, all emblematic of his hydroptic thirst to *know*, from the elegy "To his Mistris Going to Bed" through the valedictory poems. Both "A Hymne to Christ, at the Author's last going into Germany" (1619) and "A Hymne to God my God, in my sicknesse" (1623) equate voyage and experience. It is altogether appropriate that, on his ordination, Donne should have sent George Herbert a poem that contains an anchor.

> Crosses grow Anchors; Bear, as thou shouldest do
> Thy Crosse, and that Crosse grows an Anchor too.
> But he that makes our Crosses Anchors thus,
> Is Christ, who there is crucifi'd for us.[159]

Epilogue

The man whom we can with justice call "modern" is solitary. He is so of necessity and at all times, for every step towards a fuller consciousness of the present removes him further from his original *"participation mystique"* with the mass of men— from submersion in a common consciousness. Every step forward means an act of tearing himself loose from that all-embracing, pristine unconsciousness which claims the bulk of mankind almost entirely.

(Carl Jung, *Modern Man in Search of a Soul*)[1]

Man—of all ages and cultures—is confronted with the solution of one and the same question: the question of how to overcome separateness, how to achieve union, how to transcend one's own individual life and find at-onement. The question is the same for primitive man living in caves, for nomadic man taking care of his flocks, for the peasant in Egypt, the Phoenician trader, the Roman soldier, the medieval monk, the Japanese samurai, the modern clerk and factory hand. The question is the same, for it springs from the same ground: the human situation, the conditions of human existence. The answer varies. The question can be answered by animal worship, by human sacrifice or military conquest, by indulgence in luxury, by ascetic renunciation, by obsessional work, by artistic creation, by the love of God and by the love of Man. While there are many answers—the record of which is human history—they are nevertheless not innumerable. On the contrary, as soon as one ignores smaller differences which belong more to the periphery than to the center, one discovers that there is only a limited number of answers which have been given, and only could have been given by man in the various cultures in which he has lived. The history of religion and philosophy is the history of these answers, of their diversity, as well as of their limitation in number.

(Erich Fromm, *The Art of Loving*)[2]

The fear of dispossession, of being alone, while probably a continuing fixture of human experience, nevertheless finds itself aggravated in different historical moments. Donne's was such a moment of aggravation, and so is ours. His whole art is so pertinent to his own situation that it becomes pertinent to ours. The recoil from alienation, the long search for a point of convergence, the intense awareness of the reality within which convergence takes place is the design of Donne's art. While his mode of vision became Christian, the basic rhythm of his progress is adoctrinal. While he is distinctively a Renaissance poet, his poetry is para-Renaissance. While his meditative art is intensely personal, it reaches out beyond his own perplexities.

Flannery O'Connor once noted that Teilhard de Chardin's *Phenomenon of Man* is a "scientific expression of what the poet attempts to do: penetrate matter until spirit is revealed in it. Teilhard's vision sweeps forward without detaching itself at any moment from the earth."[3] With very slight adjustment, the words describe a significant theme in contemporary thought, and they describe John Donne's work. The attempt to revivify dead matter without denying it has, in our time, been made the common task of physicist, philosopher, and poet. The more difficult it becomes to touch something beyond ourselves, the more urgent becomes the need to do just that; and Sir James Jeans's mind-filled universe, Martin Heidegger's total being, and Marianne Moore's real toads in imaginary gardens are all part of the same thrust: the denial of separateness and the recovery of communion. And we have grown impatient with abstract notions of communion; the revelation of the way things converge must come through the living organism, the felt intuition, the hard-edged image.

The developing Donne is a simulacrum of modern man. In the beginning, he practices anonymity and experiences apartness. When the intolerability of separation touches him, he turns to love; at first that love is a denial of corrosive history and eroding time. But when he apprehends a love that has penetrated time, he comes to that fulfilling and participating experience toward which all his art has been mysteriously moving. And the whole experience is worked into the grainy texture of his writings, which pay strict attention to the hard existence of things. His poetry and his greatest sermons are in toto another version of his entire vision, with insight and literal detail entirely absorbed into one another. He knew too of that "secret complicity between the infinite and the infinitesimal" of which Teilhard spoke and which we are determined to perceive.

Notes

PROLOGUE.

1. Herbert J. C. Grierson, ed., *The Poems of John Donne* (Oxford, 1958), II, v–vi.
2. Pierre Teilhard de Chardin, *The Phenomenon of Man* (New York, 1959), p. 237.
3. Clyde Kluckhohn, "Myths and Rituals: A General Theory," *Myth and Literature*, ed. John B. Vickery (Lincoln, 1966), p. 43.
4. Sir James Jeans, *The Mysterious Universe* (New York, 1958), p. 181.
5. Owen Barfield, *Saving the Appearances* (New York, n.d.), p. 109.
6. Erich Fromm, *The Art of Loving* (New York, 1956), p. 9.
7. Sally M. TeSelle, *Literature and the Christian Life* (New Haven, 1966), p. 102.
8. Teilhard de Chardin, p. 276.
9. TeSelle, pp. 114–115.
10. "The Exstasie," *John Donne: The Elegies and The Songs and Sonnets*, ed. Helen Gardner (Oxford, 1965), p. 61.

CHAPTER I.

1. *Ben Jonson*, ed. C. H. Herford and Percy Simpson (Oxford, 1925), I, 135.
2. I hope this will not be interpreted as obscurantism, nor as a denial of the insights presented in such studies as Don Cameron Allen's "The Degeneration of Man and Renaissance Pessimism," *Studies in Philology*, XXXV (1938), 202–222; Herschel Baker, *The Wars of Truth* (Cambridge, Mass., 1952); S. L. Bethell, *The Cultural Revolution of the Seventeenth Century* (London, 1951); Victor Harris, *All Coherence Gone* (Chicago,

1949); Robert Ornstein, "Donne, Montaigne and Natural Law," *Journal of English and Germanic Philology*, LV (1956), 213–229; George Williamson, "The Libertine Donne," *Philological Quarterly*, XIII (1934), 276–291, and "Mutability, Decay and Seventeenth Century Melancholy," *Journal of English Literary History*, II (1935), 121–150. Certainly Donne's generation had its share of *angst*. But I suggest that while the mature Donne felt the full shock of a shaken society, the younger Donne aggravated without really having absorbed the shock.

3. Ben Jonson, *Every Man In His Humour*, III, i.
4. Edmund Gosse, *The Life and Letters of John Donne* (New York, 1899), II, 363. The painting, reproduced by Michael Strachan in *The Life and Adventures of Thomas Coryate* (Oxford, 1962) and described by Edward Le Comte in *Grace to a Witty Sinner: A Life of Donne* (New York, 1965), now hangs in the National Portrait Gallery in London.
5. Grierson, I, 141–144.
6. David Novarr, "Donne's 'Epithalamion Made at Lincoln's Inn': Content and Date," *Review of English Studies*, VII (1956), 250–263.
7. cf. Suzanne Lilar, *Aspects of Love in Western Society* (New York, 1965); and Mircea Eliade, *The Two and the One*, trans. J. M. Cohen (London, 1965).
8. "Satyre I," *The Poems of John Donne*, ed. Herbert J. C. Grierson (Oxford, 1958), I, 145.
9. *Ibid.*, I, 149–154.
10. *Ibid.*, I, 158–168.
11. *Ibid.*, I, 168–171.
12. *Ibid.*, II, cxxvii.
13. "Tutelage," *John Donne: The Elegies and The Songs and Sonnets*, ed. Helen Gardner (Oxford, 1965), p. 12. All references to the *Elegies* and the *Songs and Sonnets* are from this edition.
14. Rosamond Tuve's last work devotes considerable attention, with the thoroughness that characterizes all her scholarship, to the pilgrim figure; cf. *Allegorical Imagery* (Princeton, 1966), pp. 145–218.
15. Grierson, I, 154–158.
16. J. H. Parry has pointed out how the renaissance of cartography from mid-fifteenth to the seventeenth century stimulated the poetic imagination; cf. *The Age of Reconnaissance* (New York, 1964). See also Leo Bagrow, *History of Cartography*, revised by R. A. Skelton (Cambridge, Mass., 1966).
17. Thomas Carew, "An Elegie upon the death of the Deane of Pauls, Dr. John Donne," *The Poems of Thomas Carew*, ed. Rhodes Dunlap (Oxford, 1957), p. 72.
18. Donald Guss, first in an article ("Donne's Conceit and Petrarchan Wit," *Publications of the Modern Language Association*, LXXVIII [1963],

308–314) and then in a full study (*John Donne, Petrarchist* [Detroit, 1966], has shown how frequently Donne drew on stock Petrarchan conventions. The Ovidian and Petrarchan strains have been observed by Helen Gardner in her edition of the *Elegies* and the *Songs and Sonnets* (esp. pp. xvii–xxix).

19. cf. Gardner, p. xcvii.
20. *Ibid.*, p. 238.
21. *Ibid.*, p. 241.
22. *Ibid.*, p. 243.
23. *Ibid.*
24. *Ben Jonson*, VIII, 142, 145–146.
25. I accept Helen Gardner's argument that half of the *Songs and Sonnets* were written before the end of the century, the other half following *The Progresse of the Soule*. See her introduction, pp. lvii–lxii.
26. Gardner, pp. 145–146.
27. Grierson, I, 288.
28. *Hamlet*, III, ii.
29. Grierson, I, 175–177.
30. *Ibid.*, I, 178–180.
31. cf. Donald Ramsay Roberts, "The Death Wish of John Donne," *PMLA*, LXII (1947), 958–976: ". . . the desire for death was a permanent element in his psychic life" (959).
32. *Hamlet*, I, ii.
33. See below, Chapter V, pp. 255–256.
34. Grierson, II, 140–141.
35. Gardner, pp. 256–257.
36. Grierson, II, 104.
37. *Ibid.*
38. Donne defended the Anglican stricture, with particular reference to Machabees, in a sermon preached before King Charles on April 18, 1626. See *The Sermons of John Donne*, ed. G. R. Potter and Evelyn M. Simpson, 10 vols. (University of California Press, 1953–61), VII, 120.

CHAPTER II.

1. Evelyn M. Simpson, *A Study of the Prose Works of John Donne*, 2nd ed. (Oxford, 1962), pp. 136–137.
2. *Ibid.*, pp. 142–143.
3. Le Comte, *Grace to a Witty Sinner: A Life of Donne*, p. 253.
4. *Letters to Severall Persons of Honour*, ed. Charles Edmund Merrill, Jr. (New York, 1910), p. 173.
5. *Ibid.*, p. 196.

6. e.g., "The Character of a *Scot* at the first sight," with his "Barren-half-acre of Face." *Paradoxes and Problems,* ed. Geoffrey Keynes (Nonesuch Press, 1923), p. 69.

7. Merrill, pp. 93–94.

8. Keynes, p. 30.

9. *Ibid.,* pp. 3–4.

10. Le Comte, p. 253; cf. A. E. Malloch, "The Techniques and Function of the Renaissance Paradox," *SP,* LIII (1956), 191–220: "The office of the paradoxes themselves is not to deceive, but by a show of deceit to force the reader to uncover the truth" (p. 192).

11. The fullest treatment of paradox is Rosalie Colie's *Paradoxia Epidemica* (Princeton, 1966), in which Professor Colie distinguishes among rhetorical, psychological, ontological, and epistemological paradox in the Renaissance, in a sensitive and wide-ranging analysis of paradoxology.

12. Grierson, II, 58.

13. *Ibid.,* p. 60.

14. *Ibid.,* p. 58.

15. Mark Van Doren, *John Dryden, A Study of His Poetry* (New York, 1946), p. 145.

16. *Ben Jonson,* VIII pp. 29, 39, 46.

17. Grierson, I, 76–77.

18. *Ibid.,* p. 78.

19. *Ibid.,* I, 298.

20. In his edition of the *Parodoxes and Problems,* Professor Keynes prints this "Essay on Valour" as well as "The Character of a *Scot* at the first sight" and "The Character of a Dunce." These prose sketches were in circulation early, but were not generally ascribed to Donne; they appeared in various editions of Sir Thomas Overbury's collection of characters, *A Wife.* Cf. Simpson, *Prose Works,* p. 135.

21. Keynes, p. 77.

22. *The Courtier's Library,* ed. Evelyn M. Simpson, with a translation by Percy Simpson (Nonesuch Press, 1930). On the date of Donne's revisions, see Simpson, *Prose Works,* p. 153.

23. *Ibid.,* p. 43.

24. *Ibid.,* pp. 43, 46.

25. Gardner, pp. 251–254.

26. "A Discourse Concerning the Originall and Progress of Satire," *Essays of John Dryden,* ed. W. P. Ker (Oxford, 1926), II, 19.

27. *John Donne: The Elegies and The Songs and Sonnets,* ed. Helen Gardner (Oxford, 1965), pp. 27–28.

28. Grierson, II, xviii–xix, 219.

29. Ornstein, "Donne, Montaigne and Natural Law."

30. Williamson, "The Libertine Donne: Comments on *Biathanatos.*"

31. Grierson, II, 219.

32. W. A. Murray, "What Was the Soul of the Apple?" *RES*, n.s. X (1959), 141–155.

33. Grierson, II, 219.

34. Murray, pp. 154–155.

35. Paul Tillich, *Dynamics of Faith* (New York, 1965), p. 12.

36. *The Sermons of John Donne*, ed. George R. Potter and Evelyn M. Simpson (Berkeley and Los Angeles, 1962), VII, 138–139.

37. Grierson quotes from Josephus, *Antiquities of the Jews*, where the Seth-astronomy tradition is expressed (II, 219).

38. Grierson, I, 294.

39. Paul Tillich describes such a "boundary situation" in *The Protestant Era*, trans. James Luther Adams (Chicago, 1948), in which he also discusses the concept of the "sacred void." The dialectic of negative and positive response to the world is discussed in Tillich's *The Interpretation of History*, trans. N. A. Rasetzski and Elsa L. Talmey (New York, 1936). See especially "Faith and Doubt," in *Dynamics of Faith* (New York, 1958), pp. 16–22.

40. Potter and Simpson, VIII, 78.

41. A reviewer in the *Times Literary Supplement* suggested that without positing Ann More as the basis of these poems, "it becomes impossible to suggest for many of them a psychologically plausible explanation" (*TLS*, April 6, 1967, p. 280). This seems to me a terrible simplification, not only of Donne's psychology, but of all psychology.

42. In this, Donne shares what Harry Berger has defined as "The Renaissance imagination": "Separating itself from the casual and confused region of everyday existence, [the Renaissance imagination] promises a clarified image of the world it replaces." ("The Renaissance Imagination," *Centennial Review*, IX [1965], p. 46.)

43. The sequence I propose is slightly different from Professor Gardner's. As does she, and accepting her evidence as the most credible proposed, I assign five poems to an early and transitional stage. Beyond this, Miss Gardner cautiously declines to propose a continuum. Such caution is admirable; but critical gambles, especially when they're admittedly hypotheses and don't ignore bibliographic certainties, are sometimes necessary.

44. Gardner, pp. 256–257.

45. George Williamson, "The Convention of *The Exstasie*," *Seventeenth Century Contexts* (Chicago, 1961), pp. 63–77.

46. Merrit Y. Hughes, "The Lineage of 'The Exstasie,'" *Modern Language Review*, XXVII (1932), 1–5; A. J. Smith, "The Metaphysic of Love," *RES*, n.s. IX (1958), 362–375.

47. Gardner, p. 26; Williamson, "The Convention of *The Exstasie*."

48. "[Man is] obliged to carry with him everywhere the center of the landscape he is crossing. But what happens when chance directs his steps to a point of vantage (a cross-roads, or intersecting valleys) from which, not

only his vision, but things themselves radiate? In that event the subjective viewpoint coincides with the way things are distributed objectively, and perception reaches its apogee. The landscape lights up and yields its secrets. He sees." Teilhard de Chardin, *The Phenomenon of Man*, p. 32.

49. Cf. Mircea Eliade, *The Sacred and the Profane* (New York, 1961): "Even for the most frankly nonreligious man . . . [there] are the 'holy places' of his private universe, as if it were in such spots that he had received the revelation of a reality other than that in which he participates through his ordinary life" (p. 24). "Sacred time is indefinitely recoverable, indefinitely repeatable. From one point of view it could be said that it does not 'pass,' that it does not constitute an irreversible duration. It is an ontological, Parmenidean time; it always remains equal to itself, it neither changes nor is exhausted" (p. 69).

50. John Ives Sewall, *A History of Western Art* (New York, 1953), pp. 664–706.

51. I. A. Shapiro, "Donne in 1605–06," *TLS*, January 26, 1967, p. 76. Professor Shapiro's discovery, based on a careful examination of Donne's correspondence, whets appetites for his long-awaited edition of Donne's letters.

52. *Religio Medici*, Part I, section 10. *The Works of Sir Thomas Browne*, ed. Charles Sayle, 3 vols. (Edinburgh, 1927), I, 17.

53. Gardner, pp. 192–193.

54. *Ibid.*, pp.lviii–lix.

55. The bibliography of heterodoxy is immense; I cite only those which have some relevance to Renaissance preoccupations with the subject, and which, personally, were of considerable value. Francis Yates, *Giordano Bruno and the Hermetic Tradition* (Chicago, 1964); Joseph L. Blau, *The Christian Interpretation of the Cabala in the Renaissance* (New York, 1944); Gershom G. Scholem, *Major Trends in Jewish Mysticism* (Jerusalem, 1941); Robert Sencourt, *Outflying Philosophy* (London, n.d.); Ross Garner, *Henry Vaughan: Experience and the Tradition* (Chicago, 1959).

56. Mircea Eliade, *Patterns in Comparative Religion* (New York, 1958), p. 465.

57. G. Van Moorsel, *The Mysteries of Hermes Trismegistus: A Phenomenologic Study* (Utrecht, 1955), p. 22.

58. Gardner, pp. 177–223 et al.

59. *Hermetica*, ed. Walter Scott (Oxford, 1925–1936), 4 vols. (*The Corpus Hermeticum* is contained in Vol. I; notes and appendices, in Vol. II.)

60. My willingness to employ a musical metaphor here is encouraged by the fact that so expert a witness as John Dowland (1562–1626) imitated this poem and included it in his collection of songs, *A Pilgrim's Solace*, 1612. Cf. Gardner, p. 244. The whole structure of the poem would appeal, I think, to Charles Ives.

61. The classic discussion of the symbolism involved here is Marjorie Nicol-son's *The Breaking of the Circle* (Evanston, Ill., 1950).
62. George Williamson, "Donne's 'Farewell to Love,'" *Modern Philology*, XXXVI (1939): "Nature . . . has arranged things so that escape is pos-sible only through renunciation" (p. 303).
63. Gardner, p. 213.

CHAPTER III.

1. Gardner, p. lix.
2. *Ibid.*, p. 257.
3. Cf. W. A. Murray, "Donne and Paracelsus: An Essay in interpretation," *RES*, XXV (1949), 115–123; Louis L. Martz, *The Poetry of Meditation* (New Haven, 1954), pp. 214–215.
4. "A Sermon Upon the XV. Verse of the XX. Chapter of the Booke of Judges," September 15, 1622; "A Sermon, Preached to the Kings M^tie at Whitehall," February 24, 1625.
5. *John Donne: The Divine Poems*, ed. Helen Gardner (Oxford, 1952), pp. xlvii–xlviii.
6. See Chapter V, p. 234.
7. All references to both testaments are taken from the Authorized Version except where otherwise noted.
8. Rudolf Bultmann, *History and Eschatology: The Presence of Eternity* (New York, 1957), p. 154.
9. Grierson, I, 175–228; II, 130–177.
10. Donne's prose letters are in a state of editorial chaos, a situation that will be remedied by the appearance of I. A. Shapiro's edition. As they now stand, we have Mrs. Simpson's summary: "Most of [Donne's] correspond-ence which has been preserved was given to the world by his son in two volumes—*Letters to Severall Persons of Honour: written by John Donne* (1651), and *A Collection of Letters, made by Sr Tobie Matthews K^t* (1660). The researches of I. A. Shapiro and R. E. Bennett have shown that the younger Donne tampered with the headings of many of the letters in an attempt to curry favour with Mistress Bridget Dunch, to whom the *Letters* of 1651 was dedicated. There are also a few prose let-ters contained in the early editions of the *Poems*, and in Walton's *Life of Mr. George Herbert* (1670). During the nineteenth century about thirty fresh letters came to light, and in the first edition of the present volume I was able, by the kindness of Mr. Pearsall Smith and Sir Herbert Grierson, to print from the Burley MS. a series of letters from Donne to Wotton or to friends of Wotton, which had never before been published. Thus we have in all a collection of over two hundred letters, covering the greater

part of Donne's life, and addressed to more than forty different corre-
spondents." (Simpson, *Prose Works*, pp. 291–292.)

11. W. Milgate, the most recent editor of *The Satires, Epigrams and Verse
Letters* (Oxford, 1967), suggests that the epistles are "a legitimate kind
of complimentary and moral writing" (p. xl). Respectful commendation
seems to be the epistles' destiny.

12. "To Mr. T. W.," Grierson, I, 206.

13. "To Mr. R. W.," *ibid.*, I, 210.

14. *Ibid.*

15. Grierson, II, 133.

16. *Ibid.*, II, 209.

17. *Ibid.*, I, 280.

18. Gardner, *Divine Poems*, p. 81.

19. Simpson, *Prose Works*, p. 159; Gardner, *Divine Poems*, p. 81.

20. Gardner, *Divine Poems*, pp. xlix–l.

21. Simpson, *Prose Works*, p. 179, 179n.

22. *Ibid.*, pp. 193–194.

23. Grierson, II, 187. The poems were begun on December 13, 1610, and
December 13, 1611, respectively. They were completed in 1611 and 1612.

24. "They are vital for the understanding of Donne's position during the difficult years which preceded his entry into Holy Orders, when he was hesitating on the threshold." *Essays in Divinity*, ed. Evelyn M. Simpson (Oxford, 1952), p. ix.

25. Gosse, *Life and Letters of John Donne*, II, 321.

26. *Essays in Divinity*, pp. x–xxii; *Prose Works*, pp. 203–215.

27. Simpson, *Essays in Divinity*, p. 35.

28. Potter and Simpson, *The Sermons of John Donne*, VI, 172.

29. Helen Gardner in her edition of the *Elegies* and the *Songs and Sonnets*
remarks in a note (p. lix) that Mrs. Simpson has placed the *Essays* just
before the *Anniversaries*. I was puzzled by the note, for Mrs. Simpson is
emphatic in print that the *Essays* are later than the *Anniversaries*. But in
correspondence Miss Gardner has told me that Mrs. Simpson would now
place them just prior to the poems: the detail which prompted the new
dating is the fact that Donne's Biblical references in the *Essays* are based
primarily on the Geneva version but never the Authorized Version of the
Bible. If the *Essays* were later than 1611, Donne would surely have used
the Authorized Version. (Private correspondence, January 6, 1967. I'm
indebted to Miss Gardner for her information on this point.)

30. Simpson, *Essays in Divinity*, pp. 39–40.

31. *Ibid.*, p. 30.

32. *Ibid.*, p. 37.

33. *Ibid.*, p. 75.

34. *Ibid.*, p. 96.

35. *Ibid.*, p. 6.

36. Potter and Simpson, VII, 74–75.
37. Simpson, *Essays in Divinity*, p. 99.
38. Gosse, II, 102–103.
39. Simpson, *Essays in Divinity*, p. 76.
40. *Ibid.*, p. 85. Donne glosses the incident of the resurrected child: *Miracula Beatae Virginae*, 1581.
41. *John Donne: The Anniversaries*, ed. Frank Manley (Baltimore, 1963), p. 102.
42. Donne sided with Thomas Aquinas on the issue, who also rejected the doctrine. Cf. Gardner, *Divine Poems*, p. 84n.
43. Martz, *Poetry of Meditation*, pp. 107–112.
44. Simpson, *Prose Works*, pp. 313–315.
45. Simpson, *Essays in Divinity*, p. 50.
46. *Ibid.*, p. 41.
47. *John Donne: The Divine Poems*, ed. Helen Gardner (Oxford, 1952), p. 2.
48. Potter and Simpson, I, 235.
49. *Ibid.*, III, 190–192.
50. *Ibid.*, VII, 66. This emphasis on *Jehovah* as essence and being was repeated in the sermon of commemoration for Magdalene Herbert, Lady Danvers (Potter and Simpson, VIII, 75).
51. *Ibid.*, VII, 66–67.
52. Simpson, *Essays in Divinity*, p. 23.
53. *Ibid.*, p. 24.
54. *Ibid.*, p. 26.
55. *Ibid.*, p. 24.
56. *Ibid.*, pp. 24–25.
57. Potter and Simpson, VII, 309.
58. H. F. Stewart, *Pascal's Apology For Religion* (Cambridge, Mass., 1942), p. 160.
59. Martz, pp. 107–108.
60. Probably an early poem; cf. Gardner, *Divine Poems*, p. 92.
61. Potter and Simpson, II, 300–301.
62. Gardner, *Divine Poems*, p.28.
63. *Ibid.*, p. 30.
64. Simpson, *Essays in Divinity*, p. 24; Potter and Simpson, VII, 309.
65. Simpson, *Prose Works*, p. 159.
66. Merrill, *Letters to Severall Persons of Honour*, pp. 17–19.
67. *Ibid.*, p. 19.
68. Williamson, "The Libertine Donne," p. 286.
69. Colie, *Paradoxia Epidemica*, p. 40.
70. Joan Webber, *Contrary Music* (Madison, Wis., 1963), pp. 5, 11.
71. Cf. Potter and Simpson, IX, 177.

72. *Biathanatos*. Reproduced from the First Edition, with Biographical Note by J. William Hebel (New York, 1930), p. 18.
73. *Ibid.*
74. *Ibid.*, p. 46.
75. *Ibid.*, p. 216.
76. The history of the Lord of Misrule, in his several guises, has been interestingly charted by Enid Welsford in *The Fool: His Social and Literary History* (London, 1935; New York, 1961).
77. Charles Moore, in 1790, took exception to Donne's logic, without seeing the comic intention, in *A Full Inquiry into the Subject of Suicide*; and Joan Webber, in her study of Donne's prose, has isolated several of Donne's fallacies (*Contrary Music*, pp. 5–11). George Williamson's "The Libertine Donne" cites what have been taken as "errors" in Donne's reasoning.
78. *Rhetoric*, 1401a–1402a.
79. "The chalice of life may not be put aside in death."
80. Webber, p. 10.
81. *Biathanatos*, p. 10.
82. *Ibid.*, pp. 34–35.
83. *The Poems of John Dryden*, ed. James Kinsley (Oxford, 1958), I, 311, ll. 1–7.
84. *Biathanatos*, pp. 153–154.
85. *Ibid.*, p. 217.
86. *Ibid.*
87. *Ibid.*, p. 214.
88. Grierson, I, 198, ll. 83–86.
89. *Biathanatos*, p. 20.
90. Merrill, p. 28.
91. Gardner, *Divine Poems*, p. 83.
92. Merrill, p. 29.
93. The importance of this idea in Renaissance Christian thought has been made clear in recent studies. A strangely neglected but valuable work, G. W. O'Brien's *Renaissance Poetics and the Problem of Power* (Institute of Elizabethan Studies, 1956), has discussed the Plotinian background of the trinitarian theory; Louis L. Martz in *The Poetry of Meditation* has demonstrated how the image operates in St. Bernard and St. Bonaventure, while his study *The Paradise Within* (New Haven and London, 1964) concentrates on the doctrine as presented in St. Augustine.
94. Gardner, *Divine Poems*, p. 30.
95. *The Works of Henry Vaughan*, ed. L. C. Martin, 2d. edition (Oxford, 1957), pp. 482–483.
96. St. Augustine, *De Trinitate, The Later Works*, trans. John Burnaby (London, 1953), p. 169.
97. *Ibid.*, p. 88.

98. Undated letter to Goodyer, *A Collection of Letters, made by Sr Tobie Matthews K^t* (London, 1660), p. 34.

99. Gosse, I, 252.

100. *Pseudo-Martyr. Wherein Out of Certaine Propositions and Gradations, This Conclusion is evicted. That Those Which Are of the Romane Religion in this Kingdome, may and ought to take the Oath of Allegeance.* London. Printed by W. Stansby for Walter Burre. 1610, p. 15.

101. *Ibid.,* p. 200.

102. *Ibid.,* p. 37.

103. *Ibid.,* p. 117.

104. *Ibid.,* p. 116.

105. *Ibid.,* p. 139.

106. *Ibid.,* B2^r.

107. *Ibid.,* p. 168.

108. *Ibid.,* p. 97.

109. *Ibid.,* p. 99.

110. *Ibid.,* C^v–C4^r.

111. Gardner, *Divine Poems,* pp. xlvii–l.

112. *Ibid.,* p. 1.

113. *Ibid.,* pp. l–lv.

114. For a minority opinion, contra Martz and Gardner, cf. Stanley Archer, "Meditation and the Structure of Donne's 'Holy Sonnets,'" *ELH,* XXVIII (1961), 137–147.

115. Gardner, *Divine Poems,* pp. l–li.

116. *Ibid.,* p. lii.

117. *Ibid.,* pp. liii–liv.

118. *Ibid.,* notes on pp. xlix, li.

119. *Ibid.,* p. 5.

120. *Ibid.,* p. xl.

121. Gardner, *Divine Poems,* p. 6. All references to Donne's holy sonnets are from this edition.

122. Helen Gardner points out that the doctrine of a particular judgment is first expressed by Donne in these years (*Divine Poems,* p. xlvii). However, she implies that Donne, in accepting the idea, had to reverse himself on the matter of purgatory, which he rejects in *Pseudo-Martyr.* But the concept of a particular judgment is not dependent on the doctrine of purgatory. All souls (in the Catholic view) do not remain in purgatory in the time between particular and general judgment, but may go immediately to damnation or triumph. At the general judgment, the shame of the damned and the glory of the triumphant will be increased by their exposure to the entire assemblage of eternity: God, angels, and all humanity.

123. Potter and Simpson, IV, 45–62.

124. Certainly at least one reader misunderstood Donne's pattern, wherein "Death be not proud" is not an undervaluing of death but a celebration of the City of God's triumph over the City of Man. When Cecilia Bulstrode died at the home of the Countess of Bedford in August, 1609, Donne was quite possibly encouraged by the Countess to retract his sentiments on the destruction of death's power (cf. Gardner, *Divine Poems*, p. xlviii). His elegy on Mrs. Bulstrode thoroughly undoes the logic of his six sonnets. An impressive elegy, it nevertheless is so contrary to the spirit of the sonnets that we must suspect the influence of the little court at Twickenham. It would seem that the Countess wasn't pleased with Donne's recantation. Echoing his own sixth sonnet, it was probably she who wrote the denigration of death and celebration of Christian hope in the poem beginning "Death be not proud, thy hand gave not this blow,/Sinne was her captive, whence thy power doth flow" (cf. Grierson, I, 422–423; Gardner, *Divine Poems*, p. xlviii).

125. *The City of God*, Book XX, chapter 6 (trans. Marcus Dods [New York, 1950], p. 718).

126. *Ibid.*, p. 720.

127. *Ibid.*

128. Potter and Simpson, *Sermons*, VII, 139. cf. VII, 92–93: ". . . 4000 yeare from *Adam* to *Christ*, and 1600. from *Christ* to us."

129. *Ibid.*, IV, 45.

130. *Ibid.*, IV, 56.

131. *Ibid.*, IV, 58.

132. *Ibid.*, IV, 47.

133. Donne's reference to the "two Fathers" is unclear. He alludes immediately before his peroration to both Irenaeus and Tertullian; but in the course of the sermon he also refers to Augustine, Lactantius, and Chrysostome, all fathers of the primitive church who wrote concerning the Resurrection. Nevertheless, Donne's meaning, if not his reference, is clear: the final state of everlasting peace with God is a doctrine essential to Christianity.

134. Potter and Simpson, IV, 62.

135. Gardner, *Divine Poems*, pp. l–li.

136. *Ibid.*, p. xli.

137. Potter and Simpson, IV, 62.

138. To describe this eruption of a femaleness in Donne's poetry in psychological terms would certainly not "explain" why it occurs; but it suggests there is nothing bizarre in the phenomenon. Jungian psychology posits a "syzygy" at the center of the personality, a complex made up of a male-active and a female-passive principle, with the female anima asserting itself in the male, and vice versa. The syzygy, in Jung's system, is closely allied to the atavistic yearning for self-completion. The pertinence of this to Donne's poetry is clear enough.

139. The several theories of the Atonement have been discussed by C. A. Patrides, "Milton and the Protestant Theory of the Atonement," *PMLA*, LXXIV (1959), 7–13. It might be thought, given the tenor of this sonnet, that Donne should have chosen the most purely legalistic of the theories, the penal-substitutionary. But, as Patrides points out, this is the most aggressively "Protestant" of all the theories; and Donne is always irenic, avoiding whenever possible outright points of contention. That Donne should have adopted the ransom theory, even though the penal theory is more appropriate to the legalism of his sonnet, is an addendum to what he professed in *Pseudo-Martyr*: "[I desire] to affoord a sweete and gentle Interpretation, to all professors of Christian Religion."

140. Galileo is probably not noticed in the poem, as C. M. Coffin argued in *John Donne and the New Philosophy* (New York, 1937). Donne is referring to conservative Ptolemaists only. His suggestion is that even nonrevolutionary doctrines reveal the impermanence and flux of created matter.

141. Merrill, pp. 118–119.

142. *Ibid.*, pp. 283–284.

143. *Ibid.*, p. 61.

144. Gosse, II, 20.

145. Merrill, p. 128.

146. *Ibid.*, pp. 42–44.

CHAPTER IV.

1. *John Donne: The Anniversaries*, ed. Frank Manley (Baltimore, 1963), p. 70. Professor Grierson based his edition of the *Anniversaries* on the 1633 edition, with free adoptions from 1611, 1612, 1621, and 1625. Manley adopts the first edition of each poem as the substantive base, and all references are to Manley's edition.

2. See Chapter I, pp. 49–51, and Chapter V, pp. 236–239.

3. Cf. Simpson, *Essays in Divinity*, p. 41, Chapter III, pp. 140–141.

4. Gardner, *Divine Poems*, p. 29.

5. "Hymne to God my God, in my sicknesse," ll. 21–25 (Gardner, *Divine Poems*, p. 50).

6. Potter and Simpson, *Sermons*, VII, 78.

7. Donne evidently believed that Elizabeth died on the thirteenth; but scholarship has had to be more circumspect. The records are not clear, although "Her death is first alluded to in a letter of 13 December" (R. C. Bald, *Donne and the Drurys* [Cambridge, 1959], p. 68). Cf. John Sparrow, "Two Epitaphs by John Donne," *TLS*, March 26, 1949, p. 208.

8. Martz, *Poetry of Meditation*, pp. 211–248.

9. Cf. Nicolson, *The Breaking of the Circle*, pp. 65–66.

10. Martz, *Poetry of Meditation*, p. 221.
11. *Ibid.*, p. 223.
12. Simpson, *Essays in Divinity*, p. 46.
13. Grierson, II, 48–49.
14. Manley, p. 43.
15. William R. Mueller, *John Donne: Preacher* (Princeton, 1962), pp. 179–194.
16. Gosse, I, 305–306.
17. Manley, p. 3.
18. *Ibid.*, p. 4.
19. Merrill, p. 105.
20. Potter and Simpson, X, 418–421.
21. Neither Nicolson, Manley, nor Martz seriously considers Hall's identification; in fact, it might be said that an understanding of the *Anniversaries* must take as its starting point a denial of Hall's easy equation. A notable exception is O. B. Hardison, *The Enduring Moment* (Chapel Hill, 1962), pp. 163–186.
22. Cf. Manley, pp. 10–50: a brilliant discussion of the several manifestations of the mysterious woman.
23. On the necessary distinction between archetype and archetypal symbol, cf. Jolande Jacobi, *Complex/Archetype/Symbol* (Bollingen Foundation, 1959), pp. 74–77.
24. Jacobi, p. 74.
25. The winter solstice fell on December 13 under the old Julian calendar. The revised Gregorian calendar (which England did not adopt until 1752) placed the solstice eleven days later in the year.
26. *The Golden Legend of Lives of the Saints as Englished by William Caxton* (London, 1928), II, 130–136.
27. Potter and Simpson, III, 206.
28. Charlton T. Lewis and Charles Short, *A Latin Dictionary Founded on Andrews' Edition of Freund's Latin Dictionary*, revised and enlarged (Oxford, 1933), pp. 1188–1189, entry under *natalis*.
29. A cross for editors, not alleviated by John Donne, Jr., who paid scant attention to such exactitudes, and who left the text of the letters worse than his father had bequeathed it.
30. Merrill, p. 128.
31. Potter and Simpson, I, 236–251.
32. *Ibid.*, V, 168–183.
33. *Ibid.*, VII, 257–278.
34. *Ibid.*, VIII, 110–129.
35. Gardner, *Songs and Sonnets*, pp. 84–85.
36. Professor Martz discusses the three possible dating solutions (*Poetry of Meditation*, pp. 214–215); and Helen Gardner adds the possibility of a 1611 date (*Elegies*, p. 216). The 1611 date is very plausible, given the

resemblances between "Nocturnall" and the *Anniversaries*. But, on two points, a 1617 date of composition presents the stronger case: (1) the woman is already dead, not ill, in the poem; (2) the conclusion of "Nocturnall" is very close in mood and statement to the sonnet "Since she whom I lov'd," definitely written in commemoration of Ann. Cf. Murray, "Donne and Paracelsus: An Essay in Interpretation" (*RES*, XXV [1949], 115–123). Murray suggests that the conclusion of "Nocturnall" looks ahead to the opening lines of the sonnet: but the sequence is the other way—the "Nocturnall" recalls the sonnet, which was probably written four months earlier.

37. See Chapter V, pp. 254–255.
38. Geoffrey Keynes, *A Bibliography of Dr. John Donne* (Cambridge, 1958), p. 213. I first made the suggestion that Donne was drawing on the matins service of the breviary in an article in *Cithara*, VI (1965), 60–68. The matter was amplified in 1966 by Clarence H. Miller, "Donne's 'A Nocturnall upon S. Lucies Day' and the Nocturne of Matins," *Studies in English Literature*, VI (1966), 77–86.
39. Gosse, II, 92.
40. Beatrice explains to Dante that she was sent to guide him to Paradise and that her informant, and Dante's protectress, is St. Lucy. *Inferno*, canto II, and *Purgatorio*, canto IX.
41. cf. R. L. P. Milburn, *Saints and Their Emblems in English Churches* (London, 1949), p. 162.
42. Martz, *Poetry of Meditation*, pp. 236–248.
43. Gardner, *Divine Poems*, pp. 83–86.
44. Cf. George Williamson, "The Design of Donne's Anniversaries," *MP*, LX (1963), p. 191: ". . . in the *Second Anniversary* [Donne] . . . completed the journey of the soul from creation to its potential destiny."
45. A shorter version of this chapter first appeared as an article, "The Woman in Donne's Anniversaries," *Journal of English Literary History*, XXXIV (September, 1967), pp. 307–326. I am grateful to the editors for their permission to make this citation.

CHAPTER V.

1. Le Comte, *Grace to a Witty Sinner*, p. 156.
2. The sermon preached at the funeral of Sir William Cokayne, December 12, 1626. (Potter and Simpson, VII, 261.)
3. Potter and Simpson, VI, 69.
4. Gosse, I, 303–304.
5. *Ibid.*, I, 209, 237.
6. *Ibid.*, II, 39–41.
7. *Ibid.*, II, 59.

8. Grierson, I, 195–226.
9. An important exception is Professor Milgate: "If we will take these poems on their own terms we shall not, I think, be troubled by thoughts of a cringing poet sacrificing sincerity and artistry alike in the mercenary pursuit of a patron. The dignity of the tone seldom seriously lapses, and when it does so it is Donne's handling of this difficult genre that falters, not his self-respect" (Satires, Epigrams and Verse Letters, p. xxxix).
10. P. Thomson, "John Donne and the Countess of Bedford," MLR, XLIV (1949), 329.
11. Gosse, II, 73.
12. Ibid., I, 284.
13. Ibid., I, 314.
14. Ibid., I, 294.
15. Grierson, I, 220, ll. 1–6.
16. J. H. Wiffen, Historical Memoirs of the House of Russell (London, 1833), II, 67; Henry Ellis, Original Letters From Autographs in the British Museum (London, 1824), III, 82.
17. Wiffen, II, 63.
18. Cf. The Phoenix and The Turtle, ed. Bernard H. Newdigate (Oxford, 1937), p. xvi.
19. J. William Hebel, "'A Divine Love' Addressed by Lord Herbert to Lady Bedford?" MLR, XX (1925), 74–76.
20. Thomas Birch, The Court and Times of James the First (London, 1848), I, 262. Quoted by Grierson, II, 154.
21. The second of Donne's Problems was anti-Puritan; the first satire inveighed against the "monstrous superstitious puritan"; and later Donne twice preached against Puritan asceticism (Potter and Simpson, II, 164–178; X, 162), criticized their theories of predestination and reprobation (Ibid., III, 110), attacked their emphasis on the private pentecostal spirit (Ibid., VIII, 135), and objected to their undervaluing the state religion (Ibid., X, 144).
22. Potter and Simpson, VI, 215.
23. Grierson, I, 198.
24. Ibid., II, 132.
25. Ibid., I, 201–203.
26. Ibid., I, 224–226.
27. Simpson, Prose Works, p. 192.
28. Ignatius His Conclave: or His Inthronisation in a late Election in Hell: Wherein many things are mingled by way of Satyr; Concerning The Disposition of Iesuits, The Creation of a new Hell, The establishing of a Church in the Moone. There is also added an Apology for Iesuites. All dedicated to the two Adversary Angels, which are Protectors of the Papall Consistory, and of the Colledge of Sorbon. Translated out of Latine.

London, Printed by N. O. for Richard More, and are to be sold at his shop in S. Dunstones Churchyard. 1611, pp. 12–13.

29. *Ibid.*, p. 19.

30. Cf. Carola Oman, *Elizabeth of Bohemia* (London, 1964); and M. A. E. Green, *Elizabeth, Electress Palatine and Queen of Bohemia* (London, 1909).

31. Cf. Wiffin, *op. cit.*; and Ian Grimble, *The Harington Family* (New York, n.d.), pp. 144–147.

32. *Nugae Antiquae: Being a Miscellaneous Collection of Original Papers, in Prose and Verse, written during the reigns of Henry VIII. Edward VI. Queen Mary, Elizabeth, and King James: by Sir John Harington, Knt.* (London, 1804), I, 373–374.

33. Thomas Birch, *The Life of Henry Prince of Wales* (London, 1760), pp. 329–330.

34. *Ibid.*, p. 330.

35. *Secret History of the Court of James the First*, ed. Sir Walter Scott (Edinburgh, 1811), I, 280.

36. Birch, *Life of Henry Prince of Wales*, p. 357; Sir Anthony Weldon, "The Court and Character of King James," *Secret History*, I, 392–393.

37. Ruth Wallerstein, *Studies in Seventeenth Century Poetic* (Madison, Wis., 1950), pp. 59–95.

38. Grierson, II, 205.

39. Wallerstein, p. 68.

40. Grierson, II, 204.

41. Wallerstein, pp. 69–73.

42. Grierson, I, 267–270.

43. Gosse, I, 273.

44. Grierson, I, 127–131.

45. Bald, *Donne and the Drurys*, pp. 102–103.

46. *Ibid.*, p. 122.

47. Grierson, I, 131–141.

48. For a full account, see Grierson, II, 94, and Gosse, II, 23–28. Gosse's account needs to be approached cautiously; he misrepresents the extent to which Donne was involved in the nullity proceedings against the Earl of Essex, whereby the Countess' first marriage was dissolved and she was left free to marry Somerset.

49. Gosse, II, 68–69.

50. *Ibid.*, II, 72–73. Donne was let down by the amount of the Countess' gift, but she was in considerable financial straits herself. Cf. Thomson, "John Donne and the Countess of Bedford."

51. Gosse, II, 73.

52. Bald, pp. 122–123.

53. Wiffin, II, 96 ff.

54. Gosse, II, 20–23.

55. *Ibid.*, II, 26–27.
56. *Ibid.*, II, 32.
57. Gardner, *Divine Poems*, pp. 32–33.
58. Martz, *Poetry of Meditation*, pp. 54–56.
59. John J. Bond, *Rules and Tables For Verifying Dates of Historical Events* (London, 1866), pp. 65, 266. In 1613, Easter fell on April 4, Old Style (April 7, N.S.).
60. Izaak Walton, *The Life of Dr. John Donne*, ed. S. B. Carter (London, 1951), p. 55.
61. An interesting discussion of the doctrine of the Real Presence as it appeared in seventeenth-century poetry is Malcolm Ross's *Poetry and Dogma* (Rutgers, 1954).
62. Potter and Simpson, VIII, 351.
63. Gardner, *Divine Poems*, pp. 30–31.
64. Potter and Simpson, I, 253–254.
65. *Ibid.*, II, 170.
66. *Ibid.*, III, 210.
67. *Ibid.*, II, 72–73.
68. *Ibid.*, IV, 45.
69. *Ibid.*, IX, 383–384.
70. Martz, *Poetry of Meditation*, pp. 54–56.
71. Potter and Simpson, VII, 353.
72. *Ibid.*, IX, 176.
73. *Ibid.*, III, 359; V, 102.
74. *Ibid.*, X, 46.
75. "Since she whom I lov'd" was written in 1617; "Show me deare Christ," probably just after Donne's voyage to Germany in 1619; "Oh, to vex me," sometime after 1617 (perhaps in 1623).
76. Potter and Simpson, II, 169.
77. Walton, *Life*, p. 43: "[Donne] caus'd ["A Hymne to God the Father"] to be set to a most grave and solemn Tune, and to be often sung to the Organ by the Choristers of S. Pauls Church, in his own hearing."
78. Cf. Helen White, *The Metaphysical Poets* (New York, 1966), p. 108; Webber, *Contrary Music*, p. 183; Potter and Simpson, II, 46.
79. Grierson, I, 270.
80. *Ibid.*, I, 288.
81. *Ibid.*, I, 279, ll. 255–258.
82. Potter and Simpson, II, 172.
83. Gosse, II, 69.
84. *Ibid.*, II, 68.
85. *Ibid.*; Merrill, p. 170.
86. Gosse, II, 70.
87. Potter and Simpson, II, 49.
88. Walton, *Life*, p. 28.

89. *Ibid.*, p. 31
90. *Ibid.*, pp. 34–35.
91. *Ibid.*
92. Walton, p. 36.
93. Potter and Simpson, X, 420–421.
94. *Ibid.*, VI, 205.
95. *Ibid.*, VI, 209.
96. T. S. Eliot judged (wrongly, as it turned out) that "for the theologian even the high-sounding Bramhall and the depressive Thorndike are more important names than Donne's. His sermons will disappear as suddenly as they have appeared" (*A Garland For John Donne: 1631–1931* ed. Theodore Spencer [Cambridge, Mass., 1931], p. 19).
97. On St. Paul's emphasis on the centricity of Christ, see Ferdinand Prat, *St. Paul* (Paris, 1925); Jean Cambier, "Paul and Tradition," *Concilium: Theology in the Age of Renewal* (New York, 1967), XX, 102–104; G. Ernest Wright and Reginald H. Fuller, *The Book of the Acts of God: Contemporary Scholarship Interprets the Bible* (New York, 1906), chapter V.
98. Pierre Teilhard de Chardin, *The Divine Milieu* (New York, 1965), p. 122.
99. J. W. Blench, *Preaching in England in the Late Fifteenth and Sixteenth Centuries* (New York, 1964), pp. 1–70.
100. Dennis B. Quinn, "John Donne's Principles of Biblical Exegeşis," *JEGP*, LXI (1962), 326.
101. As Professor Quinn does in "Donne's Christian Eloquence," *ELH*, XXVII (1960), 276–297.
102. Potter and Simpson, VII, 139–140.
103. *Ibid.*, I, 308–309.
104. *Ibid.*, VIII, 161.
105. *Ibid.*, VIII, 165.
106. *Ibid.*, VIII, 332–333.
107. *Ibid.*, IX, 156.
108. *Ibid.*
109. *Ibid.*
110. Potter and Simpson, IX, 158.
111. *Ibid.*, IX, 165.
112. *Ibid.*, IX, 167.
113. *Ibid.*, IX, 168.
114. *Ibid.*, IX, 172.
115. It would be tedious to number the sermons in which Donne uses the triad as his formal principle; it is evident in the reading. But I would like to single out five sermons that seem to me to make especially effective use of the concept: that is, "A Sermon of Valediction at my going into Germany, at Lincolns-Inne, April 18, 1619" (Potter and Simpson, II,

235–249); "Preached to the King, at the Court in April, 1629" (*Ibid.*, IX, 47–67); a second sermon on the same text (Genesis 1:26), also at Whitehall (*Ibid.*, IX, 68–91); *"Death's Duell,* preached at Whitehall before the Kings Majesty in the beginning of Lent [Friday, February 25, 1631]" (*Ibid.*, X, 229–249); and the exceedingly lovely sermon "Preached at White-hall, the first Friday in Lent," 1624 (*Ibid.*, IV, 324–344), on the text of John 11:35, "Jesus Wept."

116. I'm indebted to Professor Joan Webber's perceptive discussion of the structure of the *Devotions* in her book *Contrary Music*, pp. 183–201.

117. Le Comte, p. 186.

118. See Appendix E, pp. 132–135, of Helen Gardner's edition of the *Divine Poems.* Walton said that this hymn was written eight days before Donne's death, but there is enough evidence to make it "most probably" written in 1623.

119. Gardner, *Divine Poems,* p. 50.

120. *Ibid.,* p. 51.

121. Walton, *Life,* pp. 43–44.

122. *Ibid.,* p. 41.

123. Webber, p. 197.

124. *Ibid.,* pp. 189 ff.

125. *Devotions Upon Emergent Occasions,* ed. John Sparrow (Cambridge, 1923), p. 1.

126. *Ibid.,* p. 2.

127. *Ibid.,* p. 3.

128. *Ibid.,* p. 4.

129. *Ibid.,* pp. 96–97.

130. *Ibid.,* p. 102.

131. There is nothing comparable to Donne's image in the burial service contained in the Book of Common Prayer.

132. The monumental and exemplary edition of Donne's sermons, which puts every student of Donne in the debt of its editors, Evelyn Simpson and the late George Potter, invites, for instance, a close study of Donne's theology vis-à-vis the present studies of the relationships between literature and theology. Surely there could be no better locus than John Donne for such a comparative work, and I hope to begin on such a project in short order.

133. E.g., "Two symbols which occur in the first chapters of *Genesis* and are carried on into the *Revelation* of St. John can only be mentioned here. These are the River and the Tree of Life. These two are closely linked, and they are archetypal symbols which lie deep in the subconscious of our race. They were always in the background of Donne's mind, and a long study might be made of them" (Potter and Simpson, X, 306).

134. *Ibid.,* II, 165.

135. *Ibid.,* X, 69.

136. *Ibid.*, V, 103.
137. Webber, p. 124.
138. Potter and Simpson, II, 170.
139. *Ibid.*, IV, 92.
140. *Ibid.*, III, 292.
141. The woman of the sonnet is the true Church; and Donne's wish is not to locate her, but to see her reassembled. The sonnet evidently was provoked by Donne's visit into Germany in 1619, when he was witness to the religious wars. He was not expressing any doubts about which was the true Church, as some commentators, from Gosse onward, have argued; rather, "Donne has seen a parallel between the captivity of Israel and the total collapse of the Protestants after the defeat of the Elector in the battle of the White Mountain, outside Prague, on 29 October 1620. . . . If men so naturally thought of the Protestant Church in Germany as Zion, what would be more natural than for Donne to identify it in its disasters with the afflicted Zion of Lamentations." (Gardner, *Divine Poems*, pp. 124–125).
142. Potter and Simpson, I, 164.
143. *Ibid.*, V, 113.
144. *Ibid.*, V. 325.
145. *Ibid.*, VI, 81.
146. Gardner, *Divine Poems*, pp. 48–49.
147. Potter and Simpson, I, 199.
148. *Ibid.*, II, 340.
149. *Ibid.*, III, 241–255.
150. *Ibid.*, III, 241–242.
151. *Ibid.*, VI, 82.
152. *Ibid.*, VII, 87.
153. *Ibid.*, I, 184–185.
154. *Ibid.*, I, 243.
155. *Ibid.*, VI, 113.
156. *Biathanatos*, p. 18.
157. Potter and Simpson, IX, 177.
158. *Ibid.*, VII, 71.
159. Gardner, *Divine Poems*, p. 53.

EPILOGUE.

1. Carl Jung, *Modern Man in Search of a Soul* (New York, n.d.), p. 197.
2. Fromm, *The Art of Loving*, pp. 9–10.
3. *American Scholar*, "Teilhard de Chardin," XXX (1961), 618.

INDEX

A Note About the Author

Richard E. Hughes was born in Amsterdam, New York, in 1927. He was educated at Siena College, Boston College, and the University of Wisconsin, at which he was awarded a Ph.D. Author of five textbooks, he has taught at Ohio State University and at Boston College, where he is currently Professor of English and Chairman of the Department of English. He teaches Renaissance poetry in general and John Donne's poetry in particular, and wrote *The Progress of the Soul* over a period of thirteen years.

Professor Hughes lives with his wife and five children in an ante-bellum Greek revival house in one of the few surviving New England villages, Sherborn, Massachusetts.